Critical Acclaim

Women Resist Globalization is a testimony to contemporary women's movements in different parts of the world in order to ensure dignity, justice and citizenship for the underprivileged. It documents organizing initiatives around challenges to livelihood and democracy. In the process, it affirms the crucial role of collective action for an ethical world order. The radical vision and historical imagination of Rowbotham and Linkogle give these movements, so often dismissed as sporadic or fragmentary, a rightful place in the history of resistance to hegemonic powers. Highlighting similarities as well as differences in the experiences of women in the South and in the North, the book makes an important contribution to current discourse on international feminism that needs to address the issue of gender along with questions of race, ethnicity and class.

> *Swasti Mitter, co-author of* Dignity and Daily Bread: New Forms of Economic Organisation Among Poor Women in the Third World and the First

Mobilizations against the harshest effects of globalization on people's daily lives worldwide are predominantly initiated and sustained by the visions and leadership of women. It is inspiring to read this new collection by Sheila Rowbotham and Stephanie Linkogle highlighting the breadth and creativity of women's ongoing battles to create better lives for all. A tonic for these times.

> *Lynne Segal, author of* Why Feminism: Gender, Psychology, Politics

Women Resist Globalization: Mobilizing for Livelihood and Rights

edited by Sheila Rowbotham and Stephanie Linkogle

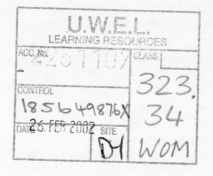

Zed Books
LONDON · NEW YORK

Women Resist Globalization: Mobilizing for Livelihood and Rights
was first published by Zed Books Ltd, 7 Cynthia Street, London
N1 9JF, UK and Room 400, 175 Fifth Avenue, New York, NY
10010, USA in 2001

Distributed in the USA exclusively by Palgrave, a division of
St Martin's Press, LLC, 175 Fifth Avenue, New York,
NY 10010, USA

Cover designed by Andrew Corbett
Set in Monotype Ehrhardt and Franklin Gothic by Ewan Smith
Printed and bound in Great Britain by Biddles Ltd, Guildford
and King's Lynn

A catalogue record for this book is available from the British
Library

Library of Congress Cataloging-in-Publication Data: available

ISBN 1 85649 876 X cased
ISBN 1 85649 877 8 limp

Contents

Acknowledgements

As both editors went down with repetitive strain injury a team of rescuers made this book possible. We are extremely grateful to Sonia Lane, Anne Morrow and Lorna Tittle, who typed parts of the manuscript, and to Gary Daniels, who helped with the editing. Thanks also to the discussions at the conference 'Towards A Global History of Contemporary Women's Movements' at Bellagio, Italy, April 2000, which helped shape this collection, and to Macalester College's International Roundtable, where Sheila Rowbotham's 'Facets of Emancipation' was presented as a paper. We are grateful for permission to print this revised version. The original was published under the heading 'Feminism and Women's Livelihood Protests' in *Macalester International, International Feminisms Divergent Perspectives*, vol. 10, Spring 2001.

Thanks too for help and advice to Jane Tate from HomeNet, Jane Turner from the Central America Women's Network, Helen Yuil from the Nicaragua Solidarity Campaign, Ros Baxandall and John Gabriel.

Biographical Notes

Meg Allen is the daughter of a mining family who were based in the north Nottinghamshire coalfield. She has been active in feminist and left politics for many years, in campaigns such as 'Fight the Alton Bill', the Anti-Poll Tax Campaign and the peace movement. She has worked on homelessness for the last 15 years and has published reports for Manchester City Council and Manchester Health Authority on homelessness, education and health. Her chapter is taken from a PhD submitted to the University of Manchester on the politics of Women Against Pit Closures.

Clara Jimeno has over twenty years' experience in social analysis in Latin America, specializing in socio-economic impact evaluation and gender equality at both the macro-economic and micro-economic levels. For over eleven years she was a professor at the Universidad de San Carlos in Guatemala, where she taught courses on economics and development. She has been involved in national planning of the industrial and co-operative sectors, particularly with artisan micro-enterprises, in Guatemala and designed and implemented participatory gender equity programmes on community development, leadership, income generation, community promotion and health. She now lives in Canada and is a social and gender consultant with CIDA's Industrial Co-operation Program in Central American countries.

Temma Kaplan an activist, historian and feminist scholar, works in decentralized grassroots movements of women in the USA, South Africa, Latin America and Spain. Her most recent books include *Red City, Blue Period: Social Movements in Picasso's Barcelona* (University of California Press, 1993) and *Crazy for Democracy: Women in Grassroots Movements* (Routledge, 1997). She works with Latino immigrants in the South Bronx and is completing a book entitled *Taking Back the Streets: Women, Popular Democracy, and Historical Memory*, which the University of California Press will publish in 2002. She is a professor of history at Rutgers University, New Brunswick, NJ.

Stephanie Linkogle has written on women's movements in *Gender Practice and Faith in Nicaragua* and in journals such as the *Bulletin of Latin American Research*, *Race and Class* and *Sociological Research On-Line*. She has recently published *Danger in the Field*, co-edited with Geraldine Lee-Treweek.

Paminder Parbha is an active management committee member of Newham Asian Women's Project and has published a report that examines the impact of domestic violence on children and its relevance to the development debate. She is currently working for Amnesty International.

Pragna Patel has been a member of Southall Black Sisters since 1982. She was a full-time case-worker for the organization until 1993. Since 1993 she has remained very active in the group. She was also the founder member of Women Against Fundamentalism.

Navtej K. Purewal teaches development and South Asian studies at the University of Manchester, UK. Her books include *Living on the Margins: Social Access to Shelter in Urban South Asia* (Ashgate, 2000) and *Teach Yourself Panjabi*, co-authored with S. S. Kalra (Hodder and Stoughton, 1999). She writes on gender and reproductive health, sex-selective technologies and development in South Asia.

Sheila Rowbotham helped to start the women's liberation movement in Britain in 1969. She is the author of many books on women's history and on women's contemporary movements and conditions, including *Dignity and Daily Bread* (Routledge, 1994) and *Women Encounter Technology* (Routledge, 1995) co-edited with Swasti Mitter. Her most recent works are *A Century of Women: The History of Women in Britain and the United States* (Penguin, 1997), *Threads Through Time: Writings on History and Autobiography* (Penguin, 1999) and *Promise of A Dream: Remembering the Sixties* (Allen Lane, 2000). She is a reader in the Sociology Department at Manchester University.

Orovu Sepoe is a lecturer in the Department of Political and Administrative Studies, University of Papua New Guinea. After completing her PhD at the University of Manchester on the role of women in the political structures of Papua New Guinea, she has continued to research and write on gender relations in Papua New Guinea.

Viji Srinavasan lived in Bihar as a child and returned while working as the Women's Programme Officer of the Ford Foundation. She settled there with her husband K. J. Srinavasan and played a crucial role in setting up the non-governmental organization Adithi in 1988. Involved in women's development work since 1962, she has been a journalist and has written several books, including *Newer Horizons* (Adithi, Bihar, India, 1999).

Sylvia Tamale is a senior lecturer in the School of Law at Makerere University Uganda, where she teaches law and gender studies. She is also an advocate of the courts in judicatur in Uganda. Her book *When Hens Begin to Crow: Gender and Parliamentary Politics in Uganda* was published by Westview Press in 1999. She is currently involved in research on gender and political processes.

Saskia E. Wieringa lectures on women and development at the Institute of Social Studies, The Hague. She is editor of *Subversive Women: Women's Movements in Africa, Asia, Latin America and the Caribbean* (Zed Books, 1995) and co-author of *Women, the Environment and Sustainable Development* (Zed Books, 1994).

1

Introduction

Sheila Rowbotham and Stephanie Linkogle

The last three decades have seen the emergence of a wide range of women's grassroots organizing, both in movements that are exclusively female and within others where women play a significant part. They have developed on a global scale, running alongside the feminist movements which have peaked and ebbed in the same period. *Women Resist Globalization* focuses on just two areas of resistance: movements asserting livelihood needs and movements around rights and democracy.

A connecting theme of this collection is that there are no hard-and-fast divisons separating activity. For example, Temma Kaplan describes North American women resisting the toxic dumping that is making their children ill and finding themselves influencing Congress, while Orovu Sepoe shows how, in the context of Papua New Guinea, ideas of women's rights are held back by poverty and inequality. Moreover, contributors show how the forms of organizing around livelihood have manifested themselves in a variety of ways and that 'rights' have acquired different meanings in diverse contexts.

During the twentieth century economic and social survival came to be associated with organization around production, trade unions bargaining for higher wages and better conditions at work. These have continued to be important aspects of material and social existence; indeed, women workers in poor countries have been part of a sustained struggle to organize in the workplace. However, the wage is only one aspect of human beings' survival, and an exclusive preoccupation with the wage imposes a false demarcation on daily existence. In the poor countries of the world many people, including the majority of women workers, are making their livings outside the regulated or organized sectors. In Chapter 6 Viji Srinivasan gives an account of a women's development network in Bihar, India, called Adithi. Set up in 1988, it reaches 40,000 women. One aspect of Adithi's work is with women in what is known as the 'informal sector', hawkers and home-based craft-workers, whose workplaces and homes are not always clearly demarcated. Adithi has worked with another women's association based in Gujarat, the Self-Employed Women's Association (SEWA). SEWA has over 200,000 members, many of whom are home-workers and vendors. They have thus taken workplace organizing into the community, showing that the capacity to earn a living cannot be conceived simply in terms of a wage but has to be seen in more holistic terms as a 'livelihood'. Both Adithi and SEWA seek to develop more social forms of production in terms of the conditions of work and the relation of work to the environment. They have also participated in global networks that aim to make the problems of women workers who are marginalized by the mainstream economy and by trade unions of the conventional kind visible. These networks, HomeNet for homebased workers and StreetNet for vendors, have exerted an influence on international and national policies that affect women in the informal sector.

Moreover, livelihood involves the cost of living, the extent of state provision, the nature of the environment, and access to financial and social infrastructure. All these have been affected by global economic policies and by politics. In response an extraordinary social phenomenon has arisen: women have mobilized in defence of their livelihoods. From the 1980s in Latin America, Asia and Africa, hundreds of thousands of women have protested around prices and rents and demanded basic social needs such as schools, day-care centres, and access to water or electricity. They have also participated in attempts to create alternative co-operative forms of social consumption – for example, the Nicaraguan Movimiento Comunal to which Stephanie Linkogle refers. Environmental devastation caused by the exploitation of natural resources by large corporations has also provoked movements of resistance in which women have played a crucial role. Temma Kaplan outlines various forms of such action in India, the USA and Africa. Another key demand has been access to credit, and Sylvia Tamale shows how women in Uganda have mobilized to create alternative forms of credit, demonstrating that livelihood also means the capacity to make a living.

The initial documenting of these movements occurred in an activist context, and originated in Latin America and to some extent in India. Left intellectuals influenced by Marxism and by socialist feminism attempted to chart these diverse forms of rebelling against poverty and inequality. In the North, interest in social movements led to an academic literature appearing *ad hoc* in several disciplines – anthropology, politics, sociology and geography – during the early 1990s. The focus of analysis was on poor countries, and 'the Third World' was seen as the site of resistance.

This interest in social movements related to debates led by feminists around development. The initial aim had been to include women in development. This was to shift to a critique of the unthinking ways in which 'modernization' short-circuited social needs and the insistence that women influenced by feminism brought alternative values to the aims of economic development. However, concern that an exclusive focus on alternative values would contain women in pockets of ethical powerlessness led to arguments for using the concept of gender and challenging the gendered bias in decisions about trade, the structure of production and distribution, finance, social and economic policy, budgets and the balance between the state and 'the market' (Porter and Judd 1999).

However, by the mid-1990s work began to appear showing that many of the struggles around livelihood being analysed in the South were also occurring in the North (Rowbotham and Mitter 1994; Naples 1998; Kaplan 1997). Examples from the USA include grassroots coalitions between African-Americans, Latino and Asian working-class people such as Direct Action For Rights and Equality (DARE) in Providence, Rhode Island, which since 1986 has mobilized low-income families in a multi-racial organization primarily of women and campaigned successfully for a playground, a supermarket and other facilities in poor areas (Anner 1996). In California immigrant Mexican and Korean workers have formed various kinds of association in sweatshops and in other low-paid jobs such as hotel work (Milkman 2000; Ross 1997). While these have not been exclusively female, women have played a vital role in such immigrant advocacy groups, and these forms of workplace organizing, which have had a big impact on organized labour, have used community networks.

Workplace struggles can span work and home, extending beyond the individual wage-earner to family, kin and neighbourhood. Opposition to changes in production can also be expressed from within communities. Again, the concept of livelihood carries not only a material aspect but an element of culture – a way of living. In Chapter 4, Meg Allen discusses the movement of women in the mining communities' support for the 1984–85 strike. In Britain these 'auxiliary' movements have been less documented than in the USA, but they have a long history, especially in mining areas.

A feature of movements around livelihood is that they are often expressed not in terms of the needs or rights of individual women but as action in relation to others, and carry an understanding of place as invested with a legacy of lived human experience. Temma Kaplan shows how women in the environmental justice movement in the USA used the notion of motherhood to express a caring interconnection and sense of responsibility for others. The integral bond is well expressed in the words of one of the forest people she quotes in the Chipko movement. He observed: 'When a leopard attacks a child the mother takes his onslaughts on her own body.' Viji Srinivasan also quotes a tribal woman from a forest area who says that 'the trees ... provide sustenance and livelihoods'. She is bitter about the disinheritance imposed by the industrialists and contractors who have cut down the forest, but says 'we have to feed our children'. Meg Allen shows how in the miners' strike women were sustained by an idea of 'community' that carried a similar sense of interconnectedness.

Sylvia Tamale questions whether gender alone is a useful framework for understanding these movements around livelihood, which are, she suggests, about poverty and race as well, and require a broad approach to social relations as a whole. They are clearly not based on a view of the individual self and the aspiration to self-determination that Sheila Rowbotham notes in Chapter 2 as one element in the history of feminism. Instead, they are rooted in organic relations to others, to kin and to community. But while they may not assert a vision of self-determination, they have frequently contained ideas of empowerment through collective action, whether through resisting at the point of production, as in the British miners' strike, through picketing or through the creation of alternative development forms such as micro-credit to enhance the conditions of life. Implicit within these are changes in daily life and in how people relate – a vision that can connect with the feminist Utopian yearning for different ways of being in relation to others. For some individuals, moreover, participation in such movements can give rise to desires for more autonomous space as women. Stephanie Linkogle in Chapter 8 documents how opposition to machismo arose from within livelihood groups in Nicaragua during the Sandinista period.

The rise of these diverse women's movements has generated a debate about their relationship to 'feminism' (Basu 1995). This is a complex and difficult issue, for women in livelihood movements sometimes express the wariness about feminism described by Meg Allen in Chapter 4. Other movements, such as Adithi, see their action as 'feminist'. It also depends partly on how the term is employed. As Sheila Rowbotham shows in Chapter 2, feminism has had many historical definitions. This is equally the case in the contemporary period, when feminism can be defined very closely as an emphasis on issues that are specific to women as women, such as reproduction, or, in contrast, in very broad terms. Gita Sen and Caren Grown state, for example, that: 'Our vision of feminism has as its very core a process of economic and social development geared to human needs through wider control over and access to economic and political power' (Sen and Grown 1987: 20).

This definition of feminism illuminates women's action around livelihood needs, which are never simply about economics. Social visions of alternative possibilities are also present within these movements (Amadiume 2000). Viji Srinivasan, for example, cites the tribal forest-dwellers' sense of a legitimate heritage in the forest that has been wrenched away. Sylvia Tamale argues that the mutual aid of micro-credit associations presents a challenge to the social and economic marginalization of poor women in Africa, and Meg Allen chronicles the ways in which women in mining communities combine the lived experience and memories of actual communities with an imaginary recreation of myths of past customary practice and reach out to new unknown forms of community. Thus movements around livelihood can carry ideas of possibilities beyond the known and contain both practical and transformational elements.

The picture is further complicated by the fact that the assumptions of the individuals who participate within them also change. In order to understand this shifting dynamic of consciousness a historical perspective in relation to social movements is vital. For example, Meg Allen shows how some women active in Women Against Pit Closures became aware of individual needs and desires through collective activity, which eventually in some cases led them to leave their communities. She observes the contradiction inherent in the process of a developing collective consciousness and sense of belonging to a community. By fostering precisely that yearning for self-determination that Sheila Rowbotham shows has been a crucial aspect of movements for women's emancipation, grassroots mobilizations can loosen the bonds of custom.

Movements around livelihood are apt to dissolve categories. Navtej Purewal explains that one reason is that women's actual circumstances are interrelated, whereas policy imposes arbitrary compartments – for example, between the means of survival and the reproduction of life. Viji Srinivasan describes how Adithi took up other issues that arose in the course of its work around livelihood. These include women's education, health, sexuality and reproduction. She stresses that Adithi defines itself as a feminist organization, yet it works closely with the Self-Employed Women's Association (SEWA), which does not call itself feminist but regards itself as part of the 'women's movement'. And SEWA, like Adithi, puts an emphasis on individual empowerment along with a sense of collective strength.

There is a growing awareness of the need to connect the personal politics of reproduction and health with a wider framework of well-being and a recognition of the obstacles that are likely to hinder such a project in practice (Petchesky and Judd 1998). Navtej Purewal shows how reproduction is integrally connected to production and consumption and has to be seen not only in terms of individual rights but also in the overall context of livelihood. She describes how structural adjustment programmes, neoliberal economic policies and population policies that aim to restrict births rather than tackle poverty have interacted, with adverse consequences for poor women. She stresses that the conditions of production have effects on reproduction and vice versa. Opposition has come not only from women's groups but from women's refusal to follow dictums on population, which do not take into account how children can ensure livelihood.

Many of the movements of poor women around livelihood have arisen in response to the impact of globalization. The version of 'modernization' that puts the stress on immediate economic efficiency has been forcing groups of women in many parts of the world onto the margins of their societies. Meg Allen's account shows how British mining communities have sunk through unemployment from the upper working class into the underclass. The consequences have been particularly severe in poor countries, as Sylvia Tamale notes in the African context. Writing on Papua New Guinea, Orovu Sepoe describes how a small percentage of the population are part of an elite, while the vast majority are illiterate, especially subsistence rural dwellers, who are being left out of the benefits of globalization. Existing inequalities are being exacerbated in many parts of the world. Viji Srinivasan demonstrates how tribal women dependent on the forest are experiencing harsher and harsher conditions because of afforestation. Stephanie Linkogle's account of the Nicaraguan Movimiento Comunal examines women's efforts to respond to the reduction of social services following the defeat of the Sandinistas.

Navtej Purewal points also to the impact of the state's retreat from social responsibility. This has had repercussions both on livelihood and on women's organizing. The gap is being filled all over the world by non-governmental organizations (NGOs) in which women play a prominent role. Many complicated questions are raised by the emergence of these NGOs, some of which are struggling to meet needs. They find themselves picking up the problems that states increasingly disdain, and present a much cheaper means of alleviating extreme poverty and social conflict than paid state employees. Since they are funded by national and international aid agencies, there is, moreover, a danger that funding priorities come to distort their programmes, meaning they become a kind of contractual bureaucracy responding to policy directives remote from the people they serve. Another criticism of NGOs is that they can be unrepresentative and not subject to democratic control. There has also been concern that they cream off and render harmless activists from campaigns and movements.

On the other hand, NGOs can indicate gaps in social provision and strengthen democracy, for they provide flexible responses to needs, as Stephanie Linkogle shows in Nicaragua. They can utilize the experience of activists on the ground to develop more democratic internal structures that can make visible and voice the needs and demands of the poor. NGOs can also combine to put pressure on the state and on international bodies to adapt and change to actual needs, as Adithi and SEWA have done.

Orovu Sepoe's positive account from Papua New Guinea shows that where representative democracy exists but is marked by a lack of participation, women's NGOs can help to awaken an awareness of rights.

Moreover, in extremely repressive situations NGOs can act as a means of organizing. Clara Jimeno relates how women's NGOs played a vital role in Guatemala during the dictatorship and later in the peace process. Another example is Indonesia before the collapse of President Soeharto's regime in May 1998, where women's NGOs asserted basic needs. Saskia Wieringa charts the bloody rise to power of Soeharto, focusing on Gerwani, the women's organization that had been close to his predecessor Soekarno. Gerwani contained a wing that emphasized a form of militant motherist politics, and it is interesting that this theme of mothers having a legitimate right to mobilize around the needs of their children was to reappear in February 1998, when a group of around twenty women, mainly from NGOs, mobilized around the 100 per cent increase in the cost of milk and were able to gain considerable public sympathy (Porter and Judd 1999). These women provide an example of women manipulating their gendered position to challenge a repressive state in the way Temma Kaplan describes of environmental movements.

However, riots and killings along with rapes occurred in the uprising against Soeharto, and women's groups in Indonesia found it extremely difficult to raise the issue of the violence directed against the mainly Chinese ethnic women (Porter and Judd 1999). These contemporary events bring an element of urgency to Saskia Wieringa's examination of the ways in which the women in Gerwani were caricatured by conservative political and religious forces in Indonesia as bloodthirsty and sexually depraved. Her contribution to this book shows how sexual politics is inseparably connected to the conservative ideological legacy of Soeharto's order.

Democracy and rights cannot be conceived simply in terms of formal representation or even collective participation: women have to challenge the terms in which they have been conceived. This collection chronicles how this is very much a realization through practice. Pragna Patel describes how, with the threat from fundamentalist Muslims to the writer Salman Rushdie, Southall Black Sisters initiated the group Women Against Fundamentalism, which deliberately involved women from a wide range of religious backgrounds, including Christians and Hindus, in order to challenge a specific interpretation of Islam. Women Against Fundamentalism saw that it was important in a British context, where hostility to Muslims is entwined with racism, to stress that all religions possess conservative strands along with democratic and emancipatory currents.

Southall Black Sisters, which was formed in 1979, found that women were coming to the group mainly because of domestic violence, although they have also been involved in cases of forced marriages. This involved them in a position of criticizing from within the Asian community.

Asian women's groups now constitute a high proportion of the grassroots groups that focus on the everyday needs and problems of women in Britain. These groups have differing emphases and outlooks in their practice and in their theory. For example, some are primarily servicing women rather than campaigning like Southall Black Sisters, and many would not identify themselves as 'feminists'. Some might be more sceptical in relation to the usefulness of human rights.

Pragna Patel, who has been active in Southall Black Sisters since its early years, shows in her interview with Paminder Parbha how issues of identity, definitions and frameworks and the languages of protest are not just academic concerns but are highly political. For example, she observes how a human rights discourse has been a means of asserting the distinct problems of women in Asian communities in Britain, who lack a voice within both the mainstream culture and their own communities. Human rights has been a way of criticizing an interpretation of multiculturalism that denies that conflict exists. Southall Black Sisters have been able to apply the idea of 'rights' to prise open a lived reality – there are differing interests and contrasting political and cultural viewpoints rather than a single 'Asian' identity.

While Pragna Patel recognizes that there are drawbacks in utilizing ideas of 'human rights' because they can lead to a focus on individual cases rather than collective social injustices, she also makes the point that the focus on the individual is extremely important for women whose individuality has been occluded. A problem that women's movements for emancipation have encountered in many countries has been that the Marxist tradition of left politics emphasized only collective resistance and was dismissive of individual rights in ways that have resembled more conservative politics. So within the traditional arguments of the left there was a dismissal of injustices in the personal and domestic sphere. Human rights arguments have thus proved a useful weapon in raising questions such as domestic violence, forced marriages and sexuality. Indeed, writing in the context of Nicaragua, Stephanie Linkogle notes how a conceptual shift in definitions occurred that rejects the differentiation of public and private.

A difficult question is raised by Clara Jimeno's contribution. In Guatemala, as in other Latin American countries, women's reproductive rights and right to sexual self-determination have been contentious issues. For this reason a theoretical distinction between demands that base themselves on existing gender relations and demands that contain a transformative aspect has had considerable political resonance, and Clara Jimeno uses this framework in relation to Guatemala. However, Sylvia Tamale, looking at women's livelihood projects in Uganda, questions the usefulness of such a distinction. She argues that transformative and strategic understandings exist within women's mobilization around economic need. Several issues lurk behind this difference in approach and explain why it has been so difficult to resolve. There is a political tension about setting a line between the values of a specific political approach to women's emancipation ('feminism') and listening to contradictory women's movements. Maxine Molyneux's effort to distinguish between differing forms of women's action and demands was not intended to set up a hierarchical structure of consciousness. (Molyneux 2001). However, in practice there has been a tendency for demands associated with Western feminism to be regarded as more 'advanced'. This can lead to imposing a set of values and assumptions that obscure ideas buried within differing kinds of women's movements (Stephen 1997).

Several contributors stress that 'women' should not be regarded as a homogeneous bloc. Clara Jimeno, for example, mentions the subordination of Mayan women within Guatemala, while Pragna Patel notes the suspicion of a predominantly white British feminist movement. On the other hand, the attempt to draw out general features of diverse movements and to reveal the points in which they go in either similar or opposing directions is vital in understanding their meanings in broader social terms, and could have a practical relevance for the kind of coalition-building many of the contributors call for. This raises the question of how to approach collective action. Are movements to be seen within a rooted and contextualized specificity, or can they be analysed in broader terms and conclusions made that relate to more than the particular? This is a problem not only for feminists but for all researchers seeking to understand human consciousness and action. The attempt to balance the two guides all the contributions in this collection. In practice, of course, it is always extremely difficult. Not only do we bring our subjective approaches to the inquiry, but social movements invariably defy classification. The contributions in this collection also suggest that there can never be some absolute answer. In certain situations it is important to stress issues of sexual and personal self-definition, in others we must recognise that the sense of 'self' also exists in relation to the needs of others and that a preoccupation with autonomy or with individual right misses the relatedness of human beings' existence. The unifying concern in this book is the effort to chart specific complexities and to draw out understandings that can have a wider implication, but the contributors approach this from differing standpoints.

Conflict about ways of seeing collective movements of protest is not simply a matter of splitting hairs over definitions. It raises the question of the impact of ways of seeing and ways of describing human action (Alvarez et al. 1998). The debate about how to approach movements is connected to a question about how to look at the ways in which a consciousness of interconnecting subordination arises. Pragna Patel makes the important point that the contemporary feminist movement has neglected how 'different systems of power can interlock'. It is becoming evident that a new paradigm is needed: rather than focusing on one key determining factor, a dynamic and interactive approach is required. A useful working metaphor is the interrelation of nerves and muscles in the body – while patterns can be observed, these vary infinitely depending on the particular circumstances.

Temma Kaplan and Paminder Parbha both refer to the vacuum left by the sidelining of socialism since the collapse of communism. It is far from clear how a new language and ideas of emancipation and well-being are to be chiselled out of all the diverse forms of global resistance to injustice and inequality. Yet the chapters in this book reveal how women have been seeking sources of power, affirming a legitimacy from their existing position in society and making use of terms such as 'rights'. They describe how, in the process of staking their claims on the basis of existing gendered activities, women have been shifting social understandings of personal and public realms. These have not only altered relations between women and men but are creating new ways of seeing communities, society and the scope of politics.

Similarly, in opening space and applying human rights strategically for women's needs, women have been interpreting abstract rights in very specific and material contexts that break out of some of the impasses within identity politics. Clara Jimeno argues for rights to be defined in relation to social needs, and also asserts the importance of alliances in the context of Guatemala with other groups campaigning for justice and equality. Sylvia Tamale is similarly interested in coalitions that would include men, adopting a gendered poverty analysis. Navtej Purewal shows how women's reproductive circumstances are affected not only by policies around population but also by economic theories of development. Structural adjustment has undermined health care and the means of livelihood. Thus a discussion of women's reproductive rights has to take on much wider material deprivation. Stephanie Linkogle cites the Women in Reconstruction Conference in Central America in 1999, which was held after the devastation of Hurricane Mitch. The participants interpreted 'reconstruction' as 'an ethical citizenship' that involves the full participation of women and other socially marginalized groups in the transformation of discriminatory structures and poverty.

It is not coincidental that movements among grassroots women overspill boundaries and seep out of existing categories. The conventional divisions between public and personal or political and social were not devised with women in mind. A fast-changing global reality has been making the lack of congruence more pronounced. The demarcations have become so evidently imprecise. Accordingly it is not really surprising that with so many of the movements in this book it is a case of one thing leading to another.

As Pragna Patel, Stephanie Linkogle and Saskia Wieringa show, the feminist redefinition of human rights to include the sexual and domestic sphere has vital consequences for women. Temma Kaplan adds that by placing the emphasis on the 'human' rather than on legal rights, women have been reinterpreting their meaning. She shows that movements around livelihood involve 'the right to a fulfilling life in which safe housing, public health conditions, housing and food, education, and clean air and water are assured'. Navtej Purewal quotes women asserting their claim to 'well-being'. And indeed, the diverse movements chronicled in this collection indicate how women have been articulating in complex ways new contours for expressing what ought to be. In charting these movements we can trace the ripples that come from innumerable unrecorded refusals of injustice and glimpse the nascent outlines of visions of emancipation.

Bibliography

Alvarez, Sonia E., Evelina Dagnino and Arturo Escobar (1998) *Cultures of Politics, Politics of Cultures: Re-visioning Latin American Social Movements*, Boulder, CO: Westview Press.

Amadiume, Ifi (2000) *Daughters of the Goddess, Daughters of Imperialism: African Women's Struggle for Culture, Power and Democracy*, London: Zed Books.

Anner, John (ed.) (1996) *Beyond Identity Politics: Emerging Social Justice Movements in Communities of Color*, Boston, MD: South End Press.

Basu, Amrita (1995) *The Challenge of Local Feminisms: Women's Movements in Global Perspective*, Boulder, CO: Westview Press.

Kaplan, Temma (1997) *Crazy for Democracy: Women and Grassroots Movements*, New York: Routledge.

Milkman, Ruth (2000) *Organizing Immigrants: The Challenge for Unions in Contemporary Capitalism*, Ithaca, NY: ILP Press, Cornell University Press.

Molyneux, Maxine (2001) *Women's Movements in International Perspective: Latin America and Beyond*, London: Palgrave.

Naples, Nancy (1998) *Grassroots Warriors: Activist Mothering, Community Work and the War on Poverty*, New York: Routledge.

Naples, Nancy (ed.) (1998) *Community Activism and Feminist Politics: Organising Across Race, Class and Gender*, New York: Routledge.

Petchesky, Rosalind P. and Karen Judd (eds) (1998) *Negotiating Reproductive Rights: Women's Perspectives Across Countries and Cultures*, London: Zed Books.

Porter, Marilyn and Ellen Judd (eds) (1999) *Feminists Doing Development*, London: Zed Books.

Rowbotham, Sheila and Swasti Mitter (eds) (1994) *Dignity and Daily Bread: New Forms of Economic Organising Among Poor Women in the Third World and the First*, London: Routledge.

Ross, Andrew (ed.) (1997) *No Sweat: Fashion, Free Trade and the Rights of Garment Workers*, New York: Verso.

Sen, Gita and Caren Grown (1987) *Development Crises and Alternative Visions*, London: Earthscan.

Stephen, Lynn (1997) *Women and Social Movements in Latin America: Power from Below*, London: Latin American Bureau.

2

Facets of Emancipation: Women in Movement from the Eighteenth Century to the Present

Sheila Rowbotham

Women's assertion of emancipation has taken many forms historically. Ideas of self-determination, visions of mutuality, the conviction of the legitimacy of claims of livelihood and the assertion of rights can be found jostling against one another and interacting in popular movements in many countries from the late eighteenth century. Taking this broad vista enables us to situate 'feminism', or indeed 'feminisms', because there have been many versions, within a wider spectrum. A historical perspective provides a useful and frequently neglected dimension not only in considering contemporary discussions of 'feminisms' but in thinking how women's specific experiences of subordination might illuminate the recreation of a vision of human emancipation.

It was not, of course, the beginning of female discontent, but the French Revolution – that extraordinary, quite unprecedented moment of upheaval in all known systems of social hierarchy – nevertheless threw up a dramatic assertion of women's right to self-determination in Olympe de Gouges' 'Declaration of the Rights of Woman and the Female Citizen', which appeared in 1791, just one year before Mary Wollstonecraft's better-known 'Vindication'. 'Woman, wake up,' demanded de Gouges, a butcher's daughter and playwright who had written the first French play against slavery in 1782. She declared: 'The tocsin of reason is being heard throughout the whole universe; discover your rights. The powerful empire of nature is no longer surrounded by prejudice, fanaticism, superstition, and lies' (de Gouges quoted in Levy et al. 1979; see also Diamond 1998; Offen 2000; Scott 1989).

Speaking from the standpoint of a constitutional monarchist, Olympe de Gouges, who was to be overtaken by the political course of the Revolution, argued for an extension of the civil rights of women. Although the Revolution presented the idea of the sovereignty of the 'people', this was in practice circumscribed. Limited civil rights were to be granted, but women were to be excluded from political rights. Along with poorer working men and servants, women remained passive, rather than active citizens who could participate in the shaping of laws.

Nevertheless, during the Revolution poor women's sense of a social responsibility legitimated by custom could overlap into the public political sphere. Poor women had taken action around consumption long before the Revolution, but their targets had usually been the bakers. During the Revolution they began to hold the king, as the head of state, responsible for supplying bread.

Prices rose dramatically amidst civil turmoil and war. In 1792 the women of Lyon seized control of the city government and raided shops for bread and meat, demonstrating through their action a moral vision of an economy of goods distributed at prices they regarded as fair and just and an alternative view of sovereignty as legitimated through its power to meet the needs of the poor.

So there appeared a startling new assertion, which, though based on time-honoured domestic activity, transcended women's allotted sphere. This was not self-determination in the sense of asserting an autonomous identity as 'women', but a collective expression of control over daily life. Because of the exceptional conditions of the Revolution, the customary realm of domestic provision and care took on an extraordinary dimension that began to impinge on the area of political decision-making. In the course of the Revolution poor women can be seen taking new historical spaces through their collective participation in crowd action. A shadowy counter-notion of what the state should do and be is documented in February 1793. A group of poor women went to the National Convention to protest about the price of basic provisions. They were told the Convention was about to adjourn for two days and would not hear their case. They were to be heard in the corridors angrily criticizing the unresponsive people's state's prevarication over the needs of their families: 'When our children ask for milk we don't adjourn them until the day after tomorrow.'[1]

It was to be the mobilization of poor women around livelihood rather than Olympe de Gouges' claim to the rights of citizenship that involved large numbers of women during the French Revolution. Action arose not from an autonomous definition of 'woman' but from the experience of being women in relation to the family. As Olwen Hufton (1992: 23) points out: 'The issue of women's equality with men ... can be allotted only a small space in the big history of the Revolution.'

With hindsight we can note that two perspectives had arrived by the late eighteenth century that were to have profound implications for the history of women's emancipation. One is this fragile sense of women's individual rights, and the second is the concept-through-action in a revolutionary context of a legitimate collective claim of poor women to shape policies that relate to the livelihood of their families. In a fascinating and prescient remark, Olympe de Gouges, commenting on the sexual power to which women had had to resort in the ancien régime, glimpsed how, through the Revolution, despite its denial of women's rights, a chink had opened: 'In this sort of contradictory situation, what remarks could I not make! I have but a moment to make them, but this moment will fix the attention of the remotest posterity (de Gouges quoted in Levy et al. 1979: 93).

After the defeat of revolutionary hope it was to take some time for a new radicalism to develop. However, the mid-1820s were to see a perceptive synthesis of issues of self-determination and livelihood concerns in 'Appeal of One Half the Human Race' (1825), the work of William Thompson, an Irish landlord with progressive views. It was an attempt to refute the Utilitarian James Mill's view in his 'Article on government' that women's interests could be included 'in that of their fathers and that of their husbands' (Mill quoted in Pankhurst 1991: 57). In rejecting this assumption that women's persons could be the property of their male kin, Thompson was influenced by a remarkable woman, Anna Wheeler, whose own life had been scarred by an unhappy and brutal marriage. Thompson argued that women's rights as individuals should be the basis for reforms that should be immediately enacted. However, he also had a longer-term perspective. Thompson and Wheeler were part of a radical circle in London who saw co-operation and association as an alternative and preferable form of development to the harshness of competition. He applied this transformatory vision of mutuality to women's economic dependence, linking his recognition of rights to an awareness of their needs.

In her study of women in the Owenite co-operative movement *Eve and the New Jerusalem* Barbara Taylor shows how both these aspects of women's emancipation were to be taken up by the co-operative movement, which developed in the 1830s among radical workers (Taylor 1993). Among the Owenites were several women lecturers and writers, and these practitioners of Robert Owen's 'New Moral World' consciously challenged the culture of the Church and their secular rulers. The Owenites' awareness that domination was not necessarily just about physical control but a matter also of values and beliefs had an obvious significance for women.

Interconnection between aspects of consciousness was matched with geographical exchanges of ideas. The socialists of the 1830s were internationalists, carrying ideas back and forth. Bonnie J. Anderson in *Joyous Greetings* charts the transmission of these international links. For instance, she records how in 1832 a small band of French Utopian socialist women, calling themselves 'New Women', wrote a 'Call to Women' in a French newspaper, asking: 'Is our condition as women so happy that there is nothing left for us to desire and demand?' Rejecting male property rights over women, they asserted, 'One half the human race cannot be made *the servants of the other*'. They called on women of all classes to unite for 'the free and equal chance of developing ... *all our faculties*' (Anderson 2000: 67; original emphasis).

Bonnie J. Anderson notes how their 'Call' was translated by Anna Wheeler and appeared in the Owenite journal *The Crisis* in 1833. Read by John Stuart Mill, among others, in Britain, it 'circulated to radicals in North America and Europe (ibid.: 68). In 1836 a Polish Jewish American, Ernestine Rose, circulated a petition for married women's property rights in the USA, which Judith Wellman (1995) says was the first time that women in North America had taken 'public action for legal reform'. Rose had emigrated to the USA from Britain as an Owenite colonist, critical of the personal paternalism of Owen himself (Anderson 2000: 51-66).

These connections have been missed by historical accounts of feminism that focus exclusively on gender or women's networks. The idea that 'feminism' can be seen apart from other political currents was, of course, the viewpoint that more conservative late nineteenth-century feminists, embarrassed by any association with Mary Wollstonecraft or Anna Wheeler, would have wished to put over. However, as Bonnie Anderson remarks (ibid.: 68), 'This international women's movement did not arise because aggrieved feminists in different nations independently decided to band together. Rather it emerged from the matrix of international socialism.' And of course this new view of society – 'socialism' – came into being in response to the massive transformations being wrought by capital and in its inception interacted with other movements such as anti-slavery, liberal nationalism, religious dissent and radical protests against censorship or for a freer sexuality.

The 'new women' of the 1830s, drawn to the ideas of mutuality, co-operation, association articulated by such thinkers as Robert Owen, Henri Saint Simon and Charles Fourier, combined the seventeenth-century radical demand for ownership of their own 'persons' with a romantic desire for self-development, through education, personal freedom and choice and public action that had its roots in both the Enlightenment and the Romantic movement. In these early texts on women's condition there are also repeated references to women's 'slavery' and the use of the word 'emancipation'. The movement for the emancipation of slaves thus not only directly inspired the American women's movement, it also provided a concept that could express an aspiration for individual self-determination, along with social, economic and political change. It differs from the more static idea of rights because it contains the notion of active personal transformation in the process of changing the old order.[2]

During the 1840s, although the free love aspect of self-ownership tended to be played down because of scandal, the connection between self-emancipation and social emancipation persisted. In the French Revolution of 1848 both were to surface through women's clubs and working women's journals where equal political and civil rights, divorce, voluntary mother-hood, male attitudes, women's feelings of inadequacy and ignorance were discussed along with co-operative households and child care. Among the demands thrown up in 1848 were: a social fund so women need not be dependent on men, a free medical service and state support for midwives, public restaurants, wash-houses, meeting rooms, libraries, and public space for recreation. Working women in the 1840s also developed a set of demands around paid work. They wanted equal pay, an end to women's low pay, long hours and exclusion from certain trades, payment of homeworkers at the same rate as workers in the workshops and the sharing of work in times of unemployment. Alternative employment for prostitutes, restaurants and crèches in all workshops, training centres for women workers including midwives, and centres for domestic workers to meet and organize were also demanded. The conviction that workers should determine their own work-ing conditions and alter the organization of production is evident in the demand for the equal participation of women on workers' committees in the National Workshops created to solve unemployment. The women of 1848 also drew up their own schemes for associations or co-operatives as producers and consumers.

In order to comprehend these claims we have to place them in the context of the pressures on working conditions and the impetus the Revolution of 1848 gave to a new vision of society, which was to remain unrealized. Working women's protests arose from a specific experience of class and gender but at a time when the sense of general transformation fed the hope that new social relationships could evolve. The writing of the minority of women who voiced this new hope is infused with a sense of becoming and of the making of an alternative culture of equality, freedom and co-operation. The year 1848 thus saw the fullest expression of an associationist idea of women's emancipation in which transforming oneself and transforming collective social existence are combined.[3]

The defeat and repression that followed resulted in a splintering of this concept of women's emancipation as the wider hope of radical change was also shattered. In a poignant letter two revolutionaries of 1848, Jeanne Deroin and Pauline Roland, wrote from prison in 1851 to the Convention of the Women of America:

Sisters of America! your socialist sisters in France are united with you in the vindication of the right of woman to civil and political equality. We have, moreover, the profound conviction that only by the power of association based on solidarity – by the union of the working-classes of both sexes to organize labor – can be acquired, completely and pacifically, the civil and political equality of woman, and the social right of all.[4]

This broad and inclusive vision of 'social right' was to be buried in oblivion.

It was evident to contemporaries that 1848 was a turning point. Not only did it send Karl Marx to the British Museum to wrestle with *Capital*, the novelist Gustave Flaubert has left us a literary testimony of the submergence of romantic dreams. His first version of *Sentimental Education* was written in 1849; his final version 20 years later aimed at sober realism. To a new generation the hopes of twenty years before were simply incomprehensible. As Flaubert himself said, 'The reaction after '48 dug a gulf between one France and the other' (Goldsmith 1941). The gulf of course extended far beyond France, and class distinctions affected how women's emancipation was seen by differing groups of women.

The discovery of social tensions between women is not peculiar to the modern women's movements. Women mobilized with very different priorities during the nineteenth century. For example, in the Chartist movement in Britain women, by and large, situated themselves in relation to their subordination as members of a class, rather than a sex. As Dorothy Thompson notes in her essay on women and nineteenth-century radical politics: 'Historians of the women's emancipation movement have observed the considerable gulf that existed between the aspirations of the middle class emancipators and those of women lower down in the social scale in Victorian society' (Thompson 1993: 77).

Even if we look at the white, middle-class feminism in Europe and the USA, which was broadly aligned with liberalism, we can see several different political assumptions and aims within the formulation of women's gender interests. In other words, the existence of 'feminisms' is not a new phenomenon either. Very familiar disputes were actually to pre-date the arrival of the term 'feminism', which Karen Offen found being first used in the early 1880s in France, arriving in the USA and Latin America in the late 1890s (Offen 1998: 126–7 and 2000: 19–26). Arguments about equality and difference for instance can be observed in the 1830s and 1840s, while the question of whether women as a group have needs and desires distinct from those of men was being discussed in the 1830s.[5]

By the time the term 'feminism' had been coined, Western capitalist society had consolidated. The impermanence and topsy-turvy fluidity of the earlier era has gone. Late nineteenth-century middle-class feminists were to focus mainly on education, access to employment and the vote. The earlier emphasis on co-operation or new social relations of mutuality becomes a sub-strand. There were, of course, notable exceptions. In the USA Elizabeth Cady Stanton, veteran of anti-slavery and early women's rights, continued to support 'association' and what she called, in 1892, 'self-sovereignty' (quoted in Offen 1988: 136).

By the late nineteenth and the early twentieth century it no longer seemed evident that an alternative 'mutuality' could evolve from and replace the capitalist economy. As industrialization demarcated aspects of daily life more sharply, this was to be mirrored in the forms of working-class resistance. The effort to improve women's livelihoods came to focus on trade unions, and on state legislation to protect workers or provide welfare. This was the approach of the socialist women who became involved in the reformist and revolutionary wings of socialist organizations (see Rowbotham 1992; Evans 1987; Hilden 1986; Hunt 1996; Hannam 1989). It was also to affect the feminists. Alongside egalitarian traditions of feminism and frequently interacting with them went what Karen Offen has called a 'relational' feminism (Offen 1988). This saw women's emancipation in terms of complementary equity rather than equality with men. From this perspective in Europe, and, to a lesser extent in the USA, both middle-class feminists and working-class labour women made gender-based claims on the state for resources for women as mothers and housewives before the Second World War.[6]

Around the time of the First World War in many countries small groups of women had also begun to define themselves as 'socialist feminists'. Both egalitarianism and ideas of women's 'difference' are present in the thinking of socialist feminists such as Crystal Eastman, Dora Russell and Stella Browne, along with an effort to combine the idea of self-determination with a wider social project. Self-determination appears in connection with what we would now call reproductive rights and runs parallel with the idea of direct democracy – 'workers' control' (Cook 1978; Russell 1975; Rowbotham 1977). Control over one's body and workers' direct action thus run in tandem, like the proverbial bicycle made for two. This anti-authoritarian socialist feminist politics was to have an increasingly bumpy ride during the Depression and the rise of fascism and Stalinism.

When the women's liberation movement emerged again, feminist historians were to rediscover many lost and buried strands in the history of women's emancipation – co-operators such as Anna Wheeler, radical feminists like Elizabeth Cady Stanton, campaigners who had struggled to define women's emancipatory needs in terms of race and class, along with the early socialist feminists who sought to link the body to labour power. This history was, of course, to extend far beyond the USA and Europe

(Johnson-Odim and Strobel 1992; French and James 1997). Feminist historians have shown how movements against colonialism in the nineteenth and twentieth centuries have raised in very different contexts the connection between the self-determination of the individual and the imagined collectivity of the nation. Radha Kumar makes this observation of Indian women in the Nationalist movement in the early twentieth century: 'Not only did they link women's rights with nationalism, they used nationalist arguments to defend demands for women's rights to equality with men.'[7] In Urmila Debi's phrase *swadhinata* meant 'the strength and power to fulfil ourselves' (quoted in Kumar 1993: 66).

The idea of the 'nation' could thus be a means of linking individual self-development and a collective project of emancipation. Nationalist women opposing imperialism, like the women of the French 1848 Revolution, had combined women's self-expression with association. Like them, too, however, women in movements for national liberation in many parts of the world were to experience strong pressures to subordinate their individual self-fulfilment and capacity to determine their own destinies to a collective goal defined by men (Jayawardena 1986, 1995; Kandiyoti 1991; Ward 1982, 1997).

The women's liberation movements that began to emerge in the late 1960s grew out of a new radicalism in which, once again, there was a convergence of self- and social emancipation. Moreover, a crucial factor was again a movement for racial equality and liberation in the USA in first civil rights and then Black Power. Both, in differing ways, created a political language that combined personal and collective liberation. Cultural and psychological attitudes were contested along with economic inequality and political rights. The processes of imposing power through control over space or, less tangibly, through definitions, assumptions and starting points were brought onto the agenda of practical politics.

In the USA many of the early women's liberation groups had a broad and inclusive scope in the early 1970s. Along with predictable issues such as equality at work, abortion rights and nurseries, they were also supporting tenants' struggles, welfare rights marchers, low-paid hospital workers' strikes and unionization drives (Baxandall and Gordon 2000: 13–16, 261–81). Similarly, in Britain in the 1970s feminist concerns included housing, prices, the democratization of public health care, the conditions of women in prison and of prisoners' wives, and family allowances (child benefit), along with support for strikes for equal pay and union recognition.

The women's liberation movement of the 1970s was to be erroneously characterized as preoccupied only with 'equality'. In fact, as in the past, aspirations for equality interacted with assumptions of women's 'difference' – for example, women were often assumed to carry alternative caring and co-operative values. Moreover, running parallel with both was a wider vision of social transformation and a commitment to personal change through activity within the movement. The feminist emphasis upon autonomous self-determination thus carried with it an aspiration to new forms of association, different kinds of collectivity that extended beyond specific gender interest (Rowbotham 1990).

In the British context it is possible to see a historic turning point by 1976. With manufacturing in decline and global financial markets beginning to exert a more pervasive influence, the International Monetary Fund exerted pressure for cuts in the public sector when the Labour government applied for a loan. The IMF loan resulted in cuts in state welfare and a much harsher political climate in relation to class and race. In this situation the women's liberation movement was to be reluctantly forced on to the defensive, and notions of a wider social transformation became harder to sustain even before the advent of Margaret Thatcher's right-wing government in 1979 (Rowbotham 1997: 398–433).

During the 1980s feminists mounted a desperate rearguard action to maintain access to social consumption. Faced with 'Thatcherism' (welfare cuts and privatization of public services), many grassroots campaigners shifted to the institutional channels of local government, where left Labour local authorities were struggling to complement and even extend the social provision that was being assailed by the Conservatives. The scope of 'feminism' was to be expanded in certain ways by the newly created 'women's committees' established by local authorities from the early 1980s. The pioneering Greater London Council's women's committee took on, for example, the design of the built environment, the provision of public transport, women's access to leisure facilities, nurseries, payment by the state to carers, cash payment for child care to council employees, grants to pay advocates for non-English-speaking pregnant women in the National Health Service, centres for child-minders, women's training, the conditions of home-workers, low-paid women, and research through women's employment centres (Rowbotham 1997: 470–505; Mackintosh and Wainwright 1987).

However, these interesting extensions of the livelihood aspect of feminism tended to shed the self-defining aspect of feminism. Domestic violence did pass into local authority feminism, but in the course of becoming a funding category the victimization of battered women rather than the earlier emphasis on empowerment came to the fore. Moreover, the early 1980s saw a pessimistic tendency gain ascendancy in the British feminist movement, which focused exclusively on power relations between men and women and regarded other concerns as diversionary. The exceptions to this narrower definition of feminism was to be the mobilization against nuclear bases and the organization of women of South Asian and Afro-Caribbean descent, which connected to anti-racist campaigns and resistance to immigration controls. Both forms of activism retained a wider perspective of social change. Nevertheless, as the 1980s drew to a close it was not clear whether a women's movement in any co-ordinated sense could still be said to exist in Britain, although groups providing services, particularly around violence, continued and a feminist awareness had reached many women through the media.

There was, however, to be an extraordinary movement of working-class women around their livelihood in this decade. The massive mobilization around the miners' strike of 1984–85 led to the formation of women's groups that interacted with feminists, including the peace demonstrators. Attempts to keep these going after the strike did not succeed, although a nucleus went on to link to women married to striking print-workers and seafarers and in the 1990s to Women of the Waterfront during the dockers' strike. These groups, formed in response to economic restructuring in defence of the needs of their families, were initially protesting against capital making their customary role impossible. Although they led to the empowerment and self-development also of individuals, they were always distinct from 'feminism'. Their existence has provoked many questions about how to understand 'women's movements'.

In the 1980s and 1990s in Britain and the USA the question of livelihood became more important for the growing numbers of women (including many women of colour) below the poverty line. In the USA this has resulted in a range of grassroots movements around housing, health, environmental dumping and low pay, which have involved significant numbers of women.[8] In Britain women's action around survival has been much less documented. However, working-class women have, for example, formed credit groups, run soup kitchens, sorted out welfare rights problems, protested over solvent abuse and drugs, and participated in tenants' struggles and campaigns around schooling. This kind of action is likely to be defined as voluntary work. It exists in a space apart from politics and bears no relation to what is popularly accepted as 'feminism' in the media, which tends now to mean women's career concerns or personal lifestyles.

The contrast is obvious with countries where the possibility of wider social change persisted into the 1990s, such as South Africa or Brazil. Indeed, in several Latin American countries an interaction between what has variously been called 'working class feminism' or 'popular feminism', focusing on empowerment and livelihood and forms of feminism that have emphasized issues of sexual identity and reproductive rights, was to continue – albeit not without conflict.[9] This important difference in the history of women's movements, along with the concentration of resources and communicative power in the USA, Europe and other rich countries, contributed to a division between 'Western' and 'Third World' feminism.

But this obscured the fact that there have been differing traditions of feminism in both the North and the South, as well as social divisions between differing groups of women historically and in the present. It also eradicated the action of poor women in the rich countries.

When Swasti Mitter and I were gathering contributions for a book on new forms of workplace organizing we called *Dignity and Daily Bread* (Rowbotham and Mitter 1994), we consciously sought to overcome this division. Over the last decade I have tried to learn about the movements around livelihood that have been appearing in so many different guises as well as trying to follow the fortunes of feminism internationally. The trickle of books has increased now, and it is hard to keep up and to span the globe.

There is, however, talk of counter-hegemonic globalization, and it seems evident to me that the ingenious forms of resistance and survival devised by millions of poor women in many lands must be recognized as a vital part of any new emancipatory project. Recognizing that women have been moved to act for broadly emancipatory aims from very different starting points historically and in the present enables us to look at movements within their own terms, rather than imposing a checklist of ideal demands upon them. In order to understand the confusing present we are living within, it is vital that we develop means of distinguishing differing kinds of rebellion that are also capable of catching the dynamic ways in which consciousness interacts and develops.

A crucial question is how ideas of individual rights, self-determination and self-fulfilment that have featured in differing contexts in the history of feminism might connect again to global livelihood movements against capitalism, reconnecting the self and the social again. It is equally important to glean the visions of association and democracy developed within these, and in many other contexts in which women have mobilized for peace or against dictatorship.

Looking backwards can reveal some unexpected kinds of illumination and, by making us aware of forgotten interconnections, shift the dimensions of how emancipation can be conceived. And for the future there is a pressing need to comprehend the sources of discontent that will trigger off forms of rebellion from which might come new definitions and contexts of human emancipation.

Notes

1. 'The women of Paris respond to the delaying tactics of the National Convention', in Levy et al. 1979. On the role of women in the crowd see also Olwen H. Hufton, 'Women and politics', in Hufton 1992; Tilly 1997; Levy and Applewhite 1980; Rendall 1985.

2. On 'emancipation' see Rancière 1989.

3. On women and personal, social and political radicalism in France in the 1840s see Anderson 2000; Rendall 1985; Goldberg Moses 1984; Scott 1988; Rowbotham 1998.

4. Jeanne Deroin and Pauline Roland (1851) in Bell and Offen 1983.

5. On these early debates in the USA, France and Britain see Rowbotham 1992: 59–63, 67–70, 144–53.

6. See Graves 1994; Scott 1998; Mink 1995; Ladd-Taylor 1994; Goodwin 1997. In relation to African-American women, see Knupfer 1996.

7. Kumar 1993: 66. On Indian nationalism, see Sangari and Vaid 1990 and Sinha 1996.

8. See Rowbotham 1997: 483–5, 539, 577–81; Kaplan 1997: 15–124; Naples 1998a, 1998b. On the uneasy relation of African-American women to feminism see also Jackson 1998. On workplace and community struggles that have included low-paid women see Ross 1997 and Milkman 2000.

9. See Basu 1995. On South Africa and Latin America see Kaplan 1997: 125–78; Stephen 1997; Jelin 1990; Alvarez et al. 1998.

Bibliography

Alvarez, Sonia E., Evelina Dagnino and Arturo Escobar (eds) (1998) *Cultures of Politics, Politics of Cultures: Re-visioning Latin American Social Movements*, Boulder, CO: Westview Press, HarperCollins.

Anderson, Bonnie J. (2000) *Joyous Greetings: The First International Women's Movement, 1830–1860*, New York: Oxford University Press.

Basu, Amrita (1995) T*he Challenge of Local Feminism: Women's Movements in Global Perspective*, Boulder, CO: Westview Press.

Baxandall, Rosalyn and Linda Gordon (2000) *Dear Sisters: Despatches from the Women's Liberation Movement*, New York: Basic Books.

Bell, Susan Groag and Karen M. Offen (eds) (1983) *Women, the Family and Freedom: The Debate in Documents. Vol. 1, 1750–1880*, Stanford, CA: Stanford University Press.

Cook, Blanche Wiesen (1978) *Crystal Eastman on Women and Revolution*, New York: Oxford University Press.

Diamond, M. J. (1998) 'Olympe de Gouges and the French Revolution: the construction of gender as critique', in M. J. Diamond (ed.), *Women and Revolution: Global Expressions*, Dordrecht and London: Kluwer Academic Publishers.

Evans, Richard (1987) *Comrades and Sisters: Feminism, Socialism and Pacifism in Europe 1870–1945*, Brighton: Wheatsheaf.

French, John D. and Daniel James (1997) *The Gendered Worlds of Latin American Women Workers: From Household and Factory to the Union Hall and Ballot Box*, Durham, NC: Duke University Press.

Goldberg Moses, Claire (1984) *French Feminism in the Nineteenth Century*, Albany, NY: State University of New York.

Goldsmith, Anthony (1974) 'Introduction to Gustave Flaubert', in Gustave Flaubert, *Sentimental Education*, London: J.M. Dent.

Goodwin, Joanne, L. (1997) *Gender and the Politics of Welfare Reform: Mothers' Pensions in Chicago, 1911–1929*, Chicago: University of Chicago Press.

Graves, Pamela (1994) *Labour Women: Women in British Working-Class Politics, 1918–1939*, Cambridge: Cambridge University Press.

Hannam, June (1989) *Isabella Ford*, Oxford: Basil Blackwell.

Hilden, Patricia (1986) *Working Women and Socialist Politics in France, 1890–1914: A Regional Study*, Oxford: Clarendon Press.

Hufton, Olwen H. (ed.) (1992) *Women and the Limits of Citizenship in the French Revolution*, Toronto: University of Toronto Press.

Hunt, Karen (1996) *Equivocal Feminists: The Social Democratic Federation and the Women Question 1884–1911*, Cambridge: Cambridge University Press.

Jackson, Shirley A. (1998) 'Something about the word': African American women and feminism, in Kathleen M. Blee (ed.), *No Middle Ground: Women and Radical Protest*, New York: New York University Press.

Jayawardena, Kumari (1986) *Feminism and Nationalism in the Third World*, London: Zed Books.

— (1995) *The White Woman's Other Burden: Western Women and South Asia During British Colonial Rule*, New York: Routledge.

Jelin, Elizabeth (ed.) (1990) *Women and Social Change in Latin America*, London: Zed Books.

Johnson-Odim, Cheryl and Margaret Strobel (eds) (1992) *Expanding the Boundaries of Women's History: Essays on Women in the Third Word*, Bloomington: Indiana University Press.

Kandiyoti, Deniz (ed.) (1991) *Women, Islam and the State*, London: Macmillan.

Kaplan, Temma (1997) *Crazy for Democracy: Women in Grassroots Movements*, London: Routledge.

Knupfer, Anne Meis (1996) *Toward a Tenderer Humanity and a Nobler Womanhood: African American Women's Clubs in Turn-of-the-Century Chicago*, New York: New York University Press.

Kumar, Radha (1993) *The History of Doing: An Illustrated Account of Movements for Women's Rights and Feminism in India, 1800–1990*, Delhi: Kali and London: Verso.

Ladd-Taylor, Molly (1994) *Mother-Work: Women, Child Welfare and the State, 1890–1930*, Urbana: University of Illinois Press.

Levy, Darline Gay, Harriet Branson Applewhite and Mary Durham Johnson (eds) (1979) *Women in Revolutionary Paris, 1789–1795*, Urbana, Chicago: University of Illinois Press, pp. 92–3.

Levy, Darline Gay and Harriet Branson Applewhite (1988) 'Women of the popular classes in revolutionary Paris, 1789–1795', in Carol R. Berkin and Clara M. Lovett (eds), *Women, War and Revolution*, New York: Holmes and Meier.

Milkman, Ruth (ed.) (2000) *Organizing Immigrants: The Challenge of Unions in Contemporary California*, Ithaca, NY: ILR Press.

Mink, Gwendolyn (1995) *The Wages of Motherhood: Inequality in the Welfare State, 1917–1942*, Ithaca, NY: Cornell University Press.

Naples, Nancy A. (1998a) *Grassroots Warriors: Activist Mothering, Community Work, and the War on Poverty*, New York: Routledge.

— (ed.) (1998b) *Community Activism and Feminist Politics: Organizing Across Race, Class and Gender*, New York: Routledge.

Offen, Karen (1988) 'Defining feminism: comparative historical approach', *Signs: A Journal of Women in Culture and Society*, 4(11).

— (2000) *European Feminisms, 1700–1950: A Political History*, Stanford, CA: Stanford University Press.

Pankhurst, Richard (1991) *William Thompson (1795–1833): Pioneer Socialist*, London: Pluto.

Rancière, Jacques (1989) 'L'émancipation et son dilemme', in Michelle Perrot (ed.), *Silence, Emancipation des Femmes entre Privé et Public*, Les Cahiers du CEDREF, La Révue des Etudes Féministes à l'Université Paris VII, CEDREF UFR, Sciences Sociales, Paris.

Rendall, Jane (1985) *The Origins of Modern Feminism: Women in Britain, France and the United States, 1780–1860*, London: Macmillan.

Ross, Andrew (1997) *No Sweat: Fashion, Free Trade and the Rights of Garment Workers*, New York: Verso.

Rowbotham, Sheila (1977) *A New World for Women: Stella Browne, Socialist Feminist*, London: Pluto.

— (1987) 'Our health in whose hands? Health emergencies and the struggle for better health care in London', in Maureen Mackintosh and Hilary Wainwright (eds), *A Taste of Power: The Politics of Local Economics*, London: Verso, pp. 326–69.

— (1990) *The Past is Before Us: Feminism in Action Since the 1960s*, London: Pandora.

— (1992) *Women in Movement: Feminism and Social Action*, New York: Routledge.

— (1997) *A Century of Women: The History of Women in Britain and the United States*, London: Penguin.

— (1998) 'Dear Dr Marx: a letter from a socialist feminist', in Leo Panitch and Colin Leys (eds), *The Communist Manifesto Now, Socialist Register 1998*, Suffolk: Merlin Press.

Rowbotham, Sheila and Swasti Mitter (1994) *Dignity and Daily Bread: New Forms of Economic Organising among Poor Women in the Third World and the First*, London: Routledge.

Russell, Dora (1975) *The Tamarisk Tree: My Quest for Liberty and Love*, London: Alex Pemberton.

Scott, Gillian (1998) *Feminism and the Politics of Working Women: The Women's Co-operative Guild, 1880s to the Second World War*, London: UCL Press.

Scott, Joan Wallach (1988) 'Work identities for men and women: the politics of work and the family in the Parisian garment trades in 1848', in Joan Wallach Scott (ed.), *Gender and the Politics of History*. New York: Columbia University Press.

— (1989 'French feminists and the rights of "man": Olympe de Gouges' Declaration', *History Workshop*, 28 (Autumn).

Sinha, Mrinalini (1996) 'Locating the Indian woman', in Joan Wallach Scott (ed.), *Feminism and History*, Oxford: Oxford University Press.

Stephen, Lynn (1997) *Women and Social Movements in Latin America: Power from Below*, Austin: University of Texas Press.

Taylor, Barbara (1983) *Eve and the New Jerusalem: Socialism and Feminism in the Nineteenth Century*, Virago: London.

Thompson, Dorothy (1993) 'Women and nineteenth-century radical politics: a lost dimension', in Dorothy Thompson (ed.), *Outsiders: Class, Gender and the Nation*, London: Verso.

Tilly, Louise A. (1977) 'Women and collective action in Europe', in Dorothy G. McGuigan, *The Role of Women In Conflict and Peace*, Ann Arbor: University of Michigan.

Ward, Margaret (1982) *Unmanageable Revolutionaries: Women and Irish Nationalism*, London: Pluto.

— (1997) *Hanna Sheehy Skeffington: A Life*, Cork: Attic Press.

Wellman, Judith (1995) 'The Seneca Falls Women's Rights Convention: a study of social networks', in Linda K. Kerber and Jane Sherron De Hart (eds), W*omen's America: Refocusing the Past*, New York: Oxford University Press.

3

Uncommon Women and the Common Good: Women and Environmental Protest

Temma Kaplan

In the spring of 2000, a movement of African American women, calling themselves Mothers Organized to Stop Environmental Sins (MOSES), took off from Winona, Texas to march from one contaminated community to another across the USA. Linking their struggle for survival to other such campaigns, the women of Winona were demanding reparations for what they had suffered and 'declaring environmental injustice a human rights abuse which must be addressed'.[1] They reported their activities to a clearing house, a loosely bonded organization called the Center for Health, Environment and Justice, made up of over eight thousand grassroots organizations in small towns and big cities all over the USA. Their activities resonated with other mobilizations ordinary women and men were pursuing throughout the world.

Although men lead many of the non-governmental organizations (NGOs) devoted to environmental causes, women have provided the mass base and leadership for the groups that have favoured direct action and civil disobedience. Women around the world have overcome quietism and have begun to confront environmental disasters and pollution, not as acts of nature but as the results of the way profits and military priorities have interfered with the common good. Performing in their capacity as home-makers and mothers in pursuit of the health and safety of their families and communities, women of all classes have alerted the public to the dangers of nuclear testing, and have insisted on the removal of pollutants from water, air and land. They have fought to preserve forests on which they depend and to plant new ones where serious erosion has occurred. Women have demanded removal from former homes that have become so contaminated that they endanger the health of all those who live there. Such women call for 'justice', by which those engaged in environmental struggles mean that governments will place human need above private profit and government expediency. Frequently these women have viewed themselves as doing just what they were raised to do – sustaining human life.

The same stereotypes that link women to nature and impede the advancement of women as individuals and as citizens sometimes provide women acting as mothers with additional rights. Paradoxically, by accepting and exploiting the contradictions of collective identities as mothers, grassroots women activists frequently gain legitimacy as women and as citizens. Exploring how motherhood has become linked to the public good raises questions about the way concepts such as 'human rights' have been developing outside the legal community.

Many non-feminist women legitimate their activities in pursuit of the common good by identifying themselves as mothers. In most contemporary cultures, that means they are responsible for preserving the health of their children, for which they depend on a safe environment. If that environment begins hurting their children, many of the women will act. As Barbara Quimby, one of the housewives who helped lead a major environmental movement in the USA, says, when you know there is a threat, 'you've got to get your kids out'.[2] When these women's initial efforts to sustain their families and communities make them conscious of more complicated reasons for why toxic wastes are being dumped near them, or why the forests upon which they depend are being sold to the highest bidder, women acting as mothers sometimes use their gender privileges to secure greater benefits.

By 'gender privileges' I mean the behaviour women who accept the division of labour by sex in their culture and historical period are allowed to exercise. If they have the obligation, as mothers do in many societies, to feed, clothe, house and nurture their families and communities, they also have the rights those obligations entail.[3]

Crises such as the death or grave illness of a child, a chemical or nuclear accident, or the widespread incidence of miscarriages sometimes galvanize women who enter movements in their capacity as mothers. That role legitimates their confrontation with public officials or managers of private enterprises. Almost every culture has some saying about what a mother can do when her child is endangered. When she behaves in extraordinary ways by expressing her anger not at the fates but at managers of multinational corporations or at government bureaucrats, she can usually be excused as an 'emotional' or 'hysterical' woman. These stereotypes, which resonate in most cultures, provide a separate space from which groups of women can mobilize outside ordinary political channels.

As such women grow over periods of protracted struggle, they can develop political strategies that are both shrewd and manipulative. Even as they figure out which corporations and government officials control a given situation, the women continue to represent themselves before journalists or television cameras as simple wives and mothers. That strategy often gives poor working-class or rural women a safer identity than they would have in demanding their rights as workers or citizens. Posing their own commitments to their family's welfare against profits, women all over the world have assumed the leadership of grassroots movements to protect the environment and to call for justice.

However limited concerns about public welfare have always been under global capitalism, the extension of the market economy to virtually every remote atoll or mountain village has revealed the ties governments have to multinational corporations. Neoliberalism, the most recent form of global capitalism, has confronted notions of the public good with plans for privatization of all productive resources.[4] Unconstrained by respect for human life, governments and corporations have often had to face the wrath of women insistent on the preservation of the health and safety of their families and communities.

Ordinary women organized into grassroots movements have increasingly confronted authorities demanding an end to deforestation or the removal of the dangerous waste products left by war, industry and daily life. These women's movements claim democratic control over resource allocations. Initially without predetermined goals, these women's environmental movements frequently challenge rights of private property and sovereignty.

These are far from being the first campaigns in which poor, rural or working-class women have engaged: environmental struggles taken up by women have a very long history. And the strategies of blocking roads, shaming men and turning traditional rituals of kinship on their heads have also been intrinsic to women's collective action when the environment is threatened. Gradually realizing that even so-called natural disasters, such as floods and climatological changes, may result from human greed, even poorly educated women who previously lacked faith in their own judgement have pitted their own rationality against that of those who seem unwilling or unable to solve the problems that endanger the women's communities.

From the Himalaya mountains of India to the tributaries of the Niagara river on the American side of Niagara Falls, to rural North Carolina, women have engaged in movements to protect or improve the quality of life of their families and friends, and in the process have raised questions about the economic, social and political priorities of their governments. These three specific campaigns only exemplify countless others, such as the Greenbelt Movement led by Wangari Maathai in Kenya, in which women have planted trees to stop erosion, and have then gone on to fight for democratic reforms; demonstrations in Poland, where women have alerted the people to the dangers of incinerating toxic waste; meetings of groups such as Women in Europe for a Common Future; and activities in Kazakhstan, where women have confronted the tragic results of open-air testing of atomic weapons.[5] Claiming in different languages and phrases to defend human life against government expediency, each movement challenges the priorities of governments that have maximized profits no matter what the human costs.

Beginning in the 1970s and continuing in some form into the twenty-first century, women who had never before assumed leadership of a social movement took action. Campaigns emerged in Latin America and South Africa,[6] where people in squatter communities and in the townships lack basic resources such as decent housing, with running water, sewerage, garbage collection and electricity. In the countryside in Asia and Africa, where women must travel up to fifteen miles a day to collect fuel and water, the environmental issues take different forms.[7] And among the Ogoni people in southeastern Nigeria, where the government-supported oil companies have destroyed the land, polluted the air and executed environmental activist Ken Saro-Wiwa, women constitute a mass movement to reclaim the land and fight for human dignity and self-determination.[8]

Chipko: Embracing One's Rights

Examination of three diverse environmental movements in which large numbers of women engage should help explain how certain fundamental beliefs in the legitimacy to speak and act as mothers galvanizes action; and how ordinary women develop the strength to denounce corporations and governments in the name of public welfare, placing social need above the claims of private property.

The connection between women and the environment has been well established in many cultures and historical periods. In Europe, women and children sent to guard the sheep or the pigs or the cows or to gather firewood were particularly dependent upon access to common land. As governments began selling off such land to private capitalists from the seventeenth through the nineteenth centuries, local people frequently rebelled. From the Rebecca Riots in Wales to the Demoiselles of France to the María das Fontes uprisings in Portugal, men dressed as women and sometimes women themselves defended the rights of the community against the interests of private property that diminished their opportunities for survival.[9]

More recently, the American Rachel Carson in *Silent Spring* called attention to the harm caused by DDT and other pesticides to wildlife, particularly birds. And Women's Strike for Peace, a group of women community activists from the USA, allied with women throughout Europe and Asia, called upon world leaders to end open-air nuclear testing in the 1950s and early 1960s because radiation had spread Strontium 90, a by-product of nuclear fission, to the breast-milk of nursing mothers and to the bones of their children (Carson 1962; Swerdlow 1993). According to a contemporary group, the Women's Environmental and Development Organization (WEDO, founded by a former member of Women's Strike for Peace, former Congresswoman Bella Abzug), the situation has only become worse. The breast-milk of women from Guatemala to Zimbabwe and from Alaska to Japan is contaminated with DDT and other pesticides far in excess of permissible levels (WEDO 1999).

One of the pathbreaking cases in which women seized the initiative in an environmental uprising was that of the Chipko movement, which began in 1973 high in the Himalaya mountains. For some time, the government had auctioned rights to cut down trees including the first-growth Himalaya (Banj) oak, the sturdy and pliable ash trees and the birch, replacing them with Chir pine, which burned too quickly to be useful for local households. And, whereas the leaves of the oak and birch formed a mulch in which grasses and bushes grew, the pine needles prevented vegetation from growing on the forest floor. Instead of the mulch and plants, which acted as sponges for the heavy rains of the monsoon, the pine needles provided a slippery watercourse or simply flowed along with mud. Landslides, which became increasingly prevalent, eroded the mountainside and led to des-tructive floods that got worse and worse. Activists such as Gandhi's disciple Mirabehn (the British-born Madeline Slade) had been arguing since the early 1950s about the need to replant birch, ash and oak. Local women, who depended on the forest for fuel and cattle fodder, found that they had to go further and further, sometimes even up steep slopes as far away as 15 kilometres from home, in order to secure the kind of slow-burning wood necessary to heat food and water and to warm their families.[10]

To the consternation of local people in Gopeshwar in the Chamoli district high in the Himalaya, in March 1973 the Forest Department auctioned off ash trees, highly prized for agricultural tools, to a sports goods manufacturer with connections to Sweden. Public meetings of men followed. At one, a disgruntled elder stood up to recall that 'When a leopard attacks a child the mother takes his onslaughts on her own body' (quoted in Weber 1988: 40), which some have suggested as one possible origin of the strategy of hugging trees, *Chipko*, to prevent their felling. As the workmen went to cut down the ash trees at the end of April 1973, they met a crowd of one hundred people. Although the company had paid in advance to cut down the trees, they couldn't risk confronting the crowd. Months later, attempting to trick the local men into letting the axe-wielders in, the government spread news that there was to be a film showing about twelve kilometres away from the village on 22 December. There was no film. But when the men returned home, five trees had already been cut down. The men guarded the trees so no more would fall to the axe (ibid.: 41–3).

A disciple of Mirabehn, Sunderla Bahuguna, travelled around the mountains, spreading the word about the need to maintain the forests and to distribute their bounty more equitably. Numerous landslides provided evidence for his arguments. The Communist Party of India also entered the fray, as did Chandi Prasad Bhatt, another activist who had been promoting resistance elsewhere in the mountains. The government announced that another forest, above the village of Reni, near the border with Tibet, would be auctioned in January 1974. As Bhatt addressed the villagers, the men said that they had already been paid to cut down 2,451 marked trees (ibid.: 44). Local women, whom no one consulted, seemed to have been listening, especially to the discussion of the tactic of 'hugging the trees'. When the government again distracted the local men on 26 March 1974, by offering to give them reparations for land the army had confiscated and to reimburse them for diminished commercial revenues at the time of the Chinese invasion, the men took the bait (ibid.: 45).[11]

In the men's absence, the woodcutters appeared. A child notified the local women, of whom Gaura Devi, a widow in her fifties, was the leader. Twenty-seven women and children confronted the workers. The men tried to cajole Devi and the other women, and then to have Devi arrested (Kumar 1993: 184–5). One of the men allegedly tried to scare the women away by making sexual threats and waving a gun. Devi told him he would have to shoot her to get to the trees. According to the historian Thomas Weber, 'She compared the forest with her mother's home. Most of the labourers were also from the hill regions and their shame at having to fight with women and their instinctive understanding of the problems Gaura Devi was explaining to them helped them to decide to withdraw' (Weber 1988: 45). Following the victory the women set up a cooperative society, which guarded the forest and supervised local use of the woods and the fields (ibid.: 97–8; Kumar 1993: 183).

Sunderlal Bahunguna set the standard that women's groups followed, by travelling to villages throughout the Himalayas calling for a moratorium on cutting trees, limiting the amount of resin that could be removed, and calling for higher wages for workers in forestry industries (Weber 1988: 46, 51). Elsewhere in the mountains the cutting continued.

In 1977, when hundreds of trees in two forests were sold, women who attacked the proceedings were arrested, and spent two weeks in jail. On 5 December 1977, a few weeks before the scheduled tree-cutting, women imitated a ceremony by which sisters show their love for their brothers by

tying thread around their wrists. The women gently put their thread around
the trees (ibid.: 52). They explained to those around them that without the
trees, they could not support their families. When an official accused them
of being too stupid to realize that trees bring commercial wealth, the
women countered by saying 'What do the forests bear? Soil, water and
pure air! Soil, water and pure air are the very basis of life!' When the
lumber company, supported by local police, tried to enter the forest, a local
woman protestor embraced a tree (ibid.: 53). Despite bad flooding in mid-
1978, the government permitted nearly one thousand trees to be auctioned
in the region of Tehri Garhwal. In 1930, an early environmental struggle
had resulted in several deaths in the village of Tilari. But villagers established their control over the forests (Kumar 1993: 183). Nearly fifty years
later, women took the lead in protecting access to the forests. In 1978, after
about two hundred women tied their silken threads around their brother
trees, thousands of men and women came from 50 villages throughout the
region, and saved the forest (Weber 1988: 54).

At another forest, where more than 2,300 trees were targeted for felling,
women taunted the workers: 'Oh brother-in-law, how brave you are that
you lift your axe to trees hugged by your sisters-in-law' (ibid.: 55). And
when the men of another mountain village wanted to accept a government
bribe of a road, employment, a clinic, a secondary school and electrification
in exchange for planting a potato seed farm where the forest stood, the
women were outraged. Since under the new circumstances the women
would have had to travel seven instead of two kilometres to get wood, they
refused. And when the men threatened the women on 9 February 1980,
the women stood their ground. The government ratified the women's
choice nine days later. Shortly afterwards, Indira Gandhi banned cutting
trees in that province for 15 years. So successful were the demonstrations
and what they achieved that the Chipko movement has found imitators all
over India, from as far away as Vindhyas in central India, Bijar to the east
and Rajasthan to the west.[12]

The empowerment of the women in the Chipko movement developed
out of their acceptance of the division of labour by sex in their culture,
but also on their insistence on their rights to fulfil their obligations to
protect their loved ones. They used gender privileges to shame the woodcutters and the authorities. Although denigrated by their opponents – and
sometimes by their allies – as being backward and conservative, the women
of Chipko persevered. The women would not have assumed the authority
that they did had they not felt legitimate in their demands. Since they
were the ones responsible for gathering wood and water, they knew the
importance of the forest and the need to have it as close by as possible.
They also understood the problems of erosion. Once the struggles

transcended women's own families and incorporated outsiders, the legitimacy of the women's struggles for their own children became even more apparent.

The Chipko movement also demonstrates the way women sometimes embrace stereotypes about themselves – as dutiful and loving sisters, who tie silken thread around their brothers' wrists or as courageous mothers, willing to risk harming themselves to save the trees upon which their children's lives depend. By challenging the outsiders sent to cut down the forests, the women placed social need above private profits. They assumed responsibility for which they had been socialized. Adapting individual feminine characteristics to social struggle has become an important strategical move women all over the world have adapted. Another common characteristic demonstrated in the Chipko movement is that of attacking the masculinity of the workmen and authorities sent to cut down the trees. The recourse to gender stereotypes should be seen not as a reactionary move, but as one showing the ways in which even previously apolitical women have learned to maximize public resources. By shaming the woodcutters, the authorities and their own husbands, the women of Chipko asserted certain cultural views about the special responsibilities of mothers – and sisters – not only to maintain their own families, but to enhance the common good.

Social Justice and Environment

The manipulation of gender stereotypes and their reversals in pursuit of public welfare has been as common in struggles against the pollution caused by industry and the military in the Northern hemisphere as in the South. By stepping into areas of conflict, as the women of Chipko did, women face not only attacks for being activists but ridicule for being 'ignorant' or 'hysterical'. Authorities accustomed to women's deference are outraged when women presume to accuse them of inadequate responses to medical emergencies.

In 1978, a young home-maker named Lois Gibbs who lived in Love Canal, a neighbourhood near Niagara Falls outside Buffalo, New York, began to worry about her son. Once he started school, he developed asthma and began having convulsions, which the doctors thought might be epilepsy. She went to the principal and tried to get him into a different school. When her requests were denied, she began to speak to neighbours. In her informal conversations, she discovered a litany of troubles ranging from respiratory diseases to skin irritations to childhood arthritis to sterility and frequent miscarriages. About 40 per cent of all pregnancies in Love Canal resulted in low birth weight, retardation or deformity; one woman in four could expect a miscarriage.[13] Moreover, Gibbs's neighbours told stories of tar-like sludge coming from their basements and of barrel rims emerging in their gardens.[14]

The city authorities and then the state officials responded to Gibbs and her neighbours in similar ways: they charged them with being 'hysterical' and accused them of misunderstanding the scientific evidence. What the women who called themselves housewives did understand was that their predictable upper working-class world, where they owned their own homes and looked forward to paying off their mortgages by the time they were in their thirties, had turned into a horror show. With the help of medical experts from the nearby State University of New York at Buffalo, the homeowners managed to discover that their housing development and the school were built over a toxic waste dump. The Hooker Chemical Company (now Occidental Chemicals) a subsidiary of Occidental Petroleum, and perhaps even the U.S. Army had dumped chemical wastes with strong components of chlorine into an abandoned canal for decades. When they had exhausted the space, they covered over approximately 20 tonnes of toxic residue in the canal. The company deeded the property to the city of Niagara for one dollar. The city built a school on the land, which, in turn, improved real estate values. Developers constructed working-class houses above the dump.

Chlorine, a widely used household chemical, is a part of most cleansers and some washing detergents since it whitens clothes and appliances. It is also the chemical basic to the formation of plastics, especially polyvinyl chloride products (PVC), and to preparing wood pulp to make paper and then to whiten that paper. Unfortunately, when chlorine interacts with organic material under heat, it forms dioxin, which some believe mimics certain hormones in the body.[15] The dioxin, a basic component in Agent Orange, the defoliant the USA used in Vietnam, is highly toxic and nearly impossible to destroy. Believed to be a powerful carcinogen, dioxin causes epilepsy, neurological damage, miscarriages, reduced sperm count, and chromosomal damage resulting in birth defects, as dioxin apparently did around Love Canal.

During the time it took to discover that dioxin (about which very few people knew anything) had formed when the chlorine mixed with underground streams that surrounded the original canal, local people formed Love Canal Homeowners' Association. With the women leaders presenting themselves as traditional mothers attempting to save their children, local women hesitantly began to take action. 'Radicals and students carry signs, but not average housewives. Housewives have to care for their children and their homes', as Lois Gibbs explained later (Gibbs 1982: 92).

As the women sought help from doctors and public officials, they managed to get some press coverage. They quickly realized that they had to be seen in order to be heard, and that their only hope of improving the situation was to cast themselves in familiar roles. Essentially they had two theatrical prototypes from which to choose: melodrama and situation comedy, and they used both over the two years it took to liberate themselves and their families from Love Canal. Gibbs and the others with whom she worked for four years, until they succeeded in getting the State of New York and the Federal Government of the United States to buy their homes from them so that they could move away, became the subjects of melodramas in which they starred. They used signs, skits and even what could be called guerrilla theatre as means by which to save their families.

Typical of the kinds of demonstrations they staged was one at the state capital in Albany. They prepared a mock coffin to demonstrate their plight, and one of the demonstrators began to sniffle with a cold as the police examined the coffin before admitting the demonstrators to the court house. Her colleagues immediately pretended that she was crying and rushed to comfort her. Presenting themselves as helpless became a key element in their repertoire even as the women became shrewd political actors.

When the government revealed in April 1979 that polychlorinated biphenyl (PCB) was concentrated in the ground at 176 per billion, the Homeowners did not at first understand its meaning. They turned to their allies at the university, who told them that PCB was a deadly chemical that originated in the USA to insulate transformers and other electrical equipment. Dyes, plastics and copying paper also use PCB. It is one of twelve pollutants, along with dioxin, that the United Nations has been trying to ban among the so-called 'deadly dozen' of persistent organic pollutants (POPs) (Brody 1998–99). It did not take long for the Love Canal Homeowners' Association to hold a rally complete with effigies of the governor and the head of the New York State Health Department. They began to chant: 'Thanks to New York State, death is our fate. We don't want to die – listen to our cry. We want out' (Gibbs 1982: 99; Levine 1982: 107). They then burned the figures of the authorities.

By dramatizing their anger and yet, at the same time, presenting themselves only as suffering women, they again won a good press. As they became more and more sophisticated, their efforts to escape the homes they could not afford to abandon became more extreme. Viewing themselves not as political actors but as desperate housewives, the Homeowners took hostage two officials who were supposed to explain the meaning of the chromosomal damage the local people had suffered. When the men showed up after a particularly harrowing weekend during which the Homeowners could get no answers, the women decided to hold the officials hostage. Seemingly unaware of how serious their behaviour might be, they called

President Jimmy Carter to demand that the government help them move
to safer homes. When, at the end of the day, the government agreed to do
something, the women released their prisoners. The two officials, relatively
sympathetic to the Homeowners' cause, kindly denied their ability to
identify their captors (Kaplan 1997: 33–6).

As Lois Gibbs recalled 20 years later in the pages of *Everyone's Backyard*, the quarterly for the Center for Health, Environment, and Justice
she had founded after the successful evacuation from Love Canal, 'Love
Canal was neither the first, nor the worst, toxic waste site identified in
1978. But it was the site that captured the media's attention, making it the
most famous' (Gibbs 1998: 4). Recognizing that the problem of pollution
went beyond Love Canal, and mindful of having developed strategies and
tactics that might work elsewhere, Lois Gibbs decided to launch an organization, at first called the Citizens' Clearinghouse for Hazardous Wastes,
which by 2000 helped co-ordinate the work of thousands of grassroots
organizations.

Fighting for Environmental Justice

The relationship between popular concepts of 'environment' and 'justice'
came together in the 1980s in the USA with the 'environmental justice'
movement that began in Warren County, North Carolina, when a group of
poor blacks resisted a government plan to put a toxic waste dump in their
district. What linked this largely Black working-class community in the
South to white working-class people in the North was the issue of PCB.

When the laws changed to prohibit the dumping of toxic wastes in city
dumps, a trucking company that had contracted to carry waste filled with
PCB from an electrical company in Raleigh, North Carolina, simply filled
tank trucks with the sludge and dribbled the toxic liquid over the back
roads of fourteen counties in North Carolina. For four years, the toxic
waste remained in the roadways, causing miscarriages, irritations and
allergies among those who lived along the roads. Without public debate,
the government secretly purchased land in Warren County, one of the
poorest, blackest counties in the state. Public hearings, scheduled to take
place when people would ignore them between Christmas and New Year,
attracted hundreds of local people, especially women who were afraid of
what the contaminated soil would do to their community.

Dollie Burwell, then a housewife and a legal secretary, who lived down
the road from the proposed dump, began talking to the ministers of the
local churches and to the women in the neighbourhood of the proposed
dump. In the rural South, black churches continue to provide a gathering
place for those concerned with the community, just as they did in the Civil

Rights movement of the 1950s and 1960s. Burwell also contacted the Southern Christian Leadership Council (SCLC), of which Dr Martin Luther King had been an early leader. And she called on her friend, Floyd McKissic, who directed the Congress of Racial Equality (CORE) and had led efforts to integrate the schools in North Carolina.

Then, taking their cue from the tactics of civil disobedience that the movement in the USA had borrowed from Gandhi, Burwell and her neighbours decided to block the roads, stalling the trucks carrying the tainted soil to the dump. On 26 September, 500 people, the majority of them women and children led by black ministers, knelt in the road, first to pray and then to chant, 'Don't spread that PCB on me'. Nearly three hundred people, among them Dollie Burwell, were arrested on the first day, the largest number ever arrested in an environmental demonstration. The crowds of women and young people returned the next day and the next, and managed to attract the cameras. One of the major national television networks had a reporter there when the police carried off the singing demonstrators, Dollie Burwell among them. Against the background of women singing 'We Shall Overcome', the reporter saw a young child crying. When he turned to Kim Burwell, Dollie's six-year-old daughter, she explained that she was crying for her people, and what she feared would happen to them as a result of having 20 tonnes of toxic waste dumped on them.

After three weeks, when interest in the demonstrations began to ebb, Dollie Burwell called on a black congressman, the Reverend Walter Fontroy, a long-time member of the SCLC, to join the demonstrators. He flew into the nearby county, and was rushing back to Washington, DC, where an important vote was to take place. Burwell persuaded him to join with the women and the ministers in prayer, arguing that he had diplomatic immunity from arrest. When the state police marched on the demonstrators, they did not believe the slightly built black man who claimed that he was a United States congressman. Not sex but race surprised the authorities in this case. While the women tried to get Fontroy released, the state troopers kept him in a metal hut for the better part of a hot September day in North Carolina. Livid, Fontroy returned to Washington and ordered a survey by the Government Accounting Office of the siting of toxic waste dumps. That report, along with one entitled, 'Toxic Wastes and Race: A National Report on the Racial and Socioeconomic Characteristics of Communities with Hazardous Wastes', issued in 1987, showed that one-third of all black, Latino and native Americans in the USA lives within 50 miles of a toxic waste dump. Another friend of Dollie Burwell, a man who had been harassed by the state police during an earlier demonstration, quipped that what they suffered was environmental racism. The trucks continued to roll in despite the demonstrators' cry for environmental justice, the watchword for a movement that began with the largely African American women of Warren County. Between 1995 and 1999, after the dump filled with water that threatened to leach the PCB into the groundwater, the organized citizens led by Dollie Burwell and the women of Warren County secured funds from the state of North Carolina to detoxify the dump.[16]

Redefining the Terms

The women of Chipko in India had considered blocking the roads that the woodcutters used to remove the timber, as the predominantly female demonstrators in Warren County had blocked the roads bringing the polluted soil to endanger them. Praying, as was done in the Civil Rights movement and then in the environmental justice movement in Warren County, was a way of contrasting a peaceful ceremony, calling for a higher good, with a more violent practice of bringing harm to people who had no other recourse except to put their own bodies on the line. The Homeowners of Love Canal could not prevent further harm; they had to get out of harm's way.

What characterized all three women's movements for environmental justice was the fact that, despite the differences, they could not delegate responsibility to political representatives, but had to take matters into their own hands. They not only demonstrated their wishes in front of an audience, but had to put their own lives in jeopardy. After the hostage incident in Love Canal, Barbara Quimby's father asked her what she had thought would happen to her children. Knowing that the children had been elsewhere at the time the government officials were held prisoner, and confident that the entire campaign was to save the children, Quimby reassured her father that they were in good hands. 'No,' he responded. 'What did you think would happen to the children while you were in jail for 20 years?' She was flabbergasted. 'I never thought of that.' Operating according to a higher law, she had never considered that she was breaking the law by kidnapping two government officials.

No one recommends permitting women to perform criminal acts in the name of the common good. And no one should have to break the law in order to save their families. Yet even police and soldiers must sometimes consider the ideas of women who are willing to defend their families with their own bodies. The diversity of the women who participate in these campaigns – ranging from largely poor, rural women in the Himalaya mountains and in Warren County, to largely urban working-class and lower-middle-class women in Love Canal or the townships of South Africa – makes consideration of the special place of women in these battles of particular interest. Despite global capitalism, and despite the advances of some women, the division of labour by sex means that most women, regardless of race, class or nationality, still are socialized to assume the principal burden of assuring the health and well-being of their family and community. Without any juridical rights to assure public welfare, large numbers of women bear the responsibility for compensating individuals in their families for the failures of the state and the economy in sustaining their lives.

Update on Environmental Movements and Justice

Waste dumps, incinerators that create dioxin by burning organic medical waste cleansed with chlorine, and abandoned factories and army bases filled with the flotsam and jetsam of war industries have become common in both the North and the South. The rich countries have turned to the poor countries and to the poor regions of wealthy countries for potential dumping grounds. In the late 1990s, a German waste removal company secretly purchased land in South Carolina to use as a nuclear waste dump. Prevented only by mass movements led by local women, European-based companies also sought out dump sites in South Africa and Namibia. As women have recognized that their children are dying from leukaemia and other diseases believed to be related to the proliferation of dioxin and PCB, and that they themselves are suffering more problems around repro-duction, they have collectively attempted as mothers to solve the medical problems that beset them. The common responses of women from Brazil to the South Bronx to threats to their families' health indicate that some-thing more systematic is occurring.

Without detracting from the achievements of women's grassroots move-ments for environmental justice, it is important to consider how gender enters these campaigns for justice. First of all, every society inculcates young girls and boys with their appropriate gender roles. So long as women and men conform to societal expectations, they achieve a certain degree of protection. When police or armies arrest women acting as mothers, it is the law that is called into question, rather than the women. If soldiers or police attack women and children, it is likely that outsiders will consider the attack a massacre. I frequently ask students why they think it is so much worse to harm women and children than to harm men. The students flounder, suggesting that women have to reproduce life and therefore their lives also incorporate potential lives. But men are also necessary to produce life, yet the decline in sperm count that accompanies the proliferation of dioxin does not seem to raise the same horror as the idea that breast-milk is contaminated with DDT and dioxin. In many cultures, motherhood is sentimentalized, an issue that women acting as mothers consciously and unconsciously use to support their struggles for public health. On the other hand, police and armies would rather confront men, who are considered worthy adversaries. Attacking women can be done, but those manoeuvres must be especially discreet, and the women must be cast as political adversaries rather than as mothers defending their children.

An underlying theme of women's grassroots environmental movements is the idea that a clean environment is a human right. As the women from MOSES and other groups all over the world claim, human rights are about what human beings need: safe food, clothing, shelter free from contaminants, dignified work in a clean atmosphere, and health care. By placing the emphasis on 'human' rather than on legal rights, the women in grassroots environmental struggles are redefining human rights to mean the common good or what socialism once meant: the right to a fulfilling life, in which safe housing, proper health conditions, nourishing food, education and clean air and water are assured. This once constituted what people hoped would be the common good.

In a so-called post-Marxist age, critics do not frequently refer to contra-dictions that may well generate new lines of thought and action. But grassroots women's movements, particularly those around the environment, seem to call for such a discussion. In pursuit of their children's and their families' health, women all over the globe have been demanding that the priorities of states and corporations be re-adjusted to take account of the ultimate goal of the common good: the achievement of a good life for all. Using their positions according to the division of labour by sex, but frequently with new insights about their place as women, as activists and as human beings, women are demanding a re-orientation of social priorities consistent with the common good. Time will tell to what length these women will go to develop the institutions that will assure that even MOSES will enter the promised land.

Notes

1. 'Action Line: Texas', *Everyone's Backyard*, vol. 18, no. 2 (Summer 2000): 25.

2. Barbara Quimby, a most reluctant activist, became one of the leaders of the effort to persuade the government to purchase the houses in her entire working-class neigh-bourhood of Love Canal in Niagara, New York. Her discussion of what a mother should do appears in my book *Crazy for Democracy* (Kaplan 1997: 43). The full text of Quimby's statement reads: 'Say you're at the shopping mall with your kids. There are clowns over here and bargains over there, and you're having a great time. And then a fire comes. Even though you'd rather stay at the mall, you've got to get your kids out, because otherwise they'll die.'

3. I have written extensively about what I call 'female consciousness' to describe the

rights that women acting as mothers and sometimes as sisters can exercise in times of crisis. Recognizing this 'right', police and soldiers are frequently reluctant to attack women who claim to be defending their children, although armed forces have no compunction against attacking the same women if they claim to defend the interests of political parties or trade unions. With greater protection acting as mothers than as citizens, shrewd women frequently cast themselves as mothers rather than as political activists, even after their abilities to strategize have developed considerably (see Kaplan 1997: 185–7). 'Gender privilege' replaces 'female consciousness' in this chapter in order to emphasize that men and women share ideas about the privileges that each can exercise because of their sex, no matter what the law decrees.

4. Even water, known in some circles as 'blue gold', has become privatized. In the spring of 2000, efforts to sell water to poor inhabitants of Cochabamba in Bolivia led to riots. But as public water supplies the world over become increasingly polluted and as supplies of clean water diminish, water is likely to become a scarce resource.

5. By teaching women to plant trees to reforest their own areas, the Green Belt movement has legitimated women's participation in political demonstrations, such as the Mothers' Hunger Strike in 1992. Fighting for the public good can be dangerous, as repeated attacks on Wangari Maathai and other women have shown. See an account of the beating of Maathai in Amnesty International 1995: 70–1; WEDO 1999a. For a discussion of how a group of women have led a struggle against a toxic waste incinerator in Bibowice, Poland, see 'Action Line: Poland', *Everyone's Backyard*, vol. 18, no. 2 (Summer 2000): 25; for information about Women in Europe for a Common Future see Yates and Chary 1999: 27 and http://www.ipen.org/pcb-workinggroup.htm. Arguments from leaders of the Union of Nuclear Test Victims about the damage to people in Kazakhstan caused by open-air nuclear testing by the former Soviet Union, not suspended until 1989, appear in Sumarakova and Igstatova 1996: 92–7.

6. For examples of the women's environmental campaigns in Latin America, see Guadilla 1993; the journal *Conspirando: Revista Latinoamerica de Ecofeminismo, Espiritualidad y Teologica*, from 1992, Santiago, Chile; for South Africa, see Cock and Koch 1991.

7. For insights into movements of women focusing on the environment in Africa and Asia, see Rodda 1991.

8. Animashaun 1998: 30. For the Royal Dutch Shell's response to criticism of its role in environmental pollution and violation of human rights, see 'How Do We Stand? People, Planet & Profits, A Summary of the Shell Report 2000', a 20-page insert in *Newsweek*, 28 August.

9. For consideration of the Rebecca Riots and the Demoiselles of the Ariège, see Rude 1964; for an interpretation of the symbolism entailed in the efforts to protect the forests in France, see Sahlins 1994; for the María das Fontes movement in Portugal, I have relied on an unpublished paper (1984) by the late Joyce Riegelhaupt.

10. Weber 1988: 26–7. Weber suggests that although women formed the mass base of the Chipko movement, men actually directed the campaign. On the other hand, he admits that the women often acted on their own, 'spontaneously' (p. 97). Other interpretations of Chipko, which place more emphasis on the importance of the women's participation, can be found in Rodda 1991: 110–11; Kumar 1993: 182–5.

11. See Kumar 1993: 184–5 for the story of the men leaving to protest to the government about the attempt to cut down the trees.

12. The Chipko Movement India: http://iiisdliisd.ca/50commdb/desc/d07.htm

13. Figures from a letter dated 15 March 1979 from Dr Haughie of the Department of Health, cited in Levine 1982: 106.

14. I have written about the mobilization of the housewives' association at Love Canal in Kaplan 1997. The world movement against toxic wastes can be said to have begun at Love Canal, about which much has been written. It is possible to trace the origins of the campaign at Love Canal in Brown 1979.

15. The most comprehensive explanation for lay people of the effects of dioxin can be found in Gibbs 1995. For an argument about how dioxin and other so-called environmental hormones affect the human body, see Lester 1997: 25–7.

16. 'Action Line: Warren County at the forefront once again', *Everyone's Backyard*, vol. 17, no. 2 (Summer 1999): 23.

Bibliography

Amnesty International (1995) *Human Rights are Women's Rights*, London: Amnesty International Publications.

Brown, Michael H. (1979) *Laying Waste: The Poisoning of America by Toxic Chemicals*, New York: Pantheon.

Carson, Rachel (1962) *Silent Spring*, Boston, MA: Houghton Mifflin.

Cock, Jacklyn and Eddie Koch (eds) (1991) *Going Green: People, Politics and the Environment in South Africa*, Cape Town: Oxford University Press.

Everyone's Backyard (2000) 'Action Line: Poland', *Everyone's Backyard* (Summer).

Gibbs, Lois Marie (1982) *Love Canal: My Story*, as told to Murray Levine, Albany, NY: State University of New York Press; updated 1998 as *Love Canal: The Story Continues*, with a foreword by Ralph Nader, Gabriola Island, British Columbia.

— (1995) *Dying from Dioxin: A Citizen's Guide to Reclaiming Our Health and Rebuilding Democracy*, Boston, MA: South End Press.

— (1998) 'Love Canal's 20th anniversary', *Everyone's Backyard*, 16(1) (Spring).

Guadilla, Maria-Pilar, Garcia (1993) '"Viva": women and popular protest in Latin America', in Sarah A. Radcliffe and Sallie Westwood (eds), *Ecologia: Women, Environment and Politics in Venezuela*, London and New York: Routledge.

Kaplan, Temma (1997) *Crazy for Democracy: Women in Grassroots Movements*, New York and London: Routledge.

Kumar, Radha (1993) *The History of Doing: An Illustrated Account of Movements for Women's Rights and Feminism in India, 1800–1990*, London and New York: Verso.

Lester, Stephen (1997) 'The truth about endocrine disrupting chemicals', *Everyone's Backyard*, 15(4).

Levine, Adeline Gordon (1982) *Love Canal: Science, Politics, and People*, Lexington, MA: D.C. Heath.

Rodda, Annabel (1991) *Women and the Environment*, London and New Jersey: Zed Books.

Rowbotham, Sheila (1997) *Crazy for Democracy: Women in Grassroots Movements*, New York and London: Routledge.

Rude, George, O. (1964) *The Crowd in History: A Study of Popular Disturbances in France and England, 1730–1848*, New York: John Wiley and Son.

Sahlins, Peter (1994) *Forest Rites: The War of the Demoiselles in Nineteenth-Century France*, Cambridge, MA: Harvard University Press.

Sumarakova, Galina and Dina Igstatova (1996) 'The human rights of nuclear test victims', in Niamh Reilly (ed.), *Without Reservation: The Beijing Tribunal on Account-*

ability for Women's Human Rights, New Brunswick, NJ: Center for Women's Global Leadership, State University of New Jersey.

Swerdlow, Amy (1993) *Women's Strike for Peace: Traditional Motherhood and Radical Politics in the 1960s*, Chicago: University of Chicage Press.

Weber, Thomas (1988) *Hugging the Trees: The Story of the Chipko Movement*, London: Penguin.

WEDO (1999a) 'WEDO condemns the brutal attack on Wangari Maathai', WEDO news release, 14 January, http://www.wedo.org/press/board statement.htm

— (1999b) *Risks, Rights and Reforms: The '99 Report*, 24 pages, http://wwwwedo.org/monitor/riskfindings.htm, pp. 17–19.

Yates, Larry and Lin Kaatz Chary, 'Global PCB contamination leads to global activism', *Everyone's Backyard*, 17(3) (Fall).

4

Women, 'Community' and the British Miners' Strike of 1984–85

Meg Allen

The 1984–85 miners' strike in Britain saw the mobilization of women in mining communities on an unprecedented scale. Although their action has resulted in several books and articles, making it among the most documented movements of working-class women, the impact of activism in the strike on the women's outlook and lives has received little attention (Barnsley WAPC 1985; Coventry Miners' Wives Support Group 1986; Seddon 1986; Miller 1986; Gibbon 1988; Allen and Measham 1995).

Between 1996 and 1999 I interviewed over 45 women who had been intensely involved in Women Against Pit Closures in Yorkshire, South Wales, the north-east and the north Midlands. They included women who had belonged to the Communist and Labour Parties and came from families with a long history of trade unionism. Others, however, had not been active in party politics though they may have had experience of community organizing.

I found that in an era of declining grassroots activity the impact of the strike had meant that the majority were more engaged in radical movements – not simply the Labour Party but campaigns and community action. Moreover, their participation in Women Against Pit Closures had also resulted in sustained reflection on alternative approaches to politics. Out of the experience of the miners' strike had come ideas of social solidarity from a gendered, working-class perspective.

A constantly recurring theme when they talked about how gender and class interacted was 'community'. The politics of WAPC did not just come out of a struggle for the preservation of pits and jobs. The most important issue for the women of WAPC was the survival of the mining community. All the women spoke at length about their communities, about how they had changed since the strike and the sense of loss they felt at this change. Their sense of community was often what motivated them. 'Community' referred not just to a geographical population, but to a sense of belonging and personal, emotive connection. The word 'community' expressed in shorthand a multitude of feelings, attitudes and beliefs that they found hard to put into political language.

The meanings of 'community' have been highly contested. The elasticity in the word 'community' makes it a slippery and difficult concept. Indeed, the women themselves interpreted 'community' in three differing ways. They often used 'community' in its most accepted sense, to describe the locality and the people in it. This definition centred on a geographical area and involved the relationships between the local people. It was about their everyday experiences of trying to get along with others in a local collective. At another level they used 'community' to describe the collective practical needs of that same local group. They spoke about resources and facilities in the area, going beyond a merely individual conception of need. This version of community was the moving force in the initial stages of the strike. It expressed the need for collective practical survival which drove the formation of the groups. They organized initially around supplying food, money and the essentials of living. The women were deeply embedded in the supportive structure of their community. Within the strike, although both men and women used the idea of community as a rallying point, it was the members of WAPC who were more closely associated with the idea of community. For example, they often argued that there would be no jobs for their children, and that they would lose both facilities and the social ties that enriched and supported their lives.

Finally, the women used the word 'community' in a more complex and ideological sense. For the women community was also an 'imagined' group, brought together by a sense of common cause and belief. This sense of shared identity and belonging drew on diverse images and ideas and was developed and strengthened as the strike progressed. It incorporated ideas of solidarity and Utopian visions of community, and specifically of mining communities, passed on from previous generations. At the same time the women I interviewed also drew on their new experiences as women in struggle, on marches and at rallies, and their involvement in other movements such as the Peace Movement or the Women's Movement. These new influences strengthened their vision of community and made it relevant to a new generation.

As the dispute progressed this imagined Utopian sense in which the women saw community was to become increasingly important. While in the early stages practical needs bonded the women and drew disparate individuals together, in the latter part of the dispute the sheer longevity of the strike meant that they needed strong and cohesive mobilizing ideas to keep up morale. The very flexibility of this 'imagined' sense of community also created an opening outwards. It enabled them to make common cause with other groups and to share a vision of collective organization and a collective future. The women of WAPC were thus able to use the gendered nature of mining communities to mobilize in positive ways. This dynamic reworking of assumptions about their responsibilities and concerns as women has implications for political activity generally and for a redefinition of what is seen as 'political' in general terms, as well as for theorizing around specifically women's activity and movements.

A gendered vision has been an important aspect of many social movements, for it is often affective ties and social networks which enable activism and make resistance possible. As Morio Diani and Ron Eyerman point out, 'if a structural component of Social Movements exists, it is to be found at the level of personal networks. Indeed these ties usually prove far less vulnerable to external conditions ... than those linking formal, bureaucratic organizations (Diani and Eyerman 1992: 110).

Although men play a role in the creation of social ties, women are more embedded in local and familial networks. Women's socialization and gendered roles mean that their small and everyday actions create the social and affective bonds that make community cohesive. Women consequently have often started from that familial and community base. The 'community' that constituted these everyday relations for the WAPC members I interviewed was very much a gendered space. It was the women who fought for local facilities for their children, who maintained the links between families and did the 'sociability' work that helped maintain solidarity in the strike.

As the notion of community broadened to include other activists it was still often the women who made and maintained links with a wider, supportive community. Thus both physical and geographical 'community' relating and 'community' in the broader sense of a shared vision were gendered. In an account of community work amongst African American women, Roberta Feldman (1998: 260) describes what she calls 'sociability work' – the unpaid provision of essential community services. Feldman's work obviously focuses on the very different American context, where services are not provided so freely by the state. Yet her description of 'sociability work' has echoes in British mining communities. Many of the women who were involved in the strike did just this kind of work. They looked after the sick or vulnerable in their villages, worked in local community centres or supported the local school. In doing this work they cemented bonds with each other and with other members of their community. Moreover, this voluntary action has continued.

In Cortonwood the group of women who run the local day centre work on an unpaid, voluntary basis providing a free service to local residents. They provide meals, advice, entertainment and a place to meet and are not funded by the local state or any charities. All the funds are raised by themselves. It is through these types of 'sociability work' that the women create and maintain social bonds that give a cohesive fabric to community life.

In their accounts the women stressed that their work was about connection and giving. One woman talks about 'giving but not getting back' (interview, Anne Brookes, Barnsley, Yorkshire, 20 May 1998). Another woman in South Wales who had been a local councillor strongly disagreed with payments for work on the local council. When they were introduced she refused to stand as a councillor, saying 'it's not something you should be paid for, it's for your community' (interview, Ann Jones, Hirwaun, S. Wales, 11 March 1999). Many of the women expressed a strong disapproval of individuals or left political groups they thought had been involved in the strike for what they could get out of it.

Work in their communities seemed to be a natural extension of their work within their families and there was a feeling that care should not be given for payment. They regarded this area of work as outside market relations. There is evidently a gendered aspect to this concern. The women carried the caring role they held in their families into their communities, into the exceptional circumstance of the year-long strike. They thus created an unalienated space that was outside economic relations – a space they were to defend fiercely.

In the context of the strike the women's sociability work took on a new public meaning. By giving their time for free during the dispute and in assisting others in their community, they made it morally harder for strikers to return to work. A shift consequently occurred between personal and public activity. Women's sense of legitimacy came from a gendered position within mining communities, but this came to impinge on the workplace. It was also to have an impact on gender relations and lead some of the women I interviewed to search for new forms of social solidarity.

The women whose lives were to be so affected by becoming active in Women Against Pit Closures came from communities that were at once closely intertwined and sharply demarcated in terms of gender. Mining communities have been marked by their geographical connection to the pit and a continuity of members and culture that has contributed to their militancy. In many areas mining was the only industry and the local pit the only chance for work if children wanted to stay close to their families or communities. This meant that mining families tended to cluster around pits, sharing the same experience of work and working life (Warwick and Littlejohn 1992). Michaela Hawkins expresses this assumed interconnectedness when she speaks about her own village, New Tredegar in South Wales:

> People just gave you things, they just did ... because we live in a mining community, well lived in a mining community, people were prepared to give because for the majority, miners, somewhere along the line, were in the family. I would say ninety-odd per cent of people round here had some connection with mining families even if it were their grandfather or someone. (interview, 22 September 1998)

Shared everyday experiences created a common culture. Jean Miller from Barnsley, Yorkshire, describes this combination of cohesion and resistance:

> There was community spirit in the villages more than there is now, although whether you remember that exactly as it was, I'm not sure whether people do. But for instance in this village we had a gala every year organized by the NUM, the Miners' Welfare put on events throughout the year and Christmas parties and all sorts of things, so there was a focal point in the village for everybody to latch on to, even if you weren't involved in that pit ... I can remember when I was a child and my father, who worked at Woolley, used to conduct the brass band and I can remember my father ... this park with the brass band, and me father's pit, they supported the band so all the miners would contribute a penny a week or whatever to keep the band going, but they also had a sports ground where they could play football and cricket and all these different things, and the NUM organized that and kept that going, and that was a whole culture. North Gawber miners, they contributed tuppence a week to the welfare which would provide cheap alcohol for the miners, plus the other events, they put on children's parties for Christmas and Easter discos and give out Easter eggs and organize a bonfire on bonfire night, and people would get pie and peas and things like that, so that was all part of the culture that surrounded it. (interview, 2 June 1998)

Another, less happy edge to that shared culture was an element of fear and danger. The men worked in an industry where injury was common and death a very real possibility. In their account of the Durham miners, *Masters and Servants* (1994), Huw Beynon and Terry Austrin describe high levels of accident and disaster, particularly in the early part of the century. Explosions, tunnel collapse and machinery accidents were a feature of the mining industry. The warning klaxon would sound the alarm and the women would gather at the pit head to hear the news of who was injured and who might be dead. This danger was not just an aspect of the early part of the century: in Easington, County Durham, the memory of a pit disaster in the 1960s in which 30 men died was fresh in the minds of the women in the village. Joan Barnes remembers it clearly:

> When I came to Easington and I joined the Labour Party I'd see the banner in the hall here and the photograph of all the men who died. There's a

constant reminder outside as well because every time I look up the window I see the memorial grave. I remember when I was little and we lived at Horden, some days I used to come over to me grandmother's in Easington and walk up to cemetery and the big grave and you'd see the mound of flowers getting bigger and bigger. The day of the Easington pit disaster was the first time I'd come home, I was ten or eleven, and my mother wasn't there. My neighbour said that I had to go in her house because my mam had gone to Easington, and I can remember I was just going down the street at Horden and this girl came and said, 'Easington pit's blown up!' Me mam had come to Easington because she had her father, her brother and her brother-in-law working in the pit, but the lady next door her family all came from away and she couldn't leave her elderly mother and father, so she asked me mother to find out what had happened for her. She had about eight or so brothers working at the pit at the time! It was horrible, it really sticks in your mind. (interview, 24 June 1998)

The danger inherent in the industry bonded men and women together. For the men there was a need to rely on fellow workers and for the women a shared fear of the loss of a loved one. For the men and the women the issues were different but related – the men faced the danger but for the women it was a case of waiting and supporting each other as best they could.

Moreover, the harshness of the men's working conditions reinforced sharp gender divisions. The family economy depended on women's domestic role. Men and women were thus connected and distinct (Colls 1987; Pitt 1979). For both men and women, female work in the home was seen as totally necessary and right in a context where men grafted so hard in the workplace. Jean Miller from Barnsley describes it well when she talks about growing up in a mining area:

When you work in an area where men labour down the pit for eight hours a day and they come home, and to be honest it's very rare that I swear, but when they come home they are knackered. (interview, 2 June 1998)

It was thus particularly difficult to question the division of male and female spheres and with this went defined notions of 'masculinity' and 'femininity'. The boundaries of those communities was very much marked by gender – what was appropriate behaviour for a woman in the city would not be so for a woman from a mining village.

The close mining communities also marked out sharp barriers according to locality. Many of the women remarked that moving to another village had been difficult and that it had taken many years to be accepted. To belong to a mining village meant to have been born there and preferably to have family there. This image of community, gendered, local, solidaristic and full of affective and class ties, was often to be mobilized during the strike.

By the time of the 1984 strike it had, however, ceased to be a lived reality in many areas. Close-knit communities still survived in places like County Durham and South Wales. For instance, when Michaela Hawkins joined a women's group she knew every face at the first meeting:

> Oh yes, I knew everybody, it's a close community here, really close, if Mrs So-and-so sneezed six doors down we'd know about it! That's not being nosey, that's being caring, like Mavis over the road, she's always on her door and she can tell you everything that's going on, but she won't interfere or gossip. (interview, 22 September 1998)

This familiarity and sense of belonging came out of long association and local ties with the pit. Moreover, many of the families in villages were also linked by blood ties. Families had been resident and working in the mine for more than one generation, and fathers, sons and grandfathers could have worked in the same pit. Kay Case from South Wales illustrates this point in her description of growing up in Treharris:

> Oh yes, we were a very close family. We laugh, and say we are all kissing cousins, because we all meet together. When I was a kid we used to come down to my Gran's and we had to stand by the Welsh dresser to eat our dinner because all the adults were sitting at the table. I mean, my father was one of six, so his sisters and their husbands were all at the table! My dad was diagnosed with bronchial asthma and he did about two years in the colliery but his chest was too bad, but all my cousins work still in the colliery. The village here is not the same without the pit. (interview, 13 March 1999)

Kay Case's grandfather, husband, sons and cousins all worked in the colliery and lived within a few miles of each other. These links between family members were to prove important during the strike.

Mining communities were, however, subject to economic change, and pit closure had already forced families to move before the 1984–85 miners' strike (Allen 1981). So by the mid-1980s, while some areas or villages managed to retain their closely knit and gendered structure, change meant that other families and women lived in larger towns, or in villages where the on-site pit had been closed. For example, Edie Woolley, living in Upton, Yorkshire, pointed out that the men in the village worked at a total of 13 different pits; that morning exodus meant that the village was not as closely linked as it had been. Similarly Anne Brookes, who came from the larger Barnsley town area, knew few of the women whose husbands worked in the mine. When groups started up in these areas women found themselves meeting new faces in groups and forming new bonds based upon the dispute.

Shared industry, shared family and shared place were not then constant, universal features of mining communities. Nor were these homogeneous entities. There was a continual shifting of miners from place to place as colliery closures proceeded, and many miners and their families were new to the areas in which they worked. Moreover, various waves of immigration from other countries occurred. For example, in South Wales in 1907 several hundred families were brought over to Dowlais by the Dowlais Iron Company, and in Abercrave to the south there was an influx of French, German and Belgian miners in the first decade of the twentieth century (Francis and Smith 1980). To some extent these 'new' miners shared a common mining culture with long-time residents, but there were conflicts. Within their apparent closeness mining communities have thus been complex, conflictual and constantly changing over time. Solidarity did emerge repeatedly from a community base, but it was not a simple or unseamed process.

Yet a sense of locality and family was there to be drawn on during the 1984–85 dispute. It ensured the survival of miners and their families and provided the infrastructure of practical aid and support to miners and their families, while the networks that existed, and were developed, during the strike provided a context of mutual support and aid. It was the women who were best placed to begin the practical task of providing for families during the dispute. To do this they drew on the networks they had established and maintained in their communities and on the skills they had as women and providers for their families. Their roles in providing for the strikers echoed their roles in the family: they worked as cooks, cleaners, shoppers and financial managers.

Both the local grassroots publications and books and articles published afterwards agree that the starting point for all of the groups was the practical need generated by the dispute. For example, in Barnsley what prompted the women to start the group was the suffering experienced by the single miners in the dispute, since they were not getting any benefits at all. Moreover, it is widely acknowledged that it was the practical, day-to-day work of the women that sustained the strike (Barnsley WAPC 1984, 1985; Coventry Miners' Wives Support Group 1986; Eppleton Miners' Wives Support Group 1985; Keating 1992; Miller 1986; Seddon 1986; Stead 1987; Withan 1986). My research confirmed the significance of both the initial mobilization around livelihood and the vital practical contribution made by the women during the strike. The women had a concern for their children and families that drew them together to provide as best they could in the strike. Their activities mirrored their usual gendered role, providing the basics of survival for the family – food, clothing and housing.

Nearly all the women I have interviewed were involved at some level with the provision of food, through the soup kitchens (or 'community cafés', as they were called in Easington), or by distributing parcels or food vouchers. The kitchens varied in size, organization and the amount of meals they provided. Some provided evening meals three or four days a week, while others provided two meals a day for the duration of the strike. Even the smallest kitchen could be feeding upwards of 150 people a day, and the largest over 600. Similarly, the distribution of food parcels and vouchers could be on a large scale. Anne Brookes remembers men queuing around the block for vouchers when they were distributed in Barnsley, and that there were often none left for workers' families at the end of the day (interview, 20 May 1998). At the height of the dispute huge amounts of food and relief were being distributed through networks that were set up within weeks of the start of the strike. For Jackie Naylor in Notting-hamshire this could mean £1,000 a week going out to individual groups at the height of the dispute (interview, 10 August 1998).

The groups also organized quickly to provide welfare rights advice, in a context where the Department of Social Security was instructed to be obstructive about benefits to strikers. This role diminished as the strike progressed as miners and their families quickly claimed what was possible and organized to fund-raise the rest. This was part of the creation of a network of alternative social services, which meant that a local union official, miner or their family might contact a group to see what it could do in case of specific needs. In the early part of the dispute Jean Miller would receive calls from union officials asking if Barnsley WAPC could supply things such as prams, nappies or children's clothing (interview, 2 June 1998). Such requests were passed on to local women's groups and in time networks were established, with officials and local miners knowing who to contact for help. In all the groups women collected and distributed children's clothes and shoes, tampons, soap – anything that was needed.

At a more overtly political level women were drawn into public speaking as a way of raising funds. Their talks appealed to the average listener. Women spoke at rallies and meetings to raise funds, and for some women this was their major activity during the strike. As the strike progressed it became obligatory for a woman from WAPC to be invited to speak at any demonstration or rally alongside NUM members or officials. Women were popular speakers, often because they tended to speak from a personal perspective and broke the mould of conventional platform speaking. WAPC members attended a multitude of marches and rallies and took part in other campaigns such as Greenham Women's Peace Camp. WAPC organized three national rallies, one in Barnsley on 12 May 1984, one in London on 11 August 1984, and a final rally in Chesterfield for International

Women's Day, 9 March 1985. They also instigated national conferences, the first of which was held on 22 July 1984 at the Northern College in Barnsley (Barnsley WAPC 1985, 1986). Even though WAPC had a relatively formal national structure, most of the activities were organized through local meetings and loose social networks, by telephone or personal contact.

In a similar way women became involved with picketing at both local and national levels. Again this could cause conflict, since it led to the women breaking out of their conventional and gendered role. The attitude of both individual men and of the NUM towards women's picketing was mixed. Some men welcomed it and saw that it brought results, while in other cases women could be told that the picket line was too dangerous, or were refused transport to pickets by local NUM officials. In South Wales and Yorkshire the women recognized early on that they needed their own transport and organized a minibus driven by one of the members to attend pickets. Activities such as speaking or picketing emerged from a genuine practical need, to stop the return to work and to raise funds for striking miners and their families. The mobilization of these activities was local – women organized from within local communities to send minibuses or arrange speakers and often picketed at local pits. Yet again, as the strike progressed these local and community-based initiatives widened and new, more national links were made. These, in turn, revealed tensions around gender and around the relation of a community-based mobilization of women to an industry-based dispute that was largely male.

What the women's experience bears out is that 'community' is a place of conflict and tension. Belonging had its privileges and its price. The paradoxical feature of the miners' strike was that the mobilization of women to defend 'community' eroded the gender relations that had sustained actual communities. A campaign that was ostensibly to defend traditional social relations was thus, by the very nature of activism and struggle, to transform those relations.

One aspect of this was that a space for criticizing ties that restricted women emerged. Some women who changed during the strike have left those communities. Lorraine Bowler, for example, left her village in Yorkshire to do a community work course with the intention that she would return to work in the mining community in which she grew up. She found the reality very different. She changed her relationship during the strike and she found after gaining qualifications as a community worker that she was no longer accepted in the village. As one of the more active, outspoken and overtly 'woman-centred' of the women, she found she had changed too much to 'fit'. She found her new life in Sheffield more satisfying than the one she left in the village, but regretted the loss of family and friends:

It's a completely different way of living to me this, I'm used to it and I love it and I didn't have to adapt to it at all. I thought I would feel like a fish out of water but I didn't and I loved it from day one. I think it's the freedom to be able to do what you want and be involved in what you want and nobody knows about it. I'm not saying I'm secretive ... but it's like the whole village knows your business and it's so liberating not to have that. I don't think I'd have settled so well if I hadn't gone to Northern College, if I hadn't gone there I'd still be living in Worsborough. I would have lived and died there. (interview, 20 June 1998)

Membership of mining communities became hotly disputed during the strike. It was defined partly in a negative sense: you are a member of a mining community because you are not a student, not a teacher or social worker. But gender also served as a way of marking out inclusion or exclusion. Just as gender can define boundaries of race and ethnicity (Anthias and Yuval-Davis 1989), it can operate similarly within working-class communities. Women are important as the social biological repro-ducers of community and so their sexual and social behaviour matters. Women who broke those rules, pursued education, changed relationships or left marriages, could be ostracized. There was a point beyond which women could not go and retain their identity as women of that community.

However, most of the women I interviewed had not cut themselves off from their communities. Instead they had managed to contain the tensions that their activism brought about. They reconciled their own needs and aims with their need to be part of their community, albeit not always comfortably.

The tension between belonging and transformation was very obvious in the women's attitude towards feminism and to feminists involved in the campaign. While they unproblematically adopted a strong class identity, their ambivalence towards feminism was (and is) apparent at all points. Because mining communities have tended to be uniformly working class, their members have had few affective ties with people not of their class. It has been class politics that have rooted them in their community. This strong sense of class meant that the women identified themselves strongly with fathers, brothers and husbands and the community, which was bounded and defined by specific gender roles. To challenge those gender roles was to challenge the organization of that community itself. However, feminism undermined the very community that gave the women a powerful feeling of identity. This was the basic problem that the women encountered again and again. Their domestic and gendered role in communities drew them into activity that challenged those very same relationships, and they carried this tension throughout their politics. Hilary Rowlands, the wife of a miner and activist in South Wales, argues that the women were 'scared of what they would become'. When asked to explain, she argued that they were scared of losing their class and connection with their communities, of 'becoming middle-class' like the feminists they worked with, but also that they were scared of having to go into the 'world' and deal with issues and life beyond the safety of that community (interview, 21 September 1998). Jean Miller in Barnsley argued that it was 'all right for middle-class women', who were seen as having money and the ability to move and live where and as they wished (interview, 2 June 1998). The community represented safety, identity and economic and emotional security.

The activists were, however, themselves somewhat apart from the other women (and men) in the mining areas, the majority of whom were not involved in the groups, despite both shared culture and locality and a shared collective need. For the activist minority, this was often hard to understand and women frequently expressed resentment against and anger with those who chose to 'free ride' through the strike. The cohesion of mining communities during the strike was thus in reality riven by tensions. Women who were active in the kitchens could find that their work created resentment and that a sense of 'obligation' was not always well received by those using the kitchens. People who ate at the soup kitchens could be critical of the women working there and accused them at times of 'skimming off the best'. The implication was that they must be getting something out of it to do the work. The women I interviewed remembered this insult very clearly, since it was so at odds with their sense of their motivations as altruistic. There were many conflicts around money, the allocation of money and its use and women often felt they had to cover themselves in the management of finances. All the women I interviewed who had acted as treasurers stressed how thoroughly they had kept the accounts and were keen to show the books as evidence. Women also commented that some members of their community had complained after the dispute that the groups had kept the strike going for an unnecessary length of time. In hindsight many of the women speak of the bitterness and backbiting that was the flipside to that solidarity.

There is a need to understand the reasons why the majority never took part in the dispute or participated more peripherally. Women who were inactive, or not as active, often expressed a reluctance to be involved in the groups because they saw them as closely knit and exclusive, or simply felt awkward going to the group for the first time. For many women the sheer work involved in keeping their families together on an emotional and practical level seemed to preclude involvement in the groups. While passivity might have been resented, however, it was tolerated. By contrast, those who chose to return to work could often face harsh sanctions. Close connections and affective ties meant that ostracism and attack could make life very difficult for strike-breakers. In Murton, County Durham, Jan Smith felt uncomfortable with the fact that scabs had been attacked and windows broken. Yet women in many of the villages had been involved in disputes with strike-breakers and their families and were often at the forefront of arguments. Jan Smith remembers an argument that happened during the strike that was very typical of conflicts in the villages:

> Once it had been going on for three, four, five months people got sick of hearing about the strike and hearing people moan about having no money. Then you see people who didn't agree with the strike would side with the people who went back to work. It created arguments, like Peter's mother, she's a very quiet woman but during the strike she went into a shop and this woman was slagging the miners off and she turned into this maniac. She'd been friends with this woman all her life and she just turned on her, going for her, like. Then this man started and she tore into him as well! In the end my sister-in-law had to drag her out of the shop and calm her down, but this fella he followed her into the Post Office and started on her again. I saw a big change because it split the village, because quite a few went back by the end of the strike. (interview, 7 October 1998)

The women's central role in maintaining community meant that they also played a part in imposing sanctions on those who broke ranks. Many of the women were involved in harassing scabs during the strike. Women were often used to 'shame' men who were crossing picket lines. In communities where gender division was clear cut, to be shouted and sneered at by a woman was seen as shaming and humiliating. Jackie Naylor in Nottinghamshire always stood at the front of the picket line. She refused to yell abuse but instead shouted her favourite expression 'You're lower than lino!' to the men going into work (interview, 10 August 1998). Women also put pressure on miners through their wives – women whose husbands had gone back to work would be barred from the conversation and company of other women in the village. There was sometimes conflict over this ostracism. In Nottingham and Barnsley the groups argued over whether to let women continue going to the group when their husbands had returned to work. It was decided in both areas that the women should not be allowed to come to the group, highlighting how women were still classed with their husbands, even though they wanted to come to the group and support the strike. They might not agree with their husbands, but, according to the established way of seeing, they were part of a partnership with a scab and solidarity had to be maintained.

Ostracism might have been a powerful tool for maintaining solidarity in some close-knit villages. But already by 1984 these traditional mining settlements were undergoing changes. In the Nottingham area and in some parts of Yorkshire, while smaller villages in more isolated areas revolved around a local mine, many other miners had moved to more urban areas or travelled out to work. Because of pit closures in Edie Woolley's village in Yorkshire the men went to work in 13 different pits in the area (interview, 26 May 1998). She still knew many of the people in her village, but this was not the case for many of the women I interviewed. But in communities that had kept their mine and a local base, there were differences that had to be worked out during the dispute. So while the image that was presented *vis-à-vis* outsiders – students, feminists or whatever – was one of uniformity and solidarity, the reality was predictably one of tensions, conflict and complexity. The miners' strike saw both the reaffirmation and re-creation of a community that had been lost over time. This was true in terms of a physical reality and mobilizing image. As David Howell observes, in many ways the bonds of community were re-created in struggle (Howell 1987). Many of the women, who had not known one another before the strike, spoke of the excitement of meeting other women and making new friendships. In the central Barnsley groups there were also many women who were not married to miners, but were students and lecturers at the Northern College. While there were conflicts between these different groups there were also to be strong alliances created as the strike progressed. 'Community', then, was not fixed but a flexible and socially created group.

Solidarity was maintained in part by personal relationships and a common need that was expressed through the day-to-day work of the soup kitchens. The practical work of the women physically drew people together, kept up morale and ensured survival. Yet despite their personal connections and despite their work to supply families with the means to exist, the pressures on families meant that men did begin to drift back to work. This drift, and the arguments that surrounded the return to work, often raised more ideological issues. In these debates, and in the need to keep the strike solid, women mobilized the idea of community as a moral entity. Community in this sense was being used more as a unifying idea, a Utopian ideal in which all could share. This ideal was opposed to the values of capitalism, it was about sharing, it was outside the market and anti-materialistic, a metaphor for common cause and belief. The women I interviewed often used 'community' in this way, as a complex and mobilizing Utopian ideal.

It was a 'hat stand' of ideology on to which both personal and collective identity was hung, and as a result it was jealously guarded.[1] As Michaela Hawkins said, it's being together through good times and bad times, loving one another, supporting one another, when we were a support group we not only supported the men, we supported ourselves … it's a bond thing, a bond thing. (interview, 22 September 1998)

While their emphases varied, 'community' was a common reference point that was described with considerable emotion as if it were a living thing, a collective organism. Thatcher, MacGregor and the Coal Board were all described as being determined to 'kill' the community. Thatcher was described as a 'murderer' by one woman. As a mobilizing and uniting metaphor there was no ambivalence: the image of life and death made the cause to save community morally just, and urgently necessary.

All the women I interviewed agreed that the fight for community was undeniably right. This belief would be reinforced by images and memories from the past. Jan Smith from Murton in Durham remembered the men walking up from the pit top after the evening shift:

They'd walk up, together like, and they'd be washed but they'd have the rings round their eyes, like mascara [laughs]. They'd be chatting like, I remember one bloke would always whistle as he went past, every morning that was. (interview, 7 October 1998)

It was not simply the women's descriptions of community that were emotive but also the tones in which they spoke. Their words were invested with an emotion that revealed the importance of the social rather than the economic issues at stake in the strike. 'Community' was turned into a means of intimating what could be possible. In Hetton-le-Hole in County Durham, Florence Anderson saw the strike and the co-operation it generated more explicitly as a different way of organizing economic and social life.

I think the community and communal wealth is more important … like during the strike, I always go back to the strike, because in the strike we took our kids with us wherever. I mean mine was 14, some had toddlers that big [lifts her hand], but your child was my child and I saw a glimpse of socialism there. Like we had the welfare kitchens and even business people in the community used to come in, a lad that had a fish and chip shop, every Tuesday and Friday he provided the fish and chips. People were emptying their gardens and bringing stuff in. A girl I know who lives down the bottom of this road, her husband's a consultant haematologist, and she's from Scotland, yet she was bringing apples from her orchards in … so what we had we shared and it was like what I call communal wealth, and that's what I believe in. (interview, 1 April 1999)

The women linked together their history as communities and their collective need to generate a vision of a future and a different way of organizing. This shared vision was one of the binding forces in the dispute: it was not about a particular line or a specific politics, it was a Utopian vision expressed through shared images.

This sense of common cause and a shared vision was reinforced by NUM organization and the social life that surrounded it. All the women in Durham have memories of the Big Meeting, a yearly march of all the miners' lodges into central Durham from the surrounding towns and villages. They remember the excitement of the marches, the beauty of the banners and the strength and exhilaration of the numbers flooding into Durham. Joan Barnes in Easington expresses this well when she talks about her childhood visits to the NUM offices to pay union subs for her father.

> But I remember really clearly going to the union and the big meeting. When you went to the big meeting you'd march in after your own banner and when you got to the meet you could put your banner down and find your relatives in other villages by looking for the banner. Horden pit had always had 'United We Stand, Divided We Fall' painted on wall and I'd see it every week when I went to pay the dues. (interview, 24 June 1998)

It was often a memory of childhood, when values were instilled in them, and the meaning of community was bound up with what community had meant to them then. Community was solidarity, laughter, sharing and a sense of something beyond the everyday grind of human existence. In this sense the strike was often about a re-creation or a reaffirmation of values that often lay dormant in those communities. Mining families in many villages had bought homes, and had cars and a reasonable income, yet the strike highlighted a less material aspect of their value system. Many of the women describe the strike as the worst and yet the best experience of their lives. While they experienced poverty during the strike, and debt in the aftermath, they also found a connection with their fellow strikers and with other communities that they felt had been lost.

It was not, then, whether such an idealized community had actually existed that came to matter, but that in the dispute they created a collective spirit based on pre-existing ideals that pointed the way towards a new way of organizing social life. In the aftermath of the strike this sense of an alternative society was dimmed but never lost. Even as the women I interviewed described the disintegrative changes that occurred after the dispute, their memory of the possibilities the strike opened up to them remained most vivid. While they have had to cope with change, many of them were to carry that vision of a communal, non-materialist community into their activism in the last 15 years.

However, the closure of the pits, the defeat of the dispute and the altered structure of mining communities continually negated this vision. The women who told me their life stories had all been forced to make major adjustments in their daily relationships and in how they work and think politically. The decline of the coal industry means that many villages are no longer made up of miners and their families.

Many women described the buying up of old NCB housing by housing associations or local landlords. This has happened to a great extent in villages in the north-east such as Easington and Murton and to some extent in the South Wales valleys. In the words of Jan Smith from Murton,

> Oh yes, I mean I can take you out there and show you the colliery houses that we used to live in and you'll see they are boarded up, the private landlords have moved in. I know one private landlord bought six houses for thirty-two thousand and rents them out for seventy pound a week and he's not bothered who he gets in. I mean we had trouble here the other night, somebody had abandoned a car up here, smashed all the windows of the car and the police had to come, it's just things like that. We had a thriving shopping centre up Market Street, it's not there no more. (interview, 7 October 1998)

The new residents have no knowledge of mining communities, and have brought new problems and a different culture. The women often view these newcomers with suspicion and they are seen as bringing problems of crime or drugs to the area. But at the same time unemployment and the deterioration of the local community has meant that people they knew are also involved in the 'trouble'. In Markham in South Wales Hilary Rowlands is a drug and alcohol worker who counsels ex-miners as well as newcomers to the area. The women struggle with this contradiction. They have a vision of the old community, yet have to admit that it is not just the newcomers who have brought problems to the area: economic change has also affected old friends and connections. Ann Jones from Hirwaun, South Wales, expresses this well:

> When I was at school I can't remember anybody's father who wasn't a miner … other than the shopkeepers' children … There's nobody ever not been a miner, I mean Tower's never been open without a member of my family working in it from the day they sunk the first shaft … but that kind of unity's gone. There isn't that kind of community spirit that there was years ago. I mean I couldn't tell you who lives in this street, you know! I lived down the street, there was two hundred houses and I could tell you every person that lived there, I could tell you now who lived in those houses but I don't know who lives in this street. We've had murders here, yes we've had

three or four murders here, and burglaries, and since that multi-storey block it's like Fagin's den. It used to be beautiful when families lived there, but now because nobody wants to live in them, anybody that can't live anywhere else is shipped over here … Mind you, saying that, that's wrong, where the murders were concerned it was local people who lived here anyway. (interview, 11 March 1999)

The change in the composition of mining communities is one they experience the most keenly. They have lost connections, friends and family, as people have moved away to find work. With the destruction of the pit the hub of the village was often lost, families no longer worked in the same locality. Kay Case in Treharris, South Wales, said:

One son, he lives in Yorkshire, but it's nice my daughter being in Blackwood. I see her on a regular basis and I have my grandson on a Tuesday, so it's lovely, but it does show what I missed with the other grandchildren going up to Yorkshire. I phone them every Sunday and speak to them, I think a family is important and that was the biggest blow about shutting the pit was that people had to move and leave their families, there must be hundreds and hundreds of people who've had to relocate. My son works in Yorkshire, but there's one section up there with people from all over Wales and other parts of the country who have moved there. I missed out so much of the children, they can never replace it with however many amenities they give me, that will never replace the fact that I didn't see my grandchildren growing up on a regular basis. That to me was the biggest upheaval. (interview, 13 March 1999)

The loss of people and jobs has meant less money circulating in the local economy and high levels of unemployment and deprivation. There has been a bleeding of population out of the areas and a deterioration in housing stock. Sandra Taylor of Church Warsop, Nottinghamshire, said:

I could take you down the street to Warsop Vale and I can show you what a community looks like now a pit is shut, it's terrible … there's houses there … there's forty-five empty houses that the Coal Board allowed a landlord – a Rachman-like landlord – to buy. (interview, 13 September 1998)

While there have been attempts to regenerate mining areas, with the loss of jobs has also come a loss of facilities and resources for local residents. In all the smaller villages women complain that shops have closed and as local businesses have moved on they find they have to travel further to shop. Not only has this meant the loss of facilities and local jobs for women, it has also meant a lessening of daily contact. Women would often meet at the local shops and if they did not know each other as friends they often knew each other by sight. Juliana Heron in Hetton-le-Hole in the north-east knew most of the women when the group started because she worked at the local Kwik Save, where all the women shopped.

Apart from the commercial resources that have gone since the strike, perhaps the greatest resource they have lost is the social life and cohesion provided by the NUM. As the pits have closed, so have miners' welfare halls. Events organized by the NUM have either faded or been transformed. The once magnificent yearly march to Durham by all the surrounding NUM local branches has become a Durham-based festival with just a few of the surviving miners' banners represented. Ann Jones regularly went from South Wales to the Durham march, but no longer does so since she now sees few faces she knows. Gwen Mellor in Nottingham, and her husband Paul, still socialize in the surviving miners' welfare club but the numbers are fewer and the atmosphere has changed.

The loss of the material resources that provided the social 'glue' to these communities has certainly undermined the women's ability to sustain the ideal they held of community. Florence Anderson in Hetton-le-Hole describes an inability to communicate this sense of community to a generation who have grown up in a completely different social and economic context:

It's 15 years, but we've got a generation that would have been educated up at Hetton pit. They would have had money in their pockets, they would have been drunk on a weekend and maybe fighting, you know, on the main street – which has always been the culture. But I'll tell you, they didn't burgle people! They didn't rob people, and that's what they're doing now, and that is part of the social repercussion. We've got youngsters who've grown up with no real job for them and they are not the type of lads who go on into higher education. But you see these days I really don't think they realize the implication of what they are doing to other people … it saddens you, you know, what it was and what it is now like. (interview, 1 April 1999)

In the context of loss it has been hard indeed for women to hold on to the Utopian vision that was so strong during the strike. Internal conflict was negotiated and minimized during the strike, and despite splits and disagreement the groups worked together. In the aftermath of the dispute the groups lost cohesion and disagreements became more open. One of the women, Maureen Stubbins from Podworth, Yorkshire, expressed a deep disillusionment with the way regional organization went after the strike:

I just feel as though I can't cope, I can't cope with the fighting. Every time you go you feel it's like a … well you walk into the room and if certain people are there you can cut the atmosphere with a knife. Quite honestly, I don't want that, and I'm sure a lot of others don't, but there's allus some that wants a bit of fight and that ... Quite honestly I don't want to go and sit around a table because if it started I would blow up and I'd say things that shouldn't be said that I've got inside ... I think I've got a lot of anger for certain folk and you've just got to keep the bloody lid on. And that's why I've had enough of politics, I don't like splits. (interview, 11 July 1998)

There is a sense in the regional and national organization that the shared vision that held the groups together has gone. Those images were mobilized in support of a dispute and at the time they seemed like a possibility. With the loss of the strike, loss of jobs, family, friends and resources, many of the women have moved on.

Yet at the same time, while many of the women have become disillusioned by the loss of the strike, others have taken what they learned during the dispute into new communities and new struggles. During the strike links were built with other organizations and individuals and many of the women have maintained those links since the dispute. The Oakdale group in South Wales made contact with a lesbian and gay group in London with whom they still have occasional contact. Many other women made friendships with miners and miners' wives from other areas and they still visit and spend time together.

Women have also made new political alliances. In Barnsley several of the women who were involved in WAPC set up a Rape Crisis Centre. Anne Brookes was one of them and she describes setting up the centre:

It was some of the women who'd been in WAPC again you see, that were in the same group as me. It were Ann, she said 'I don't know what we're going to do but we're going to have a meeting at Linda's and see, are you coming?' And that's how it began. There were some Labour Party women, but there were women from all over and women that I hadn't met before. It were like women had some energy again and said let's put this energy into something positive. And we thought about a women's centre at first and that's what we were aiming for, but there weren't funds and finding rooms and that, and then we thought what about a Rape Crisis Centre, there isn't a Rape Crisis Centre in Barnsley, nearest one were Doncaster or Sheffield – so it were quite a trek. If you think there's a woman in distress and she's got to go all that distance – so we thought let's do this, that's what we did. (interview, 20 May 1998)

After the strike Anne Brookes argued that many women needed to rest and recover from the stress and debt that had built up during the strike, but ultimately the women wanted to find a new community, to re-create the sense they had of women working together during the strike. For Anne, the Rape Crisis group gave her a new political direction and new sets of alliances and connections. The group was familiar to her in the way it worked and because its focus was on helping women:

> Well, everybody does a bit of everything, because it's a collective, with a collective they'll say no we can't do with that! I like working like that – everybody's equal. And you make space for one another. Most of the original group are there though, there's five of us which is pretty good going after eight years. We've had us ups and downs, we've had us arguments, but at end of the day, we sit down and sort it out, we should be able to clear the air, it's a collective. (ibid.)

Anne speaks for the collective regularly at fund-raising events and has launched a major campaign against rape and sexual violence in Barnsley.

The group has given her the space to express the values she fought for during the miners' strike, but finding and working with new allies has not always been easy. Anne does not describe herself as a feminist, yet uses the Rape Crisis approach developed by women who are largely feminist in her counselling work. She tries to reconcile this contradiction in her working. She also does not always feel comfortable with her new allies, who are very different from the women she worked with in the strike:

> No, no, everybody counsels in a different way, but the basics are there, they have their own style. I say I'm not a feminist but it is from a feminist perspective, that's where we differ from other services and that's why women use us, instead of statutory bodies, because we're for the women ... The majority of women, all of them except for me, in this Rape Crisis group, they've got degrees, doctorates now, many of them. They can be quite intimidating. Your stomach starts going, and it can start a few days before and I think 'why am I doing this, why am I putting myself through this?' Gets to middle of next week and I'll be in a state. Being the type of person I was I felt I couldn't do nothing, but I felt I was forced to do things no matter how difficult it was. I didn't go with the intention of getting involved, but it just happened from that one meeting. (ibid.)

While new alliances can create new contradictions, many women have focused on their own communities and the more 'traditional' work of rebuilding and sustaining the links within their communities. Many of the women who were active in the strike are at the centre of attempts to 'regenerate' their communities. Often working as local councillors, community activists and workers, they try to work to lessen the impact of economic change. The women are most often 'community' or 'parish' councillors, working at the most grassroots level to effect change in their locality. Juliana Heron from Hetton-le-Hole is in the local Labour Party,

and although she has little faith in the party hierarchy she believes that
working at a local level she can make a difference:

> Let's just say, I'm not a fan of Tony Blair! It's very difficult, I suppose you
> join because you want to change the world, but you canna. A lot of us are
> disillusioned but at the end of the day, if you want to be involved on the
> council level you can still get some of your thoughts and ideas through.
> There's a youth project being started up the road and the councillor had a
> meeting down the park with the local kids to say 'well, what do you want?',
> and it's a BMX roller park they've asked for. You see, it's the kids have come
> to him and he's said we'll give it a chance, we'll work with you, and there's
> things like that where you can work with people to make it better in your
> local area. At the minute we're trying to get this Hetton 'Centre of Excel-
> lence' set up with money from lottery bids and all that. We're hoping to get
> a brand new swimming baths and sports facilities ... a healthy living centre
> and a nursery of excellence, but we are talking three or four years' time and
> we've had a meeting today to start the process. We're going to get question-
> naires out to people, and it's people involvement. What's coming up now is
> the regeneration of the coalfields area, and our area had been pinpointed as
> an area, there could be money coming in from there, so we still do see a bit
> of light at the end of the tunnel. I'd like to see a cyber café and computers
> and that, it would be great to see the kids get trained on the computers.
> (interview, 20 April 1999)

This attitude is common among women who are still active. What we see
in Juliana Heron's thinking, and this is common to all the women who are
still active, is adaptation to a new context. Like Anne Brookes in Barnsley,
Hilary Rowlands or Hefina Headon in South Wales, they are creative in
their exploration of funding possibilities. They are realistic in their assess-
ment of what can be done in the short term and work consistently to try
to provide facilities in their local areas. Yet this is not to say that they have
abandoned the possibilities that the strike opened up to them. Juliana
makes the point that 'you join because you want to change the world, but
you canna'. The women still have a distrust of hierarchy and prefer
grassroots working, their focus is still local and they work pragmatically
with local Labour and Liberal Democrat councillors. What the women
lack is the political context in which to act on the more radical elements
of their politics.

The politics that the women held, and still hold, cannot be divorced
from their place in their communities and their vision of community. Yet
community activism is rarely acknowledged as a legitimate political arena.
The majority of the women I spoke to saw themselves as apolitical before
the strike. A few had come from political families, or were long-time Labour

Party members, but most claimed political innocence. Yet on closer inspection many of the women had been active in community politics. Sandra Taylor from Nottinghamshire had come from a conservative mining family and said she had done nothing political 'only working to keep the local nursery like, for the kids you know' (interview, 13 September 1998). It transpired that working to keep the local nursery open had involved a campaign of lobbying local councillors with local women, raising funds and running the nursery themselves. Similarly, Betty Cook from Yorkshire describes herself as apolitical before the strike, yet she had been a thorn in the side of the local council on various community issues (interview, 3 April 1998; see also Allen and Measham 1995). Because these activities were seen by the women as an extension of their domestic and caring role, they did not perceive those activities as political because they had internalized dominant ideas of 'politics', which is usually defined in a limited sense around electoral or union politics. In turn the significance of women's networking is frequently missed out of studies of social movements.

The activism of Women Against Pit Closure members both sustained and was sustained by 'community' at a variety of levels. This was an ongoing and dialectical process. They defended traditional communities and in the process created new and challenging communities. In the course of the 1984–85 strike they were to reach out to other communities and develop a wider sense of identification. Community became increasingly an ideological rather than a geographical phenomenon and the women's sense of political affiliation grew stronger during the dispute. In the process the idea of 'community' was to become encompassing; its emotional meaning and wider ideological force enabled them to act cohesively despite difference and conflict on a local level. Some of the women have tried to carry the vision of community they shared in the strike into their activities after the strike. Part of this transition has involved appropriating older conceptions of community and 'remaking' community through new alliances. This has not always been totally successful, and the women have faced great contradictions in meshing a class-based conception of community with newer alliances based around gender or other political visions. Their attempts to change and grow since the strike, changing allegiances and understandings while retaining an identity forged in a traditional community, have been continuing amid the pit closures, unemployment and social disintegration which came with defeat.

Their dynamic and complex reworking of their understanding of 'community' raises wider questions about narrow definitions of politics that exclude action around the relationships of daily life. They show how conceptions of the political are formed and reformed through reflection based on experience.

Note

1. On this ideological and symbolic dimension to community see Cohen 1985; Lakoff and Johnson 1980.

Bibliography

Allen, Sheila and Fiona Measham (1995) 'In defence of home and hearth?', *Journal of Gender Studies*, 3(1): 31–45.

Allen, Vic (1981) *The Militancy of the British Miners*, Shipley: Moor Press.

Anthias, Floya and Nira Yuval-Davies (1989) *Woman, Nation, State*, Hampshire: Macmillan.

Barnsley Women Against Pit Closures (1984) *Barnsley Women Against Pit Closures*, Vol. 1, Todmorden: Arc & Throstle Press.

— (1985) *Barnsley Women Against Pit Closures*, Vol. 2, Todmorden: Arc & Throstle Press.

Beynon, Huw and Terry Austrin (1994) *Masters and Servants – Class and Patronage in the Making of a Labour Organisation*, London: Rivers Oram Press.

Cohen, Anthony (1985) *The Symbolic Construction of Community*, London: Horwood/Tavistock .

Colls, Robert (1987) *The Pitmen of the Northern Coalfield*, Manchester: Manchester University Press.

Coventry Miners' Wives Support Group (1986) *Mummy ... What did you do in the Strike?*, Coventry: Coventry Miners' Wives Support Group.

Diani, Mario and Ron Eyerman (1992) *Studying Collective Action*, London: Sage.

Eppleton Miners' Wives Support Group (1985) *Feelings Alive 84/85*, Hetton-Le-Hole, Tyne & Wear: Eppleton Miners' Wives Support Group.

Feldman, Roberta (1988) 'The community needs to be built by us', in Nancy Naples (ed.), *Community Activism and Feminist Politics*, London: Routledge.

Francis, Hywel and David Smith (1980) *The Fed – A History of the South Wales Miners in the Twentieth Century*, London: Lawrence & Wishart.

Gibbon, Peter (1988) 'Analysing the British miners' strike of 1984/5', *Economy and Society*, 17(2) (May).

Howell, David (1987) 'Goodbye to all that', *Work, Employment and Society*, 1(3) (September).

Keating, Jackie (1992) *Counting the Cost*, Barnsley: Wharncliffe Publications.

Lakoff, George and Mark Johnson (1980) *Metaphors We Live By*, London: University of Chicago Press.

Miller, Jill (1986) *You Can't Kill the Spirit*, London: Women's Press.

Pitt, Malcolm (1979) *The World on Our Backs – The Kent Miners and the 1972 Miners' Strike*, London: Lawrence & Wishart.

Seddon, Vicky (1986) *The Cutting Edge – Women and the Pit Strike*, London: Lawrence & Wishart.

Stead, Jean (1987) *Never the Same Again*, London: Women's Press.

Warwick, Dennis and Gary Littlejohn (1992) *Coal, Capital and Culture*, London: Routledge.

Witham, Joan (1986) *Hearts & Minds*, London: Canary Press.

5

Between a Rock and a Hard Place: Women's Self-Mobilization to Overcome Poverty in Uganda

Sylvia Tamale

With a post-independence history of political strife, economic mismanagement and intense social conflict, Uganda ranks amongst the world's 20 poorest countries. Seventy per cent of its population live below the poverty line, and women constitute the majority of Ugandans who live in poverty.[1] The processes of globalization, particularly the post-Cold War economic restructuring in the area of trade and financial liberalization, have adversely affected vulnerable social groups such as women (Tamale 2000). The feminization of poverty is brought into sharp focus by the fact that despite the fact that they are the prop of Uganda's economy through the production of 80 per cent of its food production, women have far less access than men to productive means, including loan capital.[2]

Faced with gender oppression as well as economic underdevelopment, the priorities of the women's movement in Uganda include struggles for basic amenities that Western feminists, for example, take for granted. It is also important to note that the construct of 'feminization of poverty' has recently come under attack for its failure to capture adequately the nuanced dynamics at work in the creation of poverty among both men and women,. For example, in societies such as those found in Africa, where poverty is the norm, a 'feminization of gender' framework is likely to place blinders on possibilities for coalitions between men and women in their struggles to alleviate poverty. Rather than emphasize women-focused coalitions, a case has been made for a *gendered poverty analysis*. This is particularly relevant in a racialized gender analysis in order to demonstrate the impact and poverty-maintaining effects of gendered racial oppression of the life chances of African women and men (and other people of colour), albeit experienced differently (Mutua 2001; Arriola 2000; Jackson 1998).

The women themselves are not resigned to this seemingly hopeless situation. They are taking concrete measures, from the grassroots level upwards, to lift themselves out of the cycle of inter-generational poverty by tapping into their enormous potential as developers and agents of change.[3] Most significant among such measures are the self-help efforts that range from organized semi-formal groups to informal associations, all of which are built on the basis of mutual trust. Such groups function as savings, lending and borrowing associations in which individuals have access to relatively small amounts of money in an attempt to reduce the uncertainty of their lives.[4]

The phenomenon of poverty has become an issue of global concern. Indeed, the first of the twelve critical areas of concern drawn up at the 1995 United Nations Fourth World Conference on women held at Beijing obliges all member states to tackle the persistent and increasing burden of poverty on women. At the national level, the Ugandan government launched the Poverty Eradication Action Plan (PEAP) in 1997. This plan has the ambitious goal of eradicating poverty from Uganda by the year 2017. The measure of absolute poverty used under the PEAP is based on the purchasing power or self-provisioning (capacity to meet the monetary cost of certain basic needs) of a household. In other words, poverty is determined in relation to a 'minimum' food basket (Whitehead and Lockwood 1999).[5] The objective of the PEAP, therefore, is to quantitatively lift all Ugandans above this money-metric poverty line by 2017 (Tamale 2000).

There is a wide disparity between government's definition of the term poverty and that of grassroots women that I interviewed in my study on women's anti-poverty organizing. Below is a sampling of the various ways that grassroots women in Uganda define poverty.[6]

- A sense of helplessness that comes with the inability to control one's basic survival.
- Lacking the power and capacity to maintain yourself and your family; if you cannot afford to pay medical bills for your children or pay their school fees ... general inability to lift yourself up.
- Not being able to do something that generates income. Two years ago when I was still with my ex-husband, he would not let me sell samosas by the roadside to earn a few shillings. He said that it was his duty to take care of the family and yet we used to sleep hungry ... Today, I'm a different person, free to sell my samosas and I can take care of my children.
- I would refer to myself as poor if I'm not earning an income or if I don't have money to run my small charcoal-selling business.
- Poverty is self-inflicted. To be described as 'a poor person' is the worst insult anyone can throw at you ... Poverty is quite different from *enfuna entono* (i.e., income).
- Poverty comes with death; health is wealth.

- Poverty is when you cannot afford the basics in life. It's when your child attains the grades that qualify her to go to Gayaza High [a prestigious boarding school in Kampala] but you can only afford to take her to Crane High [not real name – in reference to a cheap sub-standard school].
- There are many levels of poverty: moral poverty, psychological poverty, material poverty and so on.

It is obvious that these grassroots women's view of poverty is broader than the narrow focus supplied by the Ministry of Finance, Planning and Economic Development (MFPED). While the latter views poverty through the narrow lens of per capita expenditure, grassroots women link it to disempowerment, vulnerability, lack of resources and oppression. Many of them link inability to engage in income-generating activity to their concrete positions as subservient wives or their full-time job of child-rearing and home-making. In other words, they believe that if they had the freedom, time and capital to engage in trade, it would be quite easy to escape the cycle of poverty.[7]

Most problematic about the government's characterization of poverty is that it disregards its gender implications. For instance, the poverty line is based on household expenditures, without analysis of the intra-household inequities, differences in access to income and consumption.[8] The PEAP prescriptions do not aim to dismantle the underlying structural causes of poverty and build up a strong and sustainable socio-economic base for lifting the country out of underdevelopment. Instead, the Plan seeks merely to 'adjust poverty' within existing conditions.[9] The best that the PEAP can hope to achieve is to widen the gap between the upper/middle class and the peasant/working class of Uganda.

This chapter uses the case study of Uganda to explore some of the ways in which women organize at the ground level to overcome the worst effects of poverty. The following section is a brief recapitulation of a feminist bifocal conceptualization of gender struggles into practical and strategic needs, appraising its strengths and weaknesses and linking the characterization to indigenous women's struggles in Uganda. In the subsequent section I delve into the practical efforts by grassroots women to overcome poverty. In the first half of the section I examine their confrontation with micro-finance institutions, while the latter half focuses on non-institutional self-help efforts in the form of rotating savings and credit associations (ROSCAs). The final section constitutes some concluding remarks.

Feminine or Feminist? Revisiting Practical versus Strategic Gender Needs

The dichotomization of 'practical' and 'strategic' gender needs has been a powerful conceptualization of feminist theory as well as women's mobilization since the mid-1980s (e.g. Barigg 1989; Moser 1991; Stephen 1992; Wakoko and Lobao 1996). The scholar that lent comprehensive articulation to this conception was Maxine Molyneux (1985), and she explained that practical gender interests emanate from women's day-to-day basic needs, which are closely linked to their domestic labour in the private sphere.[10] Thus women's struggles for improved access to clean water, food, healthcare, housing, clothing and credit facilities would fall into this category. Molyneux argued that while practical needs address women's subordination in society, meeting them is not sufficient to eliminate systemic gender discrimination. She contends that in order to dislodge women's subordination, there is a need to analyse such subordination deductively, identifying strategic needs that form the basis of overcoming sexism.

Examples of strategic needs include abolition of the sexual division of labour, alleviation of the burden of domestic labour and child care, and removal of institutionalized forms of discrimination. In sum, under Molyneux's conceptualization, practical interests - while mitigating the worst consequences of sexism – do not offer a lasting solution to the various forms of women's subordination; instead, they reinforce the gendered division of labour, ultimately maintaining the status quo. Strategic needs, on the other hand, politicize practical interests, challenging male domination and aiming at transforming the status quo.

More recently, the dichotomization of gender needs has been criticized for being problematic and elitist, especially insofar as it is applied to the analysis of poor uneducated women (Lind 1992; Nelson 1993; Tripp 2000). Aili Mari Tripp, who has analysed Ugandan women's grassroots organization for economic needs, has observed that:

> The dichotomization of strategic and practical gender interests ... tends to be elitist in outlook, assuming that poor women cannot transform everyday struggles for the betterment of their communities into struggles that challenge sexual subordination without the help of 'more enlightened' outside feminist influences ... While it is true that not all such mobilization leads to a new awareness about gender identity, one cannot assume this a priori without knowing the particulars of a struggle. (2000: 165–6)

Indeed, Tripp's examination of indigenous women's associations in Uganda consistently revealed that strategic gender needs were inherent in *a priori* struggles for practical interests. In other words, struggles for access were intertwined with struggles for power and control. One need only scrutinize women's definitions of poverty and the activities taken to overcome it offered in the next section to realize that their struggles are not narrowly confined to access to basic practical needs. Their consciousness is acutely aware of the nexus between their poverty (or lack of access to resources) and their subordination as women.

Poor Women's Search for Capital

The phenomenon of micro-financing[11] Uganda has joined the rest of the developing world in linking the tool of micro-financing to its poverty eradication strategy. Reminiscent of the infamous World Bank-fostered Women in Development (WID) programmes that were launched in developing countries during the 1980s, the current fascination with this new form of financing raises some concern, if not alarm. Indeed, the evangelical zeal with which donors and non-governmental organizations are embracing micro-financing leads one to believe that it is indeed the latest 'flavour of the month' in the globalization movement. Again, with the strong backing of the World Bank and other donors, micro-finance institutions (MFIs) have mushroomed in many parts of the developing world, including Uganda.[12] Micro-financing encompasses empowerment of women, financial sustainability, and working on free market principles (Wheat 1997).

From the descriptions of poverty provided by poor women in Uganda, it is clear that their expectation in relieving themselves of the burden of poverty lies in two empowering and interrelated areas: first, access to basic skills and financial resources to enable them to meet their basic needs (practical interests); second, the freedom from the socio-cultural oppression meted out to women (strategic needs). One of the NRM strategies for eradicating poverty by 2017 is to 'provide financial services to the poor through promotion of the growth of Micro-Finance Institutions (MFIs) and rural village banks (MFPED 1999: 105). Government is in the final stages of formulating a national policy on micro- and rural financing as well as a draft law for regulating MFIs. The donor community, most notably the World Bank, supplements government support to MFIs.[13] Indeed, the economic liberalization processes set in motion under the World Bank/IMF economic restructuring programmes witnessed convergence of foreign-registered MFIs towards poor developing countries.

In Uganda, several MFIs targeting women as their exclusive clientele appeared on the scene in the 1990s. Investing in women makes a lot of sense, first, because they form the largest segment of people living in poverty and second, because of their proven high debt-repayment record. Studies have shown that men are bigger defaulters than women (CEEWA

1999). Moreover, it has been established in Uganda and elsewhere that women-run businesses tend to benefit family members within their households more directly than those run by men (CEEWA 1999; Khandker 1998; Todd 1996).

How do poor Ugandan women first get to know about the availability of MFI services? Most of those I spoke to told me that they heard about it from friends and relatives. However, a good number indicated that their local female member of parliament introduced them to the MFI that they benefited from. Whether for altruistic or personal reasons, many politicians in fact make political capital out of marketing MFIs to poor women.[14]

In order to understand the concrete way that MFIs operate in Uganda, I will use the lending methodology of the Foundation for International Community Assistance (FINCA) as an example. My choice of FINCA (Uganda) is based on the fact that it is the largest affiliate of the US-registered FINCA International's network, with over 500 village banking groups and serving more than 23,000 women clients in Uganda. Under FINCA's operation structure, a group of 20 to 30 women, usually from one village, form a group (or adapt an existing one for the purpose) that acts as a conduit for administering its loan monies. FINCA loans are supposed to be used for setting up or financing small businesses. In Uganda, these include charcoal and tomato selling, retail groceries, chicken rearing, tailoring, dealing in second-hand clothing, local gin brewing and operating beauty salons and restaurants.

When they first sign up, group members are subjected to brief training in bookkeeping and other basic business skills. FINCA incorporates credit and savings in its operations and the average loan size to clients is the equivalent of US$96. More recently, it also introduced an insurance policy that absolves its clients from all FINCA liabilities at death. Thus each group must have a bank account where each member compulsorily deposits her savings. Clients are not encouraged to draw from their savings unless they are terminating their contract or are in dire need.[15]

Social collateral replaces conventional collateral whereby FINCA's loans are secured through a system of peer pressure and support. Each of FINCA's clients must guarantee a minimum of two fellow members in addition to guaranteeing the repayments of the group as a collective. This system of several and joint pledging of loans is so effective in deterring default by group members that repayment rates often stand at well over 90 per cent (Wheat 1997).[16] FINCA extends loans to the group in 16-week cycles. The interest rate stands at 4 per cent per month (i.e., 48 per cent per annum).[17] The loan carries no grace period, which means that clients have to make their first payment on the principal and interest seven days after receiving the loan. The group meets with a FINCA loan officer once a week to update all due instalments and adjust the accounts. At the end of each cycle, FINCA will recapitalize a fresh one provided the group is current with its repayments. Most other MFIs in Uganda use FINCA's village banking method or variants of it.

So, how have Ugandan women responded to the FINCA scheme? All the women said that the loans had improved their lives significantly and that they would continue using these services. Apart from expanding their small businesses, the loans have enabled many women to buy land, build houses, pay children's school fees and feed their families. Many also intimated that being part of the village-banking group has engendered feelings of empowerment and self-worth. Furthermore, the friendships that result from these groups are enduring and often sprout into new support sub-groups commonly known in Luganda as *munno mukabi* (a friend in need). Members of *munno mukabi* contribute a small amount of money (e.g., 1 dollar per month) to act as a safety-net for its members. This fund is usually kept aside for members to borrow from on a rainy day and for the general welfare of its members.

Below are some translated extracts from the narratives of women clients about the benefits that they had derived from being part of a banking group:

> The best part of being part of this group for me has been the fact that it has instilled in me an ethic of love, patience and hard work. I feel like a whole new person now … I have made lasting and invaluable friendships here.

> So why do I come back in spite of all the problems? Well, it's virtually the only source available for me to access working capital for my bakery business. It's like receiving a salary at the end of every four months [laughter].

> It is so wonderful to be able to buy milk, eggs, pay for children's fees and all that without having to beg some man. Thanks to FINCA, I got *busobozi* [empowered]. My aim is to get an even bigger loan so that I can build one-roomed houses for renting out.

However, the majority of the MFI women clients I talked to registered a litany of complaints against the micro-credit institutions that they dealt with. The most common complaints cited included the following: small loan size, high interest rates, no grace period, vulnerability created by the system of group guarantorship, difficulty accessing their savings and husbands controlling the loan monies.[18] Some of the problems were expressed to me in the following ways:

> The MFI provided *entandikwa* [seed money] and opened our eyes but it is not enough … and having to repay within only one week makes matters worse. Most of us here do not sleep, working hard to make enough for the weekly repayments.

This loan money is *kalilo* [hot]. When we joined the group it was drummed into our heads that nothing comes in the way of repayment, nothing – not sickness, a bad business week, not even the loss of a loved one! During the weekly meetings, on repayment day, the MFI does not want to hear of any such 'excuses'. You have to make arrangements for sending the money if you can't come.

I usually write off Tuesdays [meeting day] as a non-business day because we spend half the day here balancing books and making sure that repayments are up to date. Late coming and absenteeism are big problems and we're always held up by those women who don't bring their money … *Musomesa* [teacher, in reference to the MFI loan officer] will not let us disperse unless all money due has been paid. Most times, the defaulter's guarantor doesn't have the money to pay up, then the burden is passed on to the whole group; money is deducted from our savings.

I would be doing very well today if it wasn't for my husband. Most of our husbands hate it when we join women's groups but they'll salivate when we return with FINCA money. Before I joined the group he used to pay the children's school fees. But when I joined, he abdicated all his prior responsibilities. He says, 'Loan me the fees money, I'll pay you back.' He never does!

My husband persuaded me to buy a *boda boda* [motorcycle taxi] with my loan money for him to ferry passengers. That was the biggest mistake I've ever made because I never see the proceeds from the business and I struggle to meet repayments.

The women who benefited from the MFIs that I studied varied from the uneducated poor, whose families depended on their small sugar-cane selling businesses, to better off high school and college graduates who imported merchandise from various Middle and Far Eastern countries such as Dubai. This differentiation is reflected in the group membership, with similar women registering in the same group. The groups with poorer women naturally face more problems involving repayment. Trapped in the snares of poverty and subordination, many clients fight the temptation to consume rather than invest their capital.

In order for a micro-finance institution to become self-sufficient in its operations, it needs to earn enough interest from its clients to cover operating costs, loan losses, financial costs, imputed costs and its capitalization rate (CEEWA 1999). The fact that credit is advanced without collateral makes the business a high risk one. Unfortunately, the MFIs' goal towards institutional self-sufficiency is mostly fitted out at the expense of clients' needs and interests.[19] In a way, this explains the unconscionable terms under which MFI clients receive their loans. Through an elaborate lending system, MFIs structure their loans (through best practices such as group lending, weekly payments and compulsory saving) in a fashion that guarantees near 100 per cent recovery rates.

Thus the system of micro-financing confronts women with a 'Jekyll and Hyde syndrome'. On the one hand, MFIs hold potential benefit in that they fill a crucial niche in the loan and investment industry by extending small short-term loans to poor women who would never qualify for loans from the traditional financial institutions. Access to such loans allows these women to deal with the worst effects of poverty. On the other hand, however, the terms under which such loans are given are quite onerous. The interest rates demanded by MFIs are relatively high. Moreover, the formal risk-sharing arrangement proves to be quite risky for many women of good will and the terms of repayment and the conditions of default are quite stifling. However, most MFI clients are so desperate that they are willing to accept any condition to access loan monies.

So clearly, while on the one hand, micro-financing has improved the lives of most of its clients, on the other, women still feel entrapped in the twin snares of finance capital and patriarchy. Guy Winship, the country director of FINCA (Uganda) recently stated, 'No one is persuaded or coerced into utilizing the services of FINCA: the relationship we have with our clients is a voluntary, contractual business relationship.'[20] Winship does not appreciate the fact that most of his clients deal with him out of sheer desperation and really have neither the choice nor the leverage to negotiate the contractual terms under which they borrow FINCA money.

It is a no-win situation for poor Ugandan women. At national level it is multi-lateral institutions (MLIs) such as the World Bank and the International Monetary Fund that lend money to government under stringent conditions that adversely affect the local populace. At the local level, MFIs produce similar results by fostering a context where social amenities such as health care and education are no longer subsidized by the state. It is like giving with one hand and taking away with the other.

The story of micro-financing in Uganda is yet to register successes similar to those of the oft-quoted Grameen Bank of Bangladesh.[21] Although MFIs offer an escape route for some poor women in Uganda, they are increasingly the subject of debate and controversy among feminists, development economists and policy-makers. Kenneth Okello, a social analyst from Northern Uganda, writes:

Many women in Lira have become victims of micro-credit institutions like FINCA. Credit induced poverty is on the increase. 'The leading perpetrators of this misery are FINCA and Pride Africa,' says a borrower from FINCA

who sold off her property just to pay back before the repayment deadline.
... The humiliation that comes with the recovery of loans in these integrated
credit schemes, which are supposed to offer comprehensive support in
addition to credit, is driving many women away. [22]

To escape the noose of micro-credit finance institutions, poor women
have resorted to forming their own credit organizations. The most common
and popular of such self-help organizations are the Rotating Savings and
Credit Associations (ROSCAs).

ROSCAs as a coping mechanism The concept of self-help is by no
means new to African communities. It stems from a rich history of social
support networks characteristic of the so-called extended families.[23] Rural
women have always been part of loose local associations that play the role
of social insurance. Individual women rely on the solidarity of their associ-
ational members for assistance in times of sickness and death, as well as for
weddings and other family celebrations. It was therefore easy for women to
revert to traditional wisdom when faced with a situation of economic crisis.
Today, thousands of such associations exist throughout Uganda's rural and
urban poor.[24] Many poor uneducated women in Uganda choose to save
through the ROSCAs arrangement rather than deal with MFIs. One such
association – Zirindabirawa women's group[25] – consciously decided to steer
clear of MFIs because of 'their high interest rates'.

Central to ROSCAs is the concept of mutual trust. The smooth operation of the association is guided by a principle of balanced reciprocity and
dependent on individual members meeting their end of the bargain for the
general good of the group. Here, neighbours, friends or family members
form a sort of savings club whereby members pool their savings together
in a communal savings 'pot' (Wheat 1997: 21). The individual deposits are
collected on a daily, weekly, monthly, quarterly, etc. basis and, periodically,
each member in rotation takes home the consolidated fund. Who gets to
take the interest-free fund home is usually determined either on the basis
of some kind of lottery draw or through mutual agreement. Membership
varies from four to 30 members (Guwatudde et al. 1994).

Zirindabirawa is an autonomous ROSCA with a membership of 20
poor urban women operating from Busega on the outskirts of the capital
city. Every Saturday they meet and each member contributes 1 dollar
towards their savings pot. In addition to members enjoying the benefits of
a cash-go-round loan, they also run a joint piggery project. Additionally,
Zirindabirawa group exploits its natural talents in cooking traditional
cuisine by hiring itself out for outside catering services. Such ingenuity
has paid off well, as all its members have been able to improve their small

enterprises and realize a better standard of living. The group is very tightly knit and members consider themselves as siblings or special mutual friends.[26]

In spite of the fact that available working capital is small and hardly expandable, individual members of the group told me how grateful they were that Zirindabirawa had imposed a savings discipline upon them. The relentless peer pressure to be economical and save has borne fruit for all. If a member defaults on her payments she is subjected to scorn by people she knows and cares about and who are in a position to punish her for her failures. Members share with each other what they plan to do with their funds, and in the process learn a great deal (see Light 1996).

To avoid antagonizing their husbands Zirindabirawa rotates the venue of its weekly meetings to the different homes of the individual members. Here, they ensure that the spouse in that particular home is involved in their activities, even if only to listen in. In this way, they have succeeded in overcoming the hostility that many Ugandan patriarchs express against women's groups, stereotyping them as 'only good for rumour-mongering and destabilizing families'. But most important is that, rather than reject and ignore their poor husbands in their struggles against poverty, the female members of this ROSCA recognize that gender relations are deeply embedded in the operation of economic structures and bring the men on board. Although Ugandan women constitute the majority of poor people and despite the fact that they face greater vulnerability from poverty than men do, Zirindabirawa women also recognize that the conditions of their men are not necessarily better than theirs. This differs from women-only poverty alleviation strategies such as those adopted by many MFIs, which unnecessarily strain intra-community, gender-aware efforts.

Recent studies of women's ROSCAs in Uganda have recorded the liberating ways in which these associations have transformed poor women's lives (Snyder 2000; Tripp 2000; Kasente 1998). In comparison to MFIs, ROSCAs have been found to be more flexible and adaptable to local needs; they are people-centred, not institutional-centred. Most significantly, they allow women to act as agents of socio-economic change. ROSCAs to a large extent represent a type of gendered discipline on the circulation, evaluation and the uses of money (Light 1996).

Concluding Remarks

In the last two decades, the struggle to overcome extreme poverty by Ugandan women has shifted into a higher gear. The two major tools of displacing poverty for women have been found in micro-financing and ROSCAs, as evidenced by the mushrooming of such associations over the last decade. Both tools have positive and negative aspects. As poor women's self-help initiatives continue to evolve in Uganda, it is critical that the women themselves reassess each of these mechanisms, reforming and adjusting them to conform to what they consider to be the most appropriate framework for their self-actualization.

The efforts to empower women economically must necessarily go hand-in-hand with similar efforts to remove their marginalization within the socio-cultural and political spheres. This would entail radical reforms in the areas of domestic relations, land ownership, inheritance and decision-making from the household through the village and national levels.

Equally important is the need to take cognizance of the fact that both women and men in Uganda are maintained in poverty that is mediated through neocolonialism, globalization and gender oppression. Rather than women-focused poverty alleviation programmes illuminating the feminization of poverty, the interventions can borrow a leaf from Zirindabirawa and facilitate community unity, without, of course, losing sight of the gendered inequality within the socio-political structures. In other words, the phenomenon of poverty must be addressed in a multi-pronged fashion, acknowledging that poverty is not simply a factor of economic impoverishment, straddling essentialist conceptions inherent in women-only focused (or men-only, for that matter) poverty alleviation strategies.

Notes

1. Figures from the Ministry of Finance, Planning and Economic Development.

2. The United Nations Development Programme for Women (UNIFEM) reports that globally, women make up 70 per cent of the world's 1.3 billion poor. See 'Strengthening women's economic capacity', http://www.unifem.undp.org/ec_pov.htm

3. It would take a much more comprehensive study than this chapter allows for a full-blown analysis of the role of women's self-help initiatives in socio-economic changes in Uganda. However, it is quite clear, in Margaret Snyder's words, that these women 'create wealth where there was none' and do make a difference to their families (Snyder 2000: 83).

4. Similar groups have long been in existence in most developing countries around the world (see e.g. Wu 1974; Vélez-Ibañez 1983; Miracle et al. 1980; Ardener and Burman 1995). Today ROSCA users can also be found among immigrant and minority communities of advanced industrial countries such as the USA (see e.g. Light 1996; Ardener and Burman 1995).

5. Note that this is a World Bank definition that is applied across the board to all situations.

6. Unless otherwise indicated, data cited in this chapter are based on a study that I undertook during the months of August and September 2000. I attended weekly meetings of eight village banking groups around Kampala that benefited from MFIs and also conducted interviews with individual members of the group. In addition, I spent ap-

proximately three hours talking to members of one ROSCA located at Busega near Kampala. The chapter also relies heavily on data provided by recent comprehensive studies conducted by the Uganda chapter of the Council for Ecomomic Development for Women in Africa (CEEWA 1999) and Margaret Snyder (2000).

7. For an example of broader ways of measuring poverty see 'India tries to reassess its measure for poverty', *New York Times*, 8 October 2000.

8. For a feminist discussion of the gender implication of development models that treat households as a unit see Whitehead 1998; Kabeer 1994; Evans 1991.

9. Julie Hearn, 'The uses and abuses of "civil society" in Africa', *Review of African Political Economy (ROAPE)*, 28(87), 2001. In a 29 April 2000 interview Mr Keith Muha-kanizi, acting director of economic affairs in the Ministry of Finance, Planning and Economic Development, stated that he believes the structural adjustment phase ended with the advent of the PEAP. He argued that currently, Uganda is in a post-SAP phase of 'development'. For further discussion of the HIPC initiative in Uganda see Oloka-Onyango 2000.

10. The distinction between practical and strategic needs can be traced back to Latin American (particularly Brazilian) feminist theorizing of the late 1970s (Alvarez 1989).

11. Micro-financing as used in this chapter simply means the loaning of small credit (US$10 to US$250) to the poor for small businesses or micro-entrepreneurships.

12. Examples include FINCA, PRIDE, Uganda Women's Finance Trust and other smaller MFIs supported by aid agencies such as Action Aid, Oxfam, CARE and Christian Aid. Multilaterals and international agencies that have joined the bandwagon of 'allocating' funds to MFIs include USAID, the European Union, the British Department for International Development and Citibank. The entry of commercial banks into this sector has raised both ethical and moral questions.

13. In addition to funding MFIs for on-lending to the poor, donors encourage MFIs to take a business approach to ensure self-sustainability (see e.g. USAID–PRESTO Project 1998).

14. In January 1998, when US President Bill Clinton visited Uganda, his wife Hillary Rodham Clinton, together with Uganda's First Lady, Mrs Janet Museveni, visited a number of MFI borrowers, thus placing a spotlight on micro-financing in the country.

15. In reality the system of saving acts as an additional guarantee for FINCA's repayments. Its loan officers deduct all outstanding repayments from clients' savings.

16. FINCA's repayment rate in Uganda stands at 96 per cent.

17. Such an interest rate is relatively high as it stands almost 18 points higher than the commercial rate.

18. Similar complaints were registered in the CEEWA study (1999: 22–33). An interesting phenomenon common to the majority of poor women in Uganda is their strong religious belief. Every group that I visited for this study typically commenced their weekly meeting with prayers, thanking their Maker for providing the repayment monies. Prayers also close the meeting, with members imploring the Almighty to intervene by making their businesses prosperous. Indeed, desparate impoverished women consistently invoked a higher force to intervene and assist even as they engaged in self-help activities. Just as female politicians in Uganda use religion as a way of easily dealing with the patriarchal political structures (Tamale 1999), poor women find solace in a higher force to provide them with the mantle to confront all odds that arise from poverty.

19. At the 2000 international Microcredit Summit, campaigners challenged the con-

ventional wisdom that suggests that these two priorities are mutually exclusive. They commisioned courses to train practitioners in this area. The goal of the summit is to reach 100 million of the world's poorest families, especially women, with credit and other financial and business services by 2005. See 'Empowering women with microcredit', 2000 Microcredit Summit Campaign Report on-line at http://www.microcreditsummit. org/campaigns/report00.html (accessed on 17 July 2000).

20. See 'FINCA loans don't squeeze poor women', *Monitor*, 11 September 2000.

21. With over 1.8 million borrowers, the Grameen Bank, set up in 1976, is currently considered the model of poverty alleviation micro-financing stragegy for developing countries.

22. 'Micro credit forces women into hiding', *Monitor*, 5 September 2000. See also 'Money for the poor is deadly', *Monitor*, 6 September 2000; 'FINCA loans don't squeeze poor women', *Monitor*, 11 September 2000; 'Poor know where to borrow from', *Monitor*, 12 September 2000.

23. The term 'extended family' is problematic because it presupposes an extension from some norm, in this case the Western-type nuclear family.

24. But ROSCAs are by no means limited to the poor. Some middle-class people, as a means of boosting their businesses, utilize the same technique.

25. Most community-based women's groups carry empowering names that hold meaning or are shortened versions of traditional sayings, adages or proverbs. *Zirindabirawa (ennaku nga nina banange)* literally translates as 'Where will problems find me when I have friends?'

26. It was quite easy for me to sense the closeness of the members of this group during our three-hour meeting. Their ROSCA represented a space where they could open up with all their problems, and my presence did not seem to inhibit them from pouring out very personal stories.

References

Alvarez, S. (1989) 'Politicizing gender and engendering democracy,' in A. Stepan (ed.), *Democratizing Brazil*, New York: Oxford University Press.

Ardener, S. and S. Burman (1995) *Money-Go-Round: The Importance of Rotating Savings and Credit Associations for Women*, Washington, DC: Berg.

Arriola, E. (2000) 'Voices of despair: women in Maquiladoras, Latina critical legal theory and gender at the US–Mexican border,' *DePaul Law Journal* (forthcoming).

Barrig, M. (1989) 'The difficult equilibrium between bread and roses: women's organizations and the transition from dictatorship to democracy in Peru', in J. S. Jaquette (ed.), *The Women's Movement in Latin America*, London: Unwin Hyman.

CEEWA (Council for the Economic Empowerment for Women of Africa – Uganda Chapter) (1999) *Baseline Study on Lending Methodologies of Micro-Finance Institutions in Uganda*, Kampala: CEEWA-Uganda.

Evans, A. (1991) 'Gender issues in household rural economics, *IDS Bulletin*, 22(1): 51–9.

Jackson, C. (1998) 'Women and poverty or gender and well-being?', *Journal of International Affairs*, 52(1): 67–82.

Kabeer, N. (1994) *Reversed Realities: Gender Hierarchies in Development Thought*, London: Verso.

Kasente, D. (1998) 'An analysis of selected projects' progress towards improving women's social/economic status in Uganda,' (abridged research report), Nairobi: Academy Science Publishers.

Khandker, S. R. (1998) *Fighting Poverty With Microcredit: Experience in Bangladesh*, New York: Oxford University Press.

Light, I. (1996) 'A self-help solution to fight urban poverty', *The American Enterprise*, 7(4): 50–3 (July/August).

Lind, A. C. (1992) 'Power, gender, and development: popular women's organizations and the politics of needs in Ecuador', in A. Escobar and S. Alvarez (eds), *The Making of Contemporary Social Movements in Latin America*, Boulder, CO: Westview Press.

MFPED (Ministry of Finance, Planning and Economic Development (1999) *Uganda Poverty Status Report 1999*, Kampala: Government of the Republic of Uganda.

Ministry of Women in Development, Culture and Youth (1994) *Women's Informal Credit Groups: An Exploratory Study of Some Experiences in Kampala*, Kampala: Ministry of Women in Development, Culture and Youth.

Miracle, M. P., D. S. Miracle and L. Cohen (1980) 'Informal savings mobilization in Africa', *Economic Development and Cultural Change*, 28: 701–24.

Molyneux, M. (1985) 'Mobilization without emancipation? Women's interests, the state, and revolution in Nicaragua', *Feminist Studies*, 11(2): 226–54.

Moser, C. O. (1991) 'Gender planning in the Third World: meeting practical and strategic needs', in R. Grant and K. Newland (eds), *Gender and International Relations*, Bloomington, IN: Indiana University Press.

Mutua, A. (2001) 'Why retire the "feminization of poverty" construct?', forthcoming in *University of Denver Law Review*.

Nelson, B. (1993) 'Mobilizing women as women: identities, ideologies, and opportunities', paper presented at the annual American Political Science Association meeting, 1–5 September, Washington, DC.

Oloka-Onyango, J. (2000) 'Poverty, human rights and the quest for sustainable development in structurally-adjusted Uganda', *Netherlands Quarterly of Human Rights*, 18(1).

Snyder, M. (2000) *Women in African Economies: From Burning Sun to Boardroom; Business Ventures and Investment Patterns of 74 Ugandan Women*, Kampala: Fountain Publishers.

Stephen, L. (1992) 'Women in Mexico's popular movements: survival strategies against ecological and economic impoverishment', *Latin American Perspectives*, 19(72, No. 1): 73–96.

Tamale, S. (1999) *When Hens Begin to Crow: Gender and Parliamentary Politics in Uganda*, Boulder, CO: Westview Press.

— (2001) 'The state, gender policy and globalization in contemporary Uganda', in C. Dodge and N. Musisi (eds), *Transformations in Uganda* (forthcoming).

Todd, H. (1996) *Women at the Center: Grameen Bank Borrowers After One Decade*, Boulder, CO: Westview Press.

Tripp, A. M. (2000) *Women and Politics in Uganda*, Oxford: James Currey.

USAID–PRESTO Project (1998) *Business Planning Guide for Micro Finance Institutions in Uganda*, Kampala: USAID.

Vélez-Ibañez, C. (1983) *Bonds of Mutual Trust: The Cultural Systems of Rotating Credit Associations Among Urban Mexicans and Chicanos*, New Brunswick, NJ: Rutgers University Press.

Wakoko, F. and L. Lobao (1996) 'Reconceptualizing gender and reconstructing social life: Ugandan women and the path to national development', *Africa Today*, 43(3): 307–22.

Wheat, S. (1997) 'Banking on the poor', *Geographical Magazine*, 69(3): 20–2 (March).

Whitehead, A. (1998) *Women in Development (WID), Gender and Development (GAD): The New Politics of an Old Distinction*, University of Sussex Development Lectures, Brighton: IDS.

Whitehead, A. and M. Lockwood (1999) 'Gender in the World Bank's poverty assessments: six case studies from sub-Saharan Africa', UNRISD Discussion Paper DP99, Geneva: UNRISD.

Wu, D. (1974), 'To kill three birds with one stone: the rotating credit associations of the Papua New Guinea Chinese', *American Ethnologist*, 1: 565–84.

6

Adithi: Creating Economic and Social Alternatives

Viji Srinivasan

Adithi is a non-governmental organization (NGO) working predominantly with poor rural women and girl children in the state of Bihar, India. The name stands for agriculture, dairy industries, tree plantation, handicrafts and the integration of women. We started in 1988 and twelve years later are working with 40,000 women and girls throughout the state. Most of the groups with whom Adithi works are 'trade' groups – for example, *sujini* (quilt-makers) or leafplate-makers, and membership of Adithi enables them to participate in a group savings scheme that gives them access to loans. Adithi aims to empower women and girl children as well as to eradicate poverty. It also seeks to make goods that are useful, beautiful and easy to market. It promotes alternatives, highlights issues, engages in advocacy, and organizes.

One question often asked in Bihar (mostly by men) is: 'Are you feminists?' by which they mean man-haters. But we proudly say: 'Yes, we are – feminists are those who can analyse society and see that it discriminates against women and girl children; and then, most importantly, are doing something to change this ambience.'

Bihar has a patriarchal system where women have been confined to the private sphere, where illiteracy and social taboos prevail. This leads to many aberrations, from the killing of female newborn infants to enforced veiling in front of male kinsmen of the husband (as if the men cannot control themselves). Child prostitution and dowry 'murders' occur, while widows – considered unlucky for centuries – are condemned to dreary and sorrow-filled lives. Due to this semi-feudal mind set, antiquated notions of *izzat* (honour) are still expressed. There is a strong feeling of vendetta: 'I will go to Tamil Nadu and tell your family about you', 'I will kill anyone who speaks against my father.'

More general difficulties are caused by the lack of social infrastructure in Bihar, which suffers not only from extremes of inequality and poverty but from the dysfunctional government of the state. The result is a paralysis. Little-frequented by-roads are full of mud, clay and olive-green grass, with garbage rotting and piling up. Dried and rotting flowers from the temple as well as temple offerings in leafplates, pig and dog faeces, cow dung and human excreta choke the drains. Yet pigs and dogs dig into them due to hunger. The electricity lines are pilfered and not replaced. Electricity is appropriated surreptitiously everywhere – not that it helps, because the state government owes huge bills for electricity and so there is nowhere in Bihar with an uninterrupted supply of current.

Adithi's approach has been to tackle patriarchal taboos and women's livelihood needs together, adapting its approach to relate to the diverse problems of women in differing regions and trades. These groups include fisherwomen, forest workers, agricultural workers, women in dairying, home-based handicraft workers, hawkers and vendors.

Women in Inland Fisheries

Soon after its formation in 1988 Adithi became involved with the *mallahins* (fisherwomen) of Madhubani, a backward district of Bihar. In the traditional fishing communities, women, though actively involved in fish culture, net-making and selling the fish catch, were forbidden to 'throw the net' or to harvest the fish.

The *mallahins* of Riyam, a large village in the Madhubani district, formed a women's fisheries co-operative society consisting of 42 women members. A pond of 28 acres was allotted to the Riyam Co-operative Society by the deputy development commissioner (DDC) responsible for development in the district. This was the first time in Bihar that a fisher-women's group had obtained access to a pond.

After much persuasion, the district officials agreed to designate more unused ponds to the women's groups. The women weeded all their allotted ponds and prepared for stocking. The process, however, was not an easy one. There were problems of access and technical support. Not only were a number of ponds full of roots and weeds, which were detrimental to the fish culture, but the fishermen's co-operatives opposed the women gaining access to ponds.

The fisherwomen came to learn that they were stronger in groups, where they could reinforce each other, receive training, and participate in literacy and health programmes to the benefit of their whole family. By the end of 1993, an organization was evolving among them. This was registered as Sahyogini Madhubani Mahila Matsyajivi Sahyog Samiti Ltd in March 1997. However, this Samiti is still not recognized by the government bodies on the grounds that only one fishermen's co-operative society can exist. However, a state-level workshop, 'Women in Fisheries – Problems and Prospects', was organized in 1998 and the fisherwomen have asked for 50 per cent of the ponds of Bihar to be allotted to fisherwomen societies. In 2001 the government offered 849 ponds.

Problems remain. Though the fisherwomen have successfully resisted the divisive efforts of upper-caste landowners, some groups are still not very strong. The concept of 'feeding' fish has not yet taken root and consequently the yield has been affected. Nevertheless, Adithi's experience of working with poor traditional fisherwomen in north Bihar indicates an alternative model for developing fisheries resources.

Women in Afforestation

The Santal tribal people distrust outsiders, whom they call *dikus* – those who create *dikkat* (difficulties). The Santals have lost most of their land to non-tribals, and deforestation means that plant remains are not getting converted into humus. As a result the topsoil is constantly being washed away.

Tribal women headloaders carry large bundles of fuelwood to sell, while girl children fetch fuelwood, twigs and fodder, or care for siblings. They have been adversely affected by deforestation because they have to go further and further in search of fuel, while they are vulnerable as women to sexual abuse and rape by government officials, contractors, businessmen, police and forest officials. One woman described their predicament very graphically, saying that it hurt her to cut the forest.

> The trees, which provide sustenance and livelihoods. The trees in which the glorious peacocks with blue-green feathers dance and breed, and the trees around which the yellow-maned lions lope and growl. It pains me much more than any of you. Yet what can I do? We are tribal people, once the proud possessors of vast tracts of forests, we are now disinherited, the industrialists and contractors have cut out forests. The rains have stopped falling, our land has become barren, our men have migrated. We have to feed our children. Headloading is the only skill we have, the only product for which there is a market. Even for this we and our girl children walk ten kilometres carrying the fuelwood – for only nine rupees a bundle. What is our alternative?

The tribal woman's situation is unique. There is no child marriage, marriage partners can be self-chosen, there is no veiling or *purdah* and of course the Santal woman can go to the fields or forests whenever she wants. However, the customary laws of the Santals are distinctly and visibly against women. Santal men can marry up to five wives. Santali daughters cannot inherit land. If a girl does not have a brother, after the death of her parents, the father's brother's sons (*gothia*) inherit the land the girl. Moreover, Santali women are without any social or political They are not represented on traditional conflict-resolution bodies; the are called *dayens* (witches) and driven out or killed. Babies are taken away by Santali men and killed and offered to the goddess Kali.

Added to this they have a very heavy work burden, being responsible not only for fuel but for many agricultural tasks, as men only undertake ploughing. Yet tribal women are marginalized in their own economy. The Santal Parganas are full of local periodic markets called *haats*, where 'upper-' or 'middle-' caste men sell. Tribal women work on the outskirts of the *haat* selling liquor – a white fluid distilled by themselves. They pour it into leaf-cups for immediate consumption, then into glasses for savouring and gossip and fry crisp snacks.

The other major livelihood opportunity of the tribal women is making leafplates and cups for a very small income. Each woman can make around 500 leafplates a day. But they have to spend one day in collecting leaves (and the forests are 'going' farther and farther away), and half a day in marketing. Deteriorating livelihood opportunities mean that more and more women are being driven into this trade. Although the pay is very low it requires a traditional skill for, as many types of leaves are used, it is necessary to know the forest in order to find them. For example, *sal* and *palas* leaves are used for eating plates or drinking cups; teak leaves are used for leaf-cups in which flowers are kept.

A similar low-income activity is *khajoor* (date palm tree) mat-making. The *khajoor* leaves have to be collected. As they are owned by someone, either a small payment or a mat has to be given in order to obtain them. They are dried, and the leaves are removed and woven into a coil. Then the pieces are joined together to make a mat, which is eventually sold for eight rupees. This mat-making is even more time-consuming and labour-intensive than making the leafplates, and it requires more skill.

Making ropes by hand (from jute) is also common in the Santal Parganas; it gives a slightly better income than the mats or the leafplates because the product can be sold for more.

In 1994 Adithi initiated a network of ten development NGOs working among tribal and poor non-tribal women. Feedback from these stressed the need for a more systematic approach to developing better livelihoods. In 1997 the Ayodare Rural Women's 'University' was created. This is really a campus called Ayodare Jarmundi and it has identified seven key areas: tree plantation; natural resource management (including agricultural development); non-farm and off-farm income-generation; health; education; crafts; legal rights and advocacy. Our approach combines livelihood economics with social needs, regarding the two aspects as inseparable.

...ems: the community is losing access to tradi-
...d, while at the same time the outside world is
...their domain. So Adithi emphasizes that women
...of the immediate environment and how to deal with

...three years, the environment has been the most critical
is... by the Adithi groups. Our aim has been to regenerate, at
least ... the rich forests that once covered the Santal Pargana region,
providing ... oor people with excellent sources of sustenance. We have also
made the issue of environmental regeneration gender-specific, ensuring
that women obtained rights to the land on which trees were planted. As
a result we have managed to plant 500 acres of private fallow land spread
over 15 villages with a variety of species of trees.

A few projects have attempted to meet short-term economic needs.
About a hundred women have been trained in natural dyed tasar (wild silk
worm) spinning and weaving, and the fabric produced is sold in the markets
of big cities and abroad. Working capital credit has been provided to women
engaged in a number of supplementary income-generating activities such
as paddy processing, mat-weaving and food processing. One of the ten
development NGOs, Pragatisheel Mahila Sabha, has successfully upgraded
incomes in wild tasar cocoon-rearing in the forests.

More generally, Ayodare Jarmundi has built up a team of technically
and professionally qualified people to support its various activities. They
provide technical and managerial inputs to the focus teams.

Another achievement of the past three years' work has been in increasing
Santal women's awareness of their own legal rights. Very bravely, a number
of the young women are prepared to take up the fight for emancipation
and to follow it through.

Women in Agriculture

Sharecropping is illegal but widespread, especially in north Bihar. The
land of Bihar is owned mainly by Rajputs, Bhumihars and Brahmins. The
younger people from these groups migrate to the cities, leaving the landless
to work their land. Sharecropping in Bihar comes in two kinds. One is a
form of leasehold, known locally as *Mankhab*. But the more common kind
is the practice called *Bataiya*. Typically under this system the landlord and
the sharecropper share the costs of fertilizer and irrigation, plus the output,
equally. All other costs – land preparation, transplanting, harvesting and
labour – are borne by the tiller. The landlords prefer this system, as it
gives them control over deciding what crop is cultivated and how, thus
ensuring that they get higher returns.

The sharecroppers, who had been farming by the same methods for many years, faced considerable insecurity, living on the margins of subsistence. Every year they would use grain from the previous year's produce as seeds They did very little manuring, and they did transplantation and weeding in their own ways without having time to bother about productivity. As the husbands were often seasonal migrants there were large numbers of women sharecroppers.

With Adithi's help they started farming in a more organized manner. Seeds were bought from research centres in Bihar and Uttar Pradesh. *Daicha* plants for nitrogen fixation were planted in the fields, and before the ploughing started poultry feed was used as manure. By transplanting shoots they were able to increase their yield, even though they still had to give half their produce to the landlord as rent. Kusumi, one of the sharecroppers, remarked on the confidence this gave them and the irony of the landlord's change of attitude.

> Earlier we could not go near a Rajput's house wearing slippers or good clothes. If we did, our houses were set on fire, as happened in 1990. But today, the landowning Rajputs are so pleased with the increase in their share of the crop that they come to us asking us to take up more and more sharecroppers into our groups.

The paradox is that while bearing the consequences of the 'money-run' economy, the sharecroppers' livelihood struggles occur in a 'people's economy' that still bears the marks of customary social values attuned to collective need. Adithi has been concerned that interventions to improve women sharecroppers' quality of life do not hamper the functioning of the 'people's economy'.

The first necessity is to ensure that women continue to have access to land. A study done by a team of Action Aid and Adithi staff in Dumra block in Sitamarhi district found that the ability to earn cash incomes is the most important factor in reducing the disadvantages the women face as women. Availability of credit is another key area. The banks and other financial institutions are unwilling to extend credit to the sharecroppers. Adithi has taken up these issues with government and banking institutions. With assistance from SIDBI, a Women's Dairy Co-operative Society is being set up among the sharecroppers. A Revolving Fund has contributed to six crops with high yields. Only one crop has been a failure, and this was due to severe floods in 1998.

Women in Dairying

From time immemorial, rural women have played an important role in dairying activities. By and large dairying is a domestic operation that can be done by women at home. It is among the most dependable and remunerative occupations available to women, who contribute more than 70 per cent of the labour in livestock farming. In 1988 Adithi set up training programmes for women in dairying. From 1996 animal husbandry training programmes were also developed with the Bihar State Co-operative Milk Producers' Federation (COMPFED).

Women in Handicrafts

For the last few years, Adithi has been working with home-based handicraft producers of *sunjuni* (embroidery), appliqué, palm petiole, bamboo and brass, and with mat-weavers, tasar silk-rearers, dyeing and weaving workers, and jute and papier-mâché producers. All of these traditional crafts have been practised by women for whom there are few economic alternatives.

Adithi has organized more than two thousand craftswomen and up-graded their skills to bring about diversification and improvement in the quality of products. It has initiated basic training in entrepreneurship, management training, development of market strategies, support in product development and forms of credit. It has also helped to establish a federation of crafts women.

In many rural areas women are doing appliqué work (sewing coloured cloth patterns and designs onto a base material) and patchwork. They are engaged in this work for eight to ten months of the year, but they have no legal or social security, and no medical or other welfare facilities. Adithi has provided health care and non-formal education. It has also set up training and helped the women to develop innovative designs.

Adithi has encouraged a group of rural women in the Muzarffarpur district of Bihar to develop their traditional craft of *sujuni* – making babies' quilts from old saris. By reviving embroidery skills the quilts have become valuable items that can be sold abroad.

The quilts also serve as a poignant and defiant means of expression, illustrating a range of issues from dowry to the story of the 'bandit queen', Phoolan Devi, and their messages have reached all over the world. Adithi has also linked the embroiderers to other craftswomen. In 1998 *sujuni* craftswomen took part in an International Embroidery Exhibition in Delhi. This was organized by Dastkar and HomeNet. Dastkar assists groups with product development and design, while HomeNet, based in Britain, is a co-ordinating group working with home-based workers globally. The *sujuni* workers met embroiderers from other parts of India and from Pakistan, Bangladesh, Thailand, Portugal and Indonesia.

Adithi initiated a marketing wing called Mahila Harit Kala (MHK) in 1996 for all these home-based handicraft workers, opening a big showroom in Patna on 5 June, World Environment Day, as an eco-friendly sales outlet for handicraft and handloom products. The MHK showroom is located in the heart of the marketing area of Patna. It is easily accessible from all the housing and commercial complexes situated in the different parts of the city.

MHK was encouraged and supported by the Small Industries Development Bank of India (SIDBI) in Patna, which gave a grant to cover the rent of the premises and a loan to provide initial working capital. SIDBI has also supported this unique venture with a grant for entrepreneurship development training for producer groups and for participation in the Social Development Fair at New Delhi.

The showroom is run by a dedicated team of five members, of whom some are old Adithi staff and others new recruits, along with a full-time designer, a graduate in fine arts with a special interest in embroidery. Besides running the showroom the staff support the producer groups in design development, product innovation, costing and pricing, quality control, packaging and account-keeping.

The barefoot marketeers cell (Adithi Shrinkhala) consists of three craftswomen who make samples of appliqué, bamboo work, rope work and *sujuni* with guidance from the designer. Orders for the producer groups are taken on approval of these designs by the customers. The craftswomen contact individuals, boutiques, shops and exporters locally and in the cities.

Mahila Harit Kala was set up to help the craftswomen to find new channels for sales within India and also to export abroad. It strives to be a commercially viable unit and, at the same time, an empowering voice of the rural craftswomen. The attempts to improve marketing have exposed women to broader outlets for their goods but they still lack a spirit of self-reliance and enterprise.

Informal Sector Workers in the Cities

Urbanization is transforming India. Not only have the cities become the main job providers, but the informal sector has grown, intensifying the pressure on the poorest people. Most informal sector people have plied their trade in the same place and have lived in the same place (sometimes on the pavement) for many years.

Although one-third of the population are living below the poverty line, a majority of them under deplorable conditions, cities remain ill-prepared to address the problems of poverty. Moreover, there is official and social hostility towards the informal sector. Repressive policies have been developed, largely through the nexus of politicians and bureaucrats who have instituted raids preventing street selling and in some cases have evicted vendors from their living spaces too.

Adithi has facilitated an organization called Nidan, which is working with hawkers and vendors in Patna. Nidan has linked up with other groups organizing vendors nationally, including the Self-Employed Women's Association (SEWA). For several years now SEWA has been working internationally to raise the problems of street vendors through a network called StreetNet, and Nidan has supported this effort to create a visibility and voice for vendors. Although the vendors contribute to society, traffic is given greater priority and they are seen as an encroachment. In many cities around the world vendors' organizations are challenging how urban space is regarded. The mobilization of poor women vendors raises unfamiliar questions for planners about how to regulate urban space. It forces them to consider how everyone could have access to the city. StreetNet's agitation questions how legislative decisions are made, indeed the whole way in which cities are seen, and who defines these ways of seeing. It also makes vendors aware of the legitimacy of their claims. To those who seek to drive them out, the vendors say: 'Where are we to disappear?'; 'Do we not have a right to a livelihood?'

Conclusion

Inevitably we have found that our initial project of encouraging alternative means of livelihood for poor women in Bihar has led us to take up a range of economic and social problems. A key issue has been access to finance. The traditional rural credit market in Bihar is monopolized by the moneylender (the *mahajan*), who provides the necessary production and consumption loans to the rural population. The structures of formal financial institutions are not in a position to meet the credit demands of rural people, especially women. Adithi set up its credit programme in 1991 and in 1993 this evolved into a separate organisation called Nari Nidhi. Loans are made to groups, which provides a form of security, and the rate of repayment is high.

The consequent increase in the income level of the loanees means they are able to meet their consumption needs from the surplus earned through these loans. Those taking out loans include vegetable and fruit vendors, fish vendors, bangle-makers, bamboo-workers and small shop-wners. The branches of Nari Nidhi have been given considerable autonomy to run the programme at the local level. This has contributed to a proper selection of the reliable loanees and a speedy repayment of loans.

A sense of entitlement and empowerment has been crucial in Adithi's approach. A crucial element in women's empowerment is, of course, education, and Adithi has set up both adult education centres and centres for girls and boys. These not only teach literacy but provide a non-formal education that encourages participation.

Adithi members have made practical links between education and income generation as a means of resisting the widespead problem of domestic violence. Female infanticide is another difficult issue with which Adithi has had to deal. Unwanted babies have been found homes and a series of health programmes – regular check-ups, immunizations, ante- and post-natal care, including reproductive health care – has been established. Health posts have been created in a number of villages, with trained voluntary health workers in charge of them. Attempts have been made to introduce health insurance schemes at these health posts. Training of traditional birth attendants (*dais*) has been another strategy followed by Adithi. AIDS is a growing health hazard and Adithi has conducted AIDS awareness workshops and produced training manuals.

Adithi has grown organically in response to need and although women in Bihar remain poor and subordinated, the projects developed have enabled many women to change their lives and find expression for their dreams and hopes.

7

New Roots for Rights: Women's Responses to Population and Development Policies

Navtej K. Purewal

A dominant strand within development discourse has constructed Third World women as reproducers and made them targets of development. These assumptions about the relationship between reproductive patterns and the 'development' of Third World societies have been accompanied by population policies that have attempted to entwine further the productive and reproductive spheres. Little consideration has been given to the question of whether the suppositions behind either theories of development or population policies actually relate to the realities and experiences of women themselves. Women are often portrayed simply as passive recipients who carry the weight of maintaining the livelihood of the household. Contrary to this portrayal, there is an abundance of documented and undocumented examples of women organizing, reacting and responding to these policies and the accompanying processes (Petcheskey and Judd 1998; Correa 1994; Hartman 1995). Structural adjustment programmes (SAPs) and population programmes have provoked contention from women because of their failure to respect their reproductive decisions.[1] Although this has been recognized by feminists writing on reproductive rights, an underlying factor has been less noted. These approaches have exacerbated the tension between the households' livelihood activities in terms of sustaining itself, and choice over fertility. It is here that the discrepancy within development discourses that promote economic efficiency, through liberalization and privatization, while simultaneously advocating a strict code of population reduction is most clearly exposed. Despite the rhetoric which espouses the idea that there exist rights to economic opportunity, such policies have actually resulted in a denial of a right to make a livelihood. So, on the one hand economic development has required women's reproductive roles to support the household unit, while on the other hand it has denied women reproductive rights through fixed notions of family size, fertility and population control.

The experiences of women in various countries that have undergone 'development' under the auspices of the World Bank and its structural adjustment programmes tell an important story about the relationship between population control and wider development policies. Too often the connections made between the two are misunderstood by policy-makers. Population control and increased economic productivity are not only insufficient guidelines in themselves for improved social development, but also have a range of interconnected points that show the often contradictory effects of development upon population patterns and perceptions. Prescriptive approaches to population have maintained that (over)population has been an obstacle to unrealized development potential. However, when one looks beyond the jargon of quantitatively defined development indicators and listens to the voices of women and grassroots organizations, perceptions of how population and development relate to one another are often quite different from the policies to which they are responding. Furthermore, critical responses to population and development adopting the notion of reproductive rights have been neither uniform nor united on how they define and determine reproductive rights. Opposition to the impact of population mandates and the multi-variable effects of SAPs has not only been mounted by socialists or feminists.[2] It is the many movements of women (see Rowbotham 1992) rather than any monolithic women's movement who are responding and speaking out against the denial of reproductive rights by development and population policies. This resistance can be traced not only in the meetings and policies of actual groups but in the refusal of many poor women to accept economic agendas that deny their social reality.

Development Discourse and Women: Population – the Ulterior Motive

Central to the underlying ethos of structural adjustment is the notion that population growth reduction is a necessary prerequisite for improved economic performance. It is here that the thoughts of Thomas Malthus, the eighteenth-century economist, have continued to resonate within population and development policies.[3] Strains on limited resources by the world's steadily growing population, it is commonly argued, will have catastrophic effects on global stability. The characterization of the 'population problem' within this line of thought attributes declines in social development to the effects of overpopulation rather than to the system of production and management of resources within this system.[4] This argument is a common example of the international development establishment's preoccupation with population, choosing not to question the operations of international capitalism but rather to support it.[5] This also represents an ideological position from which the poor, specifically women, have consistently been targeted throughout the Third World, with population control and economic growth seen as the panaceas. Abidance with World Bank-prescribed population control has more recently been tagged on as one of the conditions attached to a country receiving an IMF (International Monetary Fund) loan.[6]

The policies attached to structural adjustment entail cuts in public spending, accentuation of free market principles and, more recently, strict population control policies. The end result of these policies, in isolation and in combination, have sometimes had unexpected results. In many cases, population growth, not decline, has resulted contrary to the aims of the policies from the onset. The history of international development discourse has capitalized upon and emphasized the utility of women in propagating capitalist development through institutions such as the World Bank and the IMF. Women, as the primary contributors to the 'caring economy', have been at the centre of both poverty and development policies (Harcourt 1997) and as a result have been most affected by policies dealing with social welfare as well as those relating to improved economic performance. The utilization of women in international development discourse illuminates the undertones of population reduction under the guise of various development themes.

The main discourse throughout the 1960s and early 1970s in development planning was that poverty and population were inherently linked with one another, and that if poverty was to be addressed, then the Third World would have to take drastic measures to reduce its population. The physical survival of poor families was emphasized through smaller families and in the distribution of food aid from developed to developing countries. The means by which such 'overpopulation' and poverty were to be tackled was seen to be through women as the carers of the household. During the 1960s and early 1970s women were a specific target group, albeit in a passive capacity, of anti-poverty policies through a variety of programmes including relief distribution, voluntary work, nutritional education and population reduction (Moser 1989). The underlying assumption was that, given adequate information and aid, women would see that smaller families and improved nutrition were an important part of improving poverty indicators at the household level. The analysis of the relationship between poverty, women and fertility fell short of supporting improved distribution of income and instead argued for family planning to decrease family sizes. Crucially, the incidence of poverty was seen as a result not of the structural marginalization of the poor from economic processes, but of ignorance on the part of poor women.[7] This analysis failed to consider the logic behind large families and the fact that more children can be a means of survival for the poor, and not necessarily a result of misinformation or women's subordination. That population, not poverty, was identified as the cause of poor development indicators is a point that will be addressed in the last section of this chapter.

With the declaration of the UN Women's Decade in 1976, there was a dramatic shift in international development discourse that saw the recognition of women as active participants in development through their productive and reproductive roles. During this period the 'equity approach' was adopted, locating the subordination of women in the family but also in relations between men and women in the marketplace. Women's independence became synonymous with equity, and women's needs were positioned with their rights to earn a livelihood. In the context of the rise to dominance of the World Bank and the IMF in formulating the consensus on development policy, it became widely accepted that economic strategies had had negative impacts on women because they had failed to include them. What was needed was a means of drawing women into the development process through access to employment and the marketplace. This period marked the 'women in development' (WID) approach, which maintained that women had been left out of development whereas their 'invisible role' or unacknowledged contributions had actually formed the basis for all development reliant upon the household unit. The inclusion and integration of women into mainstream economic policies began with WID. Crucially, this period formulated the equation of development equalling access to the marketplace, a concept at the core of structural adjustment policies today.

The variety of roles that women play is most commonly cited in terms of reproductive and productive activities (Boserup 1970; Beneria and Sen 1997). The merging of the reproductive and productive spheres of women's contributions to the economy has been a point of contention among feminist economists, particularly in their analysis of structural adjustment (Beneria and Feldman 1992; Elson 1989; Dalsimer and Nisonoff 1984). Reproductive activities are those that sustain the household and the labour force, while productive activities are those that involve income generation either through employment outside the household or production within the household economy for the market. The gender and development approach (GAD) arose out of the criticism of previous development policies that targeted women without attempting to question social relations. GAD maintains that the roles that women and men are assigned in any given society are socially constructed and not 'natural' in any way (Young 1997). It is critical of the effects of development upon women and argues that reproductive activities have historically been taken for granted and have been unmeasured in terms of women's contributions to the household economy, hence the 'invisibility' of women in the economy (Elson 1994). The GAD approach is particularly poignant when examining reproduction and population issues, challenging assumptions about women's biological ability to bear children with the analysis that the roles of men as providers and women as carers are socially constructed (Hartman 1995; Pearson and Jackson 1998).

While the various approaches to women's roles in development have all been exposing the international development establishment's adherence to sexist assumptions about gender roles, little attention has been paid to the interactions of other policies. Even with the Convention on the Elimination of All Forms of Discrimination Against Women (CEDAW) in 1979 and in South Asia the declaration of the Decade of the Girl Child in the 1990s, there has been little connection made between the notion of reproductive 'rights' and the contradictory anti-rights effects that development discourses have imposed. However, in contrast, women's groups on the ground have become all too aware of the links. The meetings and discussions surrounding the International Conference on Population and Development (ICPD) in Cairo in 1994 and the parallel NGO forum that took place saw the emergence of a powerful yet diverse force of women's groups and non-governmental organizations from around the world.[8] If anything, the show of force at ICPD and the articulation by women's groups and NGOs displayed a united opposition to the eugenics agenda of population control under the guise of 'reproductive rights' (Haynes 1999). The 'New Global Racism' is perhaps more apparent in the language and philosophies of international population organizations working directly with population and fertility issues. The founder of Planned Parenthood, Margaret Sanger, argued in favour of the sterilization of 'genetically inferior races' (Sanger 1922), while Jan Fransen, a former United Nations Fund for Population Activities (UNFPA) representative, in a speech to the European Parliament in 1999, stated that population growth on the African continent could be limited by an increase in mortality rates, not to mention the AIDS virus (Ruse 1999). Such statements, while resonating with the sentiments of the eugenics movement of the early twentieth century, have been unashamedly woven into the policy approaches to population. While such organizations as the UNFPA, the Population Council and Planned Parenthood International have dedicated their attentions to tackling the so-called population problem in developing countries, a potent reference to consumption patterns in Western countries shows that the amount of money needed each year to provide reproductive health care for all women in developing countries ($12 billion) is the same as the amount of money actually spent annually on perfumes in Europe and the USA.[9] This comparison reveals the misguided priorities of development policies in light of the social issues at stake. It raises the fundamental question of why population control, rather than better and more effective reproductive and general health services, has been such a priority of development policies.

'SAPping' Social Welfare

As part of the process of adjustment, women's reproductive and productive efforts in the household have become increasingly entwined with the market, a process that has had an impact on social welfare. As a result, structural adjustment programmes have generally resulted in the reversal of social improvements that had been achieved in previous decades (Bandarage 1994; Shiva 2000). In assessing the effects of SAPs on social welfare, there are two main areas that have emerged. The first is how shifts in market production have affected women's working lives. The second is how cuts in government spending on social services and subsidies have affected social development and welfare. Both areas reveal the social dimensions of structural adjustment. While the causality between declines in social welfare and structural adjustment is an issue for evaluating the social dimensions of structural adjustment, there is a small but growing body of longitudinal household-level empirical studies that have explored the 'before and after' effects of SAPs (Sparr 1994; Afshar and Dennis 1992). In the immediate term, analytical studies have provided a depth of comparative perspectives on the effects of structural adjustment while women researchers, NGOs and activists have collected data and evidence that cumulatively show some of the negative repercussions of SAPs. Indeed, groups such as Women's Eyes on the World Bank have specifically examined the gender implications of the World Bank's reform programmes in areas such as education and health, strengthening the international pressure put upon the World Bank.[10]

Cuts in government expenditure on social services and subsidies form an important element of structural adjustment packages in which evidence of a significant decline in social development can be seen. In Zambia, for example, expenditure on health fell by 22 per cent from 1982 to 1985 (Stewart 1992: 27). In many other countries health centres were closed down and those that remained suffered from poor resources and cuts in funding. For women this has had a particularly negative effect, with the burden of family health care generally falling on their shoulders. In sub-Saharan Africa households with declining real incomes have had to absorb the costs of health and education, with a resulting decrease in average birth intervals and shortening of breast-feeding (Ofosu 1994). This in turn has had profound effects upon women's health. Immunization, pre-natal care and unavailability of medicines have led to increased infant and child mortality rates, the spread of diseases and a further strain on the productive activities of the household.[11] In Sri Lanka, a country renowned for its relatively high-quality of life compared to other Third World countries, childhood mortality rose substantially when food subsidies were withdrawn in the 1980s (Stewart 1992). A study of reproductive tract infections in Africa found that half of the infertility cases were caused by such infections, and that this was largely due to government inaction and unwillingness to see its role as fulfilling its citizens' rights to basic health-care (Germain et al. 1992).

There has also been a marked shift in health policies by governments undergoing SAPs, from basic health care to contraceptive service delivery.[12] The privatization of health services is a further more recent trend in both developing and developed countries alike, making it even more difficult for people to claim rights to basic health care. Resistance has come from women's movements in the Third World. In opposition to the global dimensions of this phenomenon, the Third World Women's Conference against APEC (Asia Pacific Economic Cooperation) made a statement that:

> Privatisation of health care is a violation of women's basic human rights to total well-being by denying them access to safe, appropriate, affordable, high quality preventative and curative health care. It also commodifies reproductive health needs. The population control policies and methods together with the dumping of harmful and experimental contraceptives have increased the risk to women's lives. (*Statement of the Third World Women's Conference Against APEC*, Kuala Lumpur, November 1998)

One impact of the privatization of health care has also been an increase in the influence of transnational corporations over other health-related issues. The Swiss-based company Nestlé is one of the largest food companies and a major producer of infant formula. It has actively promoted its formula products worldwide as a substitute for breast-feeding, which has provoked consumer boycotts of its products in many countries around the world. The health implications of the adoption of infant formula in place of breast-feeding have been profound. A 1995 UNICEF report entitled *The State of the World's Children* estimates that more than one million infants died because they had not been exclusively breast-fed for the first six months of their lives.

Education is another sector that has been affected by cuts in government expenditure with illiteracy and drop-out rates rising. Decreasing numbers of girl children attending school have been an inevitable knock-on effect of government cuts on education.[13] Reductions in school enrolment for girls often result in earlier marriages of girls in South Asia, for example, where more educated girls tend to get married later and have fewer children (Jeffery et al. 1989; Caldwell 1982). Illiteracy also disempowers women from gaining information about child-rearing and reproductive and general health services and has obvious repercussions upon the household's awareness of its choices, reducing its chances of ensuring the best quality of life for its family members.

The impacts of cuts on social welfare have been far-reaching, and critiques of SAPs have exposed the multiplicity of their social effects. The imposition of market forces in the reproductive and productive spheres of women's lives has put extra pressure upon women's capacities to earn livelihoods and to maintain the family unit. Through public sector cuts, which are a core feature of adjustment packages, formal sector employment opportunities for both men and women have been reduced, but evidence indicates that women's employment rates have suffered proportionately more. Unemployment figures in adjusting economies during the 1980s clearly exhibited the disadvantaged position of women in the labour market. In Peru real wages for women fell by 15 per cent from 1976 to 1984 while men's wages fell by 11 per cent (Stewart 1995). During times of recession and stabilization women sustain household incomes through their activities in the local job market. The need for waged incomes has forced women, particularly in low-income families, into the labour force in addition to the day-to-day running of the household unit and is often supplementing household production of goods for market sale. Two identifiable patterns are evident within this shift. The first is that female labour participation has increasingly become concentrated in the informal sector. This sector has multiplied alongside the reduction in public sector employment and offers lower wages, less security and no formal rights. The second is that women have become even further entrenched into the sexual division of labour, which increasingly relies upon women's subsistence production.[14]

Maria Mies (1986) takes the argument a step further when she terms the labelling of women as dependents in the household as 'housewifization', a concept that points out the fact that women's market activities have actually been on the increase, though not in the recognized formal sectors where they would be accounted for. A further squeeze on women's contributions to the subsistence economy has been caused by the abolition of subsidies and the end of price controls on agricultural production. Poor households rely upon the production of crops for household consumption as well as selling in the market to supplement household income. Women in these households have had to arrange their time around the consumption of food, often being forced to grow more profitable crops and then having to buy food from the market (Elson 1994). An employment survey of Mexico in 1995 illustrates the significance of these trends: it was found that 90.5 per cent of economically active women were also carrying out unpaid work at home, compared to 62.4 per cent of economically active men (UNIFEM/CONMUJER 1999).

Within a dominant development discourse cuts to government spending by means of ending subsidies and reducing public spending on social welfare are seen as part of shifting resources from non-productive services to more 'productive', tradeable activities. Social welfare and subsidies are defined as 'unprofitable' and 'unproductive' and it is argued that they do not directly contribute to the national GNP (Afshar and Dennis 1992; Elson 1989). This has been accompanied by a shift towards labour-intensive manufacturing for export, most commonly epitomized in the garment and electronic industry 'sweatshops' of many Third World countries. The concentration of women in these 'sweatshops' is no coincidence considering the declining employment opportunities in the formal sector. Maternity rights are generally non-existent in these forms of production, particularly notorious in free trade zones, where a tacit understanding that if a woman becomes pregnant she will lose her job prevails. Women have been organizing around this issue and have lobbied for improved maternity rights. Activists from Latin American and East European countries have been lobbying the International Labour Organization (ILO) for an international maternity protection treaty to include codified benefits such as longer leave and paid breast-feeding breaks. This global coalition of women activists has been calling for a review of the existing ILO convention of 1952, which after 50 years is to be revised in 2002, to include more generous terms for pregnant women and nursing mothers. The activists have accused the governments of Australia and the USA of not offering paid maternity leave rights in their own countries and of opposing improved terms of employment during maternity in a global context in which more women are having children while being in paid work (Cyber-fem 2000).

Amid the far-reaching impacts of SAPs on social welfare, there is an implicit assumption that the services formerly provided by the state will be absorbed by women, who are somehow 'naturally' equipped with the skills to take over the responsibility of sustaining the population. As a result, the household responsibilities of many women have been increased as support from the social sectors have been withdrawn. At the same time, the demand for women's increased labour participation in the local economy has been matched by the need for extra incomes to sustain the household. This has meant an overall increase in working hours for women alongside domestic responsibilities, often assisted by younger female members of the family. The deterioration of social welfare due to economic reforms has evoked active opposition. In the context of declining basic services within the framework of SAPs, non-governmental organizations, including feminist and women's organizations, have become a significant force in negotiating access to services. An example is Isis International, an international organization that has disseminated information on access to health care, women's rights and the right to mass education, helping to create a basis for national campaigns for improved public services (Jacobson 1993). In Brazil Sempreviva Organizacao Feminista (SOF) has been active in lobbying around women's health and reproductive rights in the context of the inadequate health and social services available to low-income communities (Faure 1994).[15]

Women's experiences of policies under SAPs have shown that there has been an overall deterioration in the quality of life of poor households through increased pressures on and expectations of women's paid and unpaid work. This, in turn, has affected perceptions and practices of fertility at the household level. While shifting policies towards economic productivity and decreased population growth has been central to SAPs, it has not necessarily been in the immediate interests of women in poor households to follow the population mandates passed on to them *vis-à-vis* the economic reforms. In numerous cases where this conflict of interest has been apparent or even subtly apparent, women have resisted population control strategies that have impinged on their rights both to livelihood and to the right to make their own fertility choices.

Rights of Action

The acceptance of an overarching patriarchal ideology and reliance on women's reproductive and productive contributions provides the basic skeletal structure of SAPs. The implicit expectation is that women will continue to serve as the 'safety-net' for the decline in public services while also scaling up their input of unpaid and paid work. Assumptions about fertility within both SAPs and population control programmes similarly view Third World women's reproductive patterns as misguided and un-informed. However, when one looks at the stark discrepancy between national and international policies and the practices and patterns at the household and regional levels, and even more importantly at the responses of women's organizations, the evidence suggests that it is the policy-makers, not the Third World poor, who are uninformed.

Population programmes have shown a consistently unapologetic commit-ment to population reduction at any cost which have, by and large, failed to take into account the importance of social and economic development in defining population targets and have remained prescriptive in their approach. Because inequalities, including gender imbalances, have largely been ignored, existing social inequalities have been reified. An example of this uncritical acceptance of unequal social relations was in Nigeria in 1989 where a population policy was formulated as part of the adjustment package. The policy affirmed patriarchal norms outright and targeted women by stating that 'the patriarchal family system in the country shall be recognized for stability of the home' (Hartman 1995: 126). Women were called upon to reduce the number of children they have, while men were merely encouraged to limit their number of wives.

In fact, the traditional patriarchal household has not been completely unchanged by the effects of SAPs. As wage labour and the participation of women and children in the market economy have been one side-effect of SAPs on poor households, in some cases control by male elders of older children has been undermined by the wage-earning activities and the potential economic autonomy of children from their parents. This has a bearing on population, for in some contexts it has had a weakening effect upon the cost benefit of having more children (Folbre 1998: 122). Likewise, extended families that previously acted as old-age security are increasingly being replaced by nuclear families.[16] However, these effects of the market have not necessarily been translated into a demise of the patriarchal household, which continues to define women's roles as carers as well as breadwinners, though within the 'housewife' model.[17] Indeed, male migration has been one outcome of market pressures on the household and has certainly added a new dimension to our understanding of the hierarchical base of the household (Chant 1992). The rise in female-headed households[18] will not be examined here but is an interesting angle from which to critique the patriarchal household, namely in terms of how women's changing structural position within the household impacts upon their fertility and decision-making power (Chant 1997).

On the other side of the coin, the cost benefit of more children has continued to be found to offset the economic strains on the household. Under pressures to increase household incomes, more children can translate into increased income where wages are pooled within the household unit (Caldwell 1982). For the poor, additional children can mean high economic returns with only marginal costs. The Indian economist Ashok Mitra inadvertently criticizes the two-child and one-child models of India and China respectively in pointing out that a majority of economic activity relies upon uncompensated family labour (quoted in Bandarage 1997: 161). Nevertheless it is also widely recognized that the household itself is not unified in terms of income and decision-making around household expenditure (Sen 1987).[19] Perhaps even more important is the fact that in the absence of social security, children provide an immense sense of long-term security because they can look after parents in their old age. Beyond the more economically calculated fertility choices that people make, for many of the poor in the Third World, in addition to being a means of survival, children are a source of happiness and hope (Bandarage 1997). A study of migrants in the Indian states of Uttar Pradesh and Tamil Nadu found that the percentages of women who expressed contentment with their lives increased with the number of children they had (Basu 1992). This study highlights the important human dimension of population frequently dismissed by prescriptive policy-makers as ignorance and misguidance. Another study of reproductive choices in Egypt concluded that having children empowered women and enabled them to negotiate and to stand up to their husbands (El-Dawla et al. 1998).

The tendency for uncritical prescription has also resulted in a denial of choice for the recipients of population policy. This has ranged from incentive and disincentive schemes, selective 'encouragement' of particular types of contraception to the more extreme cases of coercive tactics. Incentive payments for sterilizations have been a recurring feature of campaigns for population control. A government scheme in Bangladesh during the mid-1980s used financial incentives and was heralded as a success story of fertility decline by the World Bank. Emergency measures were called upon through government and high-ranking army personnel to increase sterilization incentives (Hartman 1995: 225). Poor men and women were given several months wages in return for undergoing the sterilization operation. Wider poverty and development indicators in Bangladesh during this period deteriorated rather than improved, showing how such policies have avoided addressing the social and economic factors surrounding people's population choices.[20] In other cases, politicians have 'bartered sterilisations for votes' (Salles 1992), a popular practice particularly in the favelas in the state of Maranhao in the north-east of Brazil, where poor women are persuaded to have sterilization operations in return for voting for political candidates.[21] In return for the votes and the sterilizations, a brighter future with fewer children is offered as a campaign promise. As a young woman in her early twenties with four children said 'I spoke to the candidate and it was very simple … He fixed me up with a visit to the Santa Lucia Hospital and I was sterilized. After all, you can't keep filling your house with children, can you?' (quoted in Salles 1992). The targeting of poor, predominantly black, women for these 'bartered sterilizations' in north-eastern Brazil has caught the attention of women's groups in Brazil such as the Mae Andrezza Women's Group, who have campaigned against what they identify as the sexist, classist and racist agenda of mass sterilizations (Salles 1992). These methods of controlling the fertility of the poor is by no means exclusive to the Third World. The USA was the first country to actually permit mass sterilizations as part of its drive to 'purify the race' (Forte and Judd 1998). Native Americans, African Americans and immigrant communities, as well as epileptics, the mentally disabled and criminals were targeted by the US government's eugenics agenda, and by the end of the Second World War it is estimated that 50,000 sterilizations had taken place (DeFine 1997). The Native American Women's Health Education Resource Center has documented abuses by the Indian Health Services (IHS) and other agencies delivering health care services to Native American women. Even as recently as the 1990s sterilization abuse was found to be still occurring in Native American reservation health centres (ibid.) In addition to forced sterilizations, there is evidence of extensive promotion of Depo-Provera and Norplant as routine methods of birth control.

Disincentives have similarly been used to discourage people from having more children. In July 1999 a population control bill was introduced in India in the Delhi State Assembly to penalize families exceeding the two-child 'norm' by denying them ration cards (IPS, July 11 1999).[22] The author of the bill argues that the bill is justified on the grounds that Delhi's rate of population growth cannot be sustained and that the poor need to be deterred from having more children. This is another example of where disincentives rather than improved social sector programmes have been used to address the question of population.[23] The bill has met with intense opposition from women's groups, including the All India Democratic Women's Association (AIDWA), who argue that Delhi's population has experienced such a rapid rate of growth not because of high fertility but because of in-migration from other parts of India. This argument exposes the weakness in the supposition that population concentration is solely due to fertility increase.

The selective 'encouragement' of contraceptives in the Third World is a phenomenon that incorporates developing countries into the marketing and research objectives of large pharmaceutical companies in the West. Population control advocates argue that 'the poor are ignorant and irrational about their own needs and that they need to be educated and motivated to use modern contraceptives' (Bandarage 1997: 88), an attitude that has opened the door to big business interests in the promotion of contra-ceptives. Invasive contraceptive drugs such as Norplant 6, Depo-Provera,[24] and vaccines against pregnancy have been tested and promoted in the Third World, often without the appropriate follow-up, information dis-semination or medical support required (Shrivastava 1994; Hardon 1994). Such long-acting methods limit user control while posing a threat to women's health.[25] India, the country that implemented the first family planning programme in 1951, inadvertently integrated these methods into its Family Planning Programme in 2000 by relaxing drug regulations in order to encourage the adoption of long-acting contraceptives to help meet its population targets under the direction of the World Bank (*Indian Express*, 18 October 2000). Women's groups and NGOs have been critical of these methods as there is evidence of dangers to immunity and hormonal levels where correct and longitudinal procedures are not followed. An absence of controls to regulate the use of these drugs has made Third World women vulnerable to the dangers of fertility drug experimentation. Such methods have positioned women as guinea-pigs rather than em-powering them with choice and control over their fertility (Melrose 1982; Mies 1986).

The pharmaceutical industry's targeting of women is merely the tip of the iceberg amid much wider processes of declining social development and the commodification of population issues that are emerging. During the period when many countries underwent SAPs, namely the 1980s and 1990s, sex ratios in strongly patriarchal regions were seen to become further skewed in favour of males due to the discrimination against female foetuses as well as babies. Discussion of the economic value of bearing children becomes further complicated by social and cultural constructions of gender. Son preference has historically contributed to the maintenance of high fertility: families continue to conceive until they produce a son. Particularly against the socio-economic backdrop of the patriarchal household unit in South Asia, girls are seen as liabilities due to the dowry system[26] while a son is seen as an asset. Historically, incidences of female infanticide in India, though largely unreported, have been predicted as one of the most severe in the world due to particularly strong preferences for sons.[27] Although this practice is thought to be decreasing, there is evidence to show that its decline may be offset by new technologies facilitating sex-discriminating abortions (Das Gupta and Bhat 1997). Amartya Sen (1992) estimates that one hundred million women are 'missing' from population statistics globally, while Das Gupta and Bhat (1997) pose that approximately one million women are missing in India from the 1991 census. As the household model modifies itself to the demands of the market, families have become in-creasingly conscious of the value and costs attached to children. While this raised 'consciousness' may have led to steadily declining fertility in many countries,[28] another result has been the discrimination against girl children.

Ultrasound scanning services from private medical clinics have become more accessible since the early 1980s, although it is not yet clear how widespread their impact has been. There is evidence too that amniocentesis, meant for detecting foetal abnormalities, has also been used for sex identi-fication. Access to such sex-selective technologies, while colluding with population reduction objectives, is thus contributing to a more masculine population.[29] The short-term costs to poor couples of visiting a private clinic for sex-selective services could be perceived as an investment offset by the long-term savings from potential dowries by aborting a female foetus. Indeed, this argument has been capitalized upon in advertisements for sex-selective services. A clinic offering pre-natal scanning appealed to patriarchal tendencies to discriminate against female children by advertising '500 Rupees now or 50,000 later' (Gandhi and Shah 1992). Such advertisements have been opposed by women's groups in India, who have spoken out against the fact that these practices remain legal, but, more crucially, have campaigned against the discrimination against the female child, born and unborn. On Children's Day in 1986 a march of parents and daughters carried banners and shouted slogans 'girls are not inferior to boys' and 'we too want to live' (ibid: 131).[30] Despite pre-natal sex determination techniques being made illegal in India in 1994, it has become clear that legal stipulations alone cannot address the issues surrounding the (mis)use of medical procedures for such ends. The multitude of ways in which cultural perceptions of women and girls relate to the economics and politics of gender make the task of opposing anti-women practices a particularly challenging one (Razzouk 2000).

The utilization of sex-selective technologies is not merely limited to the poor; the more affluent in the West and in Third World countries have been found to use these services to tailor the gender balance of their families to meet their own requirements. Further scientific developments have more recently made it possible to 'produce' a boy or girl child through the Ericsson Method, which separates the x and y chromosomes before conception to increase the chances of having either a boy or a girl. Advertisements by private clinics offering the service in the USA and Europe expound that the method 'has an 80 per cent success rate of resulting in males' but that 'procedures for girl children are also available', implying that most potential customers would be interested in the former rather than the latter. Certainly these developments within reproductive technology have added a new dimension to the notion of 'choice' within reproductive health and women's rights debates and will no doubt be a point of contention in the future.

Conclusion

From the experiences of women having undergone development and population policies, a visible pattern has become evident showing that rights of population and development have deteriorated rather than improved. With population being at the centre of Western institutional notions of development, women have consistently been targeted by international development discourse for their roles as mothers and carers. SAPs have extended this to instruct Third World women to have fewer children while also becoming more active producers and workers in the market economy. There has not been one distinct fertility response emerging from the impacts of SAPs; the diversity of socio-economic realities of the Third World poor has resulted in a range of fertility responses. A common characteristic is, however, that the so-called logic of population control and SAPs imposes contradictory pressures upon the household and women. On the one hand, the increased economic productivity of the household has frequently led to the perceived need for more children, while on the other hand, women's augmented participation in the market economy has made it more difficult for them to raise and support their children.

Concomitantly, there is also evidence of poverty-induced fertility decline in areas of the Third World that experience famines or where land pressure or unemployment have increased poverty within households, with specifically adverse effects upon women (Jeffery et al. 1989; Das Gupta and Shuzuo 1999). The ways in which fertility decline has occurred under SAPs (distress reduction, coercive sterilization and sex-discriminatory terminations, to name a few) expose the unwillingness of policy-makers to take into account sufficiently the needs and realities of people outside the 'population-reduction-at-any-cost' framework. Why, for instance, have SAPs induced declines in female schooling and women's health, which quite clearly have a direct relationship to high fertility? Largely ignored by the vision of SAPs and population control, the fertility experiences of Sri Lanka and Cuba present, in contrast, exemplary cases of countries where improvements in social development have resulted in a transition to low fertility.

Fertility decline requires that issues of gender equity, poverty and wealth distribution be seriously addressed. However, the World Bank has taken the position that 'it is possible for fertility to decline ... without much change in those social, economic, and health variables generally believed to be crucial pre-conditions for demographic change' (World Bank 1992). The most potent evidence against the impact of SAPs and upon social well-being is in the reversal of social development indicators. Child mortality, girls' schooling, pre-natal health care and child nutrition, which had previously improved, have now deteriorated as government support in these areas has been withdrawn. The boundaries of the political space in which women's organizations and activists have confronted these issues continue to be expanded to redress the notion of reproductive rights and its linkages with livelihoods. The example of trade unionists lobbying the ILO for an international charter recognizing universal rights to paid maternity leave and breast-feeding breaks cogently illustrates this transcendence of reproductive rights (or at least the demand for reproductive rights) between the home and the public sphere. However, as Diniz et al. (1998) note in their examination of women activists (and non-activists) in Brazil, 'the road to activism is not an easy one', for women making challenges to the status quo meet resistance from male family members and the community, who see them as a threat for challenging prescribed gender norms. Not only does women's resistance challenge population and development policies, but it also poses a threat to the patriarchal household and community structure upon which such policies stand. While the connection between reproductive rights and the household's livelihood is inadequately construed by development and population planners, women activists and women's organizations continue to face these challenges and speak out, react and respond to the 'SAPping' of well-being, economic livelihoods and reproductive rights.

Notes

1. The World Bank became a major funder of population control from the 1970s onwards, when its expenditure increased from $278 million on population programmes during the decade 1969–79 to an estimated $2.5 billion in 1995. See Shiva 1994.

2. For an insightful analysis of women's activism and its relationship to Gandhian, socialist, communist and Maoist traditions in India see Kumar 1993.

3. Thomas Malthus wrote that 'overpopulation' would ultimately result in the depletion of natural resources and in a potentially explosive social disorder due to heightened inequality. His writings went as far as to argue that the poor are a drain on society and that any system of state welfare merely encouraged higher fertility among the poor. This type of thinking became particularly popular in Europe among the ruling classes soon after the French Revolution and has since evolved to the modern form of 'neo-Malthusianism'.

4. Paul and Anne Ehrlich's book *The Population Explosion* (1990) was one of the many Malthusian-influenced contributions to this hysteria and cited masses of people in overpopulated Third World cities as one of the biggest potential threats to global social and economic stability.

5. Michel Chossudovsky (1997) argues that the global economic establishment's campaign is to eliminate the poor rather than to eliminate poverty.

6. During the 1980s the World Bank worked closely with the UNFPA to persuade African countries to accept population control. Eventually population control became part and parcel of SAPs.

7. A comprehensive study concludes that food production over the past few decades has overtaken population growth, debunking the neo-Malthusian 'people versus the Earth's resources' perspective. See Dyson 1996.

8. The ICPD conference marked an international recognition of the reproductive rights of women, diverting attention away from a simplistic 'population problem' to one that takes into account and promotes women's agency in reproductive and sexual relations (Correa 1994; Sen et al. 1994).

9. http://www.worldwatch.org/mag/1999/99-1b.html. Reprinted from UNDP *Human Development Report 1998*, New York: Oxford University Press, pp. 30–7.

10. In response, the World Bank has set up an External Gender Consultative Group (EGCG) made up of 14 women from around the world to give advice on gender issues.

11. According to Malthus, who wrote in the eighteenth century, such tragedies as child mortality and food shortages acted as a 'positive check' on overpopulation.

12. Population control in India has been an even higher priority than basic health services in terms of public expenditure.

13. National education statistics do not show the kind of education that girls and boys receive and whether it exacerbates or reifies existing gender inequalities or stereotypes. See UNIFEM 2000.

14. For in-depth examinations of the international sexual division of labour see Mies 1986; Beneria and Feldman 1992; Standing 1989.

15. Despite the fact that Brazil's Federal Constitution recognizes health care as a universal right, putting the state in a position of accountability to fulfil this right, actual expenditure on services has been far from adequate. Also, as abortion remains illegal in Brazil the state's commitment to reproductive rights falls short of addressing the full range of women's needs and concerns (see Diniz et al. 1998).

16. See Lynn Duggan 'Households and Families: Introduction to Part 2' in Vishvanathan et al. 1997 for a comprehensive overview of some of the issues surrounding poor households and capitalist development.

17. Deniz Kandiyoti (1984) dissects the changes to the 'patriarchal bargain' that new market forces have imposed on classic patriarchy and some of the implications for women.

18. Lise Ostergaard (1992) estimates that approximately one-third of all households are female-headed at some point or other.

19. In the same vein, there is evidence to show that while women tend to share and pool their income men's earnings are commonly saved for personal spending (see Elson 1994).

20. This took place despite the widespread criticism of the emergency in India a decade earlier when the central government put pressure on family planning workers to meet their sterilization quotas. Police are said to have rounded up women for forced sterilizations (see Kabeer 1994). There were even stories of older women being sterilized as a means of meeting these quotas.

21. According to figures from UNICEF, Brazil's sterilization rate rose from 11.3 per cent in the late 1960s to 45 per cent in 1990, showing how widespread sterilization is as a means of contraception. In the north-eastern state of Maranhao 79.8 per cent of women have been sterilized.

22. Ration cards in India are essential for receiving entitlement to subsidized food and also serve as a vital proof of identity and residence.

23. Contrary to this logic, in the southern Indian state of Kerala, social sector programmes, in addition to the declining perception of children as an economic asset, have resulted in a dramatic drop in family size and population.

24. Depo-Provera was banned in the USA because of its carcinogenic content. It was found to cause cancer in animals and to cause menstrual problems.

25. There have been cases in Indonesia, Egypt and Bangladesh where women were refused removal of the hormonal implant Norplant. See Mintzes et al. 1993.

26. Payment and gifts are expected from the bride's family to the groom and his family.

27. The state of Punjab in India has the highest sex ratio against females, 875:1,000 (Census of India 1991).

28. Population growth rates have been on the decline in nearly all regions of the world.

29. In 1973 the biologist Postgate defended the use of new technologies for sex selection in his claim that birth control was not effective in the Third World and that sex-selective technologies capitalized on an already existing preference for boy children.

30. Rather than banning sex-selective procedures, the government called for regulation of these services through appropriate health and medical bodies that further professionalized and legitimized these services.

Bibliography

Afshar, Haleh and Carolyne Dennis (1992) *Women and Adjustment Policies in the Third World*, New York: St. Martin's Press.

Bandarage, Asoka (1997) *Women, Population and Global Crisis: A Political-Economic Analysis*, London: Zed Books.

Bannerjee, Nirmala (1998) 'Household dynamics and women in a changing economy', in M. Krishnaraj, R. M. Sudarshan and A. Shariff (eds), *Gender, Population and Development*, New Delhi: Oxford University Press.

Basu, Alaka M. (1992) *Culture: The Status of Women and Demographic Behaviour: Illustrated with the Case of India*, Oxford: Clarendon Press.

Beneria, Lourdes and Gita Sen (1997) 'Accumulation, reproduction and women's role in economic development: Boserup', in N. Visvanathan et al. (eds), *The Women, Gender and Development Reader*.

Beneria, L. and S. Feldman (1992) (eds), *Unequal Burden: Economic Crises, Persistent Poverty and Women's Work*, Boulder, CO: Westview Press.

Boserup, Ester (1970) *Women's Role in Economic Development*, New York: St. Martin's Press.

Caldwell, J. C. (1982) *Theory of Fertility Decline*, New York: Academic Press.

Chant, Sylvia (1992) *Women and Survival in Mexican Cities: Perspectives on Gender, Labour Markets and Low-income Households*, Manchester: Manchester University Press.

— (1997) 'Single-parent families: choice or constraint? The formation of female-headed households in Mexican shanty towns', in Vishvanathan et al., *The Women, Gender and Development Reader*.

Chossudovsky, Michel (1997) *The Globalization of Poverty: Impacts of IMF and World Bank Reforms*, London: Zed Books.

Cook, Rebecca J. (1995) 'International human rights and women's reproductive health', in Julie Peters and Andrea Wolper (eds), *Women's Rights, Human Rights*, London: Routledge.

Correa, Sonia (ed.) (1994) *Population and Reproductive Rights: Feminist Perspectives from the South*, London: Zed Books.

Cyber-fem (2000) 'Activists seek stronger maternity rights treaty', www.obgyn.net/reuters/200000607pub1002.htm

Dalsimer, Marilyn and Laurie Nisonoff (1997) 'Abuses against women and girls under the one-child family plan in the People's Republic of China', in N. Visvanathan et al. (eds), *The Women, Gender and Development Reader*.

Das Gupta, Monica and Li Shuzhuo (1999) 'Gender bias in China, South Korea and India 1920–1990: effects of war, famine and fertility decline', *Development and Change*, 30(3).

Das Gupta, Monica and P. N. Mari Bhat (1997) 'Fertility decline and increased manifestation of sex bias in India,' *Population Studies*, 51.

El-Dawla, Aida Seif, Amal Abdel Hadi and Nadia Abdel Wahab (1998) 'Women's wit over men's: trade-offs and strategic accommodations in Egyptian women's reproductive lives', in Petchesky and Judd (eds), *Negotiating Reproductive Rights*.

DeFine, Michael Sullivan (1997) 'A history of governmentally coerced sterilisation: the plight of the Native American woman', wysiwyg://64/http://www.geocities.com/CapitolHill/9118/mike2/htm

Diniz, Simone Grilo, Cecilia De Mello E Souza and Ana Paula Portella (1998) 'Not like our mothers: reproductive choice and the emergence of citizenship among Brazilian rural workers, domestic workers and housewives', in Petchesky and Judd (eds), *Negotiating Reproductive Rights*.

Dixon-Mueller, Ruth (1993) *Population Policy and Women's Rights: Transforming Reproductive Choice*, Westport, CT: Praeger.

Dyson, Tim (1996) *Population and Food: Global Trends and Future Prospects*, London: Routledge.

Ehrlich, Paul and Anne Ehrlich (1990) *The Population Explosion*, London: Hutchinson.

Elson, Diane (ed.) (1994) *Male Bias in the Development Process*, Manchester: Manchester University Press.

Elson, Diane (1989) 'The impact of structural adjustment on women: concepts and issues', in B. Onimode (ed.), *The IMF, the World Bank and the African Debt, Vol. 2*, London: Zed Books.

Faure, Denise (1994) 'Women's health and feminist politics' in Caroline Sweetman with Kate de Selincourt (eds), *Population and Reproductive Rights*, Oxford: Oxfam.

Folbre, Nancy (1998) 'Patriarchy and fertility decisions', in Paul Demeny and Geoffrey McNicoll (eds), *Population and Development*, London: Earthscan.

Forte, Diane and Karen Judd (1998) 'The South within the North: reproductive choices in three US communities', in Petchesky and Judd (eds), *Negotiating Reproductive Rights*, p. 269.

Gandhi, Nandita and Nandita Shah (1992) *The Issues at Stake: Theory and Practice in the Contemporary Indian Women's Movement in India*, Delhi: Kali for Women.

Germain, A., K. K. Holmes, P. Piot and J. N. Wasserheit (eds) (1992) *Reproductive Tract Infections: Global Impact and Priorities for Women's Reproductive Health*, New York: Plenum Press.

Harcourt, Wendy (ed.) (1994) *Feminist Perspectives on Sustainable Development*, London: Zed Books.

— (1997) 'An analysis of reproductive health: myths, resistance and new knowledge, in Wendy Harcourt (ed.), *Power, Reproduction and Gender: The Intergenerational Transfer of Knowledge*, London: Zed Books.

Hardon, Anita (1994) 'The development of contraceptive technologies: a feminist critique', in C. Sweetman with K. de Selincourt (eds), *Population and Reproductive Rights*, Oxford: Oxfam.

Hartman, Betsy (1995) *Reproductive Rights and Wrongs*, London: Zed Books.

Haynes, Mary Meaney (1999) 'The latest alibi', *Population Institute Review*, 1(21) (October–December).

Jacobson, Jodi (1993) 'Women's health: the price of poverty', in Marge Koblinsky, Judith Timyan and Jill Gay (eds), *The Health of Women: A Global Perspective*, Boulder, CO: Westview Press.

Jeffery, Patricia, Roger Jeffery and Andrew Lyon (1989) *Labour Pains and Labour Power: Women and Childbearing in India*, London: Zed Books.

Kabeer, Naila (1994) *Reversed Realities: Gender Hierarchies in Development Thought*, London: Verso.

Kumar, Radha (1993) *The History of Doing: An Illustrated Account of Movements for Women's Rights and Feminism in India, 1800-1990*, Delhi: Kali for Women.

Melrose, Diana (1982) *Bitter Pills: Medicines and the Third World Poor*, Oxford: Oxfam.

Mies, Maria (1986) *Patriarchy and Accumulation on a World Scale: Women in the International Division of Labour*, London: Zed Books.

Mintzes, Barbara, Anita Hardon and Jannemieke Hanhart (eds) (1993) *Norplant: Under Her Skin*, Amsterdam: Women's Health Action Forum.

Moser, Caroline (1989) *Gender Planning in the Third World*, London: Routledge.

Mu, Aiping (1996) 'Social politics and rural women's fertility behaviour in the People's Republic of China, 1979–1990', in H. Afshar (ed.), *Women and Politics in the Third World*, London: Routledge.

Ofosu, Yaw (1994) 'Breast-feeding and birth spacing: erosion of West African traditions', in Aderanti Adepoju and Christine Oppong (eds), *Gender, Work and Population in Sub-Saharan Africa*, Geneva: International Labour Organization.

Lise Østergaard (1992) *Gender and Development: A Practical Guide*, London: Routledge.

Pearson, Ruth and Cecile Jackson (1998) 'Introduction: interrogating development, feminism, gender and policy', in C. Jackson and R. Pearson (eds), *Feminist Visions of Development: Gender Analysis and Policy*, London: Routledge.

Petcheskey, Rosalind and Karen Judd (eds) (1998) *Negotiating Reproductive Rights: Women's Perspectives Across Countries and Cultures*, London: Zed Books.

Petchesky, Rosalind (1990) *Abortion and Woman's Choice: The State, Sexuality, and Reproductive Freedom*, Boston, MD: Northeastern University Press:.

Razzouk, Christine (2000) 'The SAARC Decade of the Girl Child: the girl child's destiny?' Women's Coalition, Centre for Women's Development Studies (CWDS) Library, http://www.hsph.harvard.edu/grhf/SAsia/discussion/discussframe.html

Rowbotham, Sheila (1992) *Women in Movement: Feminism and Social Action*, London: Routledge.

Ruse, Austin (1999) 'UNFPA briefing makes light of high mortality in Africa', 15 October, C-FAM, cited in Haynes 1999.

Salles, Vera Lucia (1992) 'Bartering fertility for votes', in *The Power to Change*, Delhi: Women's Feature Service.

Sanger, Margaret (1922) *Pivot of Civilization*, New York: Brentano.

Sen, Amartya (1987) 'Gender and co-operative conflicts' (mimeo), World Institute of Development Economics Research: Helsinki.

— (1992) 'More than 100 million women are missing,' *New York Review of Books*, 20 December, 1990.

Sen, Gita, A. Germain and L. C. Chen (1994) *Population Policies Reconsidered: Health, Empowerment and Rights*, Cambridge, MA: Harvard Centre for Population and Development Studies.

Shiva, Vandana (1994) 'Women's rights reduced to reproduction issue', Third World Network Features, http://www.mbnet.mb.ca/linkages/Cairo/twnpop.txt, 1 September.

Shrivastava, Jaya (1994) India: SAPping women's roots and resources', in *People vs. Global Capital: Report of the International People's Tribunal to Judge the G-7*, Japan: Pacific Asia Resource Center.

Sparr, Pamela (ed.) (1994) *Mortgaging Women's Lives: Feminist Critiques of Structural Adjustment*, London: Zed Books.

Standing, G. (1989) 'Global feminization through flexible labor', *World Development*, 17(7): 1077–96.

Stewart, Francis (1992) 'The many faces of adjustment', *World Development*, 19(12).

— (ed.) (1995) *Adjustment and Poverty: Options and Choices*, London: Routledge.

UNICEF (1995) *The State of the World's Children 1995*, New York: UNICEF.

UNIFEM (2000) *Progress of the World's Women 2000*, UNIFEM Biennial Report, New York: United Nations Development Fund for Women.

UNIFEM/CONMUJER (Comision Nacional de la Mujer) (1999) *Mujeres Mexicanas: Avances y Perspectivas*, Mexico: UNIFEM/CONMUJER.

Vishvanathan, Nalini, Lynn Duggan, Laurie Nisonoff and Nan Wiegersma (eds) (1997) *The Women, Gender and Development Reader*, London: Zed Books.

World Bank (1992) *Population and the World Bank: Implications from Eight Case Studies*, Washington, DC: World Bank.

Young, Kate (1997) 'Gender and development', in Vishvanathan et al. (eds), *The Women, Gender and Development Reader*.

8

Nicaraguan Women in the Age of Globalization

Stephanie Linkogle

Human rights are being reconceptualized by Nicaraguan women working for social change. Politics, both within Nicaragua and in the world at large, have shifted dramatically in the past 20 years and activists have made the conceptual shifts to function strategically in these new circumstances. Globalization has extended the reach of capitalist institutions and further secured the hegemony of 'the market'. In poor countries such as Nicaragua one of the main instruments of the globalization process has been structural adjustment programmes, which have stipulated the scaling down of the state through the privatization of services such as health and education. For Nicaraguan women, who are primarily responsible for supporting their families, this has meant the employment of individual and household strategies to maximize income. In a highly organized and politicized society like Nicaragua it has also provided the imperative for livelihood movements in which women work together to meet their economic needs. These include communal kitchens, health clinics, etc. The extent to which these movements define their remit beyond a particular neighbourhood or the provision of a particular service to encompass the gender and class dimensions of the problems they address varies.

As has been argued throughout this volume, there is no template for studying women's movements. The great diversity of women's activism in Nicaragua demonstrates the futility not only of attempts to formulate a picture of an ideal-type women's movement at the global level but also of providing a model of what a women's movement looks like in the more localized setting of the nation-state. There is a huge breadth of work being undertaken by women in Nicaragua, some of it with the explicit aim of advancing gender-specific aims, some of it with a class-based focus where participants are seeking ways to fulfil their gendered roles. With this in mind it is possible to identify some relevant political and socio-economic factors that shape the context of activism for Nicaraguan women.

Furthermore, despite differences in class background and political and religious orientation, women's movements have made alliances on particular issues. Such alliances demonstrate how class and gender issues are inter-woven and inseparable. Violence against women has been one such issue and has united diverse groups of women around a specifically feminist analysis of this problem. This chapter will look at themes of women's activism in relation to: the rise of the NGO sector, the alliance challenging violence against women and the increasing importance of human rights discourses. These are taking novel forms but display some continuities with other kinds of action and debate. They are strategically utilizing both the resources and the conceptual tools of the globalization agenda to advance the gender-specific and class-based interests of women.

The Changing Context of Women's Activism: From Revolution to Neoliberalism

From 1936 to 1979 Nicaragua was ruled by the Somoza dynasty, which enriched itself at the expense of the country's economic development. A lack of social services and infrastructure particularly affected poor women, who had fewer income-generating opportunities than men. Physical and sexual violence within the home was not recognized as a matter of public concern and there was no forum, state or otherwise, for women to seek help in understanding and challenging such abuses.

In July 1979, Somoza was overthrown in a popular revolution and the Sandinista National Liberation Front (FSLN) came to power with the aim of transforming the gross inequalities of Nicaraguan society and the legal and institutional framework that sustained these. Particularly in the early years of the revolutionary government, living standards and social provision in the areas of health education and housing improved for all Nicaraguans. Many of these initial ameliorations particularly benefited women and enabled them to provide for their families better (Harris 1987: 16). More-over, women not only benefited from social welfare programmes, but outnumbered men as participants in the early literacy and health care campaigns (Collinson 1990: 97, 124).

The emancipation of women was part of the revolutionary platform, and in the war to overthrow Somoza over 25 per cent of the Sandinista guerrilla forces were women. Shortly after the Sandinistas came to power, the recently founded women's organization AMNLAE (Asociación de Mujeres Nicaragüenses Luisa Amanda Espinosa) was incorporated into the structures of the new state. As the official women's organization, AMNLAE became the channel through which women's interests were meant to be articulated. This official status and subsequent legislative and constitutional changes gave activists 'a certain moral authority' in organizing around gender-specific issues (Envio 1987: 30).[1] Yet the Sandinista leadership often conceived of women's roles as supporting players on the revolutionary stage and commitment to the transformation of gender relations was equivocal and contradictory. A valorization of women as mothers dovetailed with the notion of women's interests based on an unproblematized gender division of labour. Furthermore, the US-financed Contra war, and the decision (contested by AMNLAE) to draft men only, recast women not as fighters for liberation but as mothers supporting conscripted men (Chinchilla 1985–86). As the ferocity of the war intensified 'controversial' demands put forward by the women's movement, such as the legalization of abortion, were seen by the state as less critical priorities than national defence and indeed potentially a rallying point for opponents of the revolution. In this way the women's movement and AMNLAE in particular were placed under great moral pressure to suppress or delay the pursuit of overtly feminist demands.

After 1987 the women's movement began to diversify and organize increasingly outside of the AMNLAE framework (Blandón 1994). The ATC (Rural Workers' Association) and the CST (Sandinista Workers Central) established women's sections. Here a much more autonomous feminist agenda developed, which addressed many of the issues that AMNLAE had side-stepped. The Matagalpa Women's Collective was the first women's organization to declare independence from AMNLAE. In addition, Ixchén, an independent women's clinic offering gynaecological, legal and mental health care, began to operate in January 1989. Further, AMNLAE's *casas de la mujer*, or women's centres, often pursued a more radical agenda than the national organization. Some centres provided gynaecological services as well as support and advice on issues such as domestic violence and family planning.

Since 1990, when the Sandinistas left office, the women's movement has been coming to terms both with the new political and economic realities and with a greater independence and autonomy from an increasingly fragmented FSLN. This has been against the backdrop of attempts to reassert and legally endorse the traditional notions of family and womanhood.[2] One of the most dramatic examples of this is the establishment in 1998 of the Ministry of the Family, a new 'super-ministry' merging the Institute of the Family and the Nicaraguan Women's Institute. The remit of the Ministry is to support the 'traditional family', described as 'a man, a woman and their children' (Hadgipateras 1997: 8). The Ministry has garnered much opposition from the women's movement, who see it as an 'attempt to extend the principles of Catholic morality to the entire Nicaraguan populace' (*Envio* 1997: 15) and to roll back many of the legislative and institutional gains that women made in the 1980s. An editorial in the conservative daily *La Prensa* maintained that those opposed to the new ministry were 'radical feminists, far removed from the interests of real women', which were defined as 'children and husbands' (Hadgipateras 1997: 8).

The Fluidity of Movements and Consciousness

This narrow invocation of 'real women' and their interests raises the question, 'What are women's interests?' It has become apparent that answers to such questions are far from being self-evident.

A pioneering analysis that sought to define different kinds of activism was made by Maxine Molyneux in the early 1980s. She produced a cogent critique of the Nicaraguan revolutionary government's validation of demands based on 'practical' or class-based interests over 'strategic' or 'gender-specific' sets of interests. She did not say this was a static or absolute distinction, noting how movements focused on 'practical' agendas had the potential to take on a wider more 'strategic' set of interests (Molyneux 1984).

Indeed, this transformatory aspect of struggles around daily survival was borne out by work on women's movements coming out of Latin America (Jelin 1990). It was also being documented historically. Temma Kaplan's analyses of women's crowd actions in early twentieth-century Barcelona showed how a 'female consciousness', invoking existing assumptions of gender, could bring women into public spaces where they acted in ways contrary to accepted gender norms. Through their activism their consciousness could be transformed (Kaplan 1992).

The attempt to understand these kinds of women's rebellions around livelihood in their own terms and assess their strengths and weaknesses, historically and in the present, was unfortunately to be subsumed in the political conflicts between feminists and increasingly beleaguered left groupings who refused to take on issues such as reproductive rights, male violence and the personal and domestic subordination of women.

In 1992 Saporta Sternbach et al. noted a distinction common in the Latin American left, where instances of women working collectively to advance their class-based interests within a traditional gender division of labour were being seen as examples of 'good feminism'. In contrast, movements that problematized such gender hierarchies and organized for sexual and reproductive autonomy were located in the category of 'bad feminism' (Saporta Sternbach et al. 1992: 212).

During the 1990s, amid a global retreat from attempts to redistribute wealth on egalitarian lines, an alternative valorization was to arise in which an exclusive application of a gender lens came to predominate. This ironically reproduced the tendency to dichotomize movements by simply reversing the order. The division between strategic and practical was to harden, implicitly setting up a hierarchy of consciousness whereby organizing around 'strategic' interests was posited as a more evolved and informed type of activism than organizing around 'practical' class-based interests.

There is a tacit power in the act of naming, and the distinction between and definition of categories such as strategic and practical were to prove problematic when they came from outside the movements themselves (Wieringa 1994). The political implications of definitions have, however, also provoked argument among activists themeselves. Innumerable agonized debates have taken place about what constitutes a 'women's movement' and how 'feminism' is to be understood. These are at once theoretical and political issues. For example, in a recent debate in the pages of the leading Nicaraguan feminist journal, *La Boletina*, a broad range of women's groups from all over the country have been invited to air their views on a number of questions including:

> What would you say must be in the category 'feminist'? Is there a danger that opening up the category will dilute it and make it meaningless? Is it better to have fewer criteria and a broader movement? Is the word 'feminist' relevant in defining ourselves? (*La Boletina* 2000)

Theoretical examinations of women's activism need to take account of the ways in which activists themselves are grappling with such questions. Moreover, definitions have to be continually reviewed in relation to the actual fluidity of movements and forms of organizing. Rather than a universal model of a feminist consciousness to which all women and movements should aspire, a dynamic and historical approach is needed. As Allison Drew, in her analysis of women's movements in sub-Saharan Africa, argues, 'female consciousness and feminism cannot be fully understood as polarized ideal-types but should be viewed as historically evolving and interpenetrating types of consciousness' (Drew 1995: 27).

Women's Movements and the Rise of the NGO Sector

A new development that has forced a re-examination of the meanings of 'activism' and 'movements' globally has been the growth of non-governmental organizations. Since 1990 there has been a huge proliferation of national and international NGOs in Nicaragua. While this development is in keeping with a trend throughout Latin America, in Nicaragua NGOs offered a legitimate and fundable status for the organizations and institutions that had been displaced by the Sandinistas' electoral loss. Throughout the era of revolutionary government (1979–90) there had been a lack of clarity between civil society, the state and the Sandinista political party. As a result institutions of civil society were included in a quasi-corporatist structure whereby a range of civil society organizations were simultaneously part of the state and the Sandinista party structure.

After 1990 popular movements have had to redefine their role in Nicaraguan society; many became NGOs, which took over when the Sandinista government projects closed down (Randall 2000: 28). Furthermore, new NGOs emerged and existing ones adapted their roles to address the shortfall in public services that accompanied the contraction of the state. In response to the progressive agendas of many NGOs, the state questioned their status and attempted to introduce taxation and greater regulation of these bodies, accusing them of being 'businesses' (Nitlapan-Envio Team 1999).

Feminism has played an important role in the growth of this sector in two key ways. First, the number of NGOs that concern themselves primarily with gender-specific issues has increased dramatically. These organizations have tapped into international and global institutions and organizations that have provided contacts and funding. This has been especially important given the reactionary character of post-1990 governments. Second, many other NGOs have introduced gender perspectives into their work, often supported by international NGOs in this task.

Clearly 'having a gender perspective' and meaningfully implementing it are not the same thing. Moreover, the feminist agenda advanced by many international NGOs is selective (Alvarez 1998) and often devoid of a critique of the capitalist social relations in which gender inequalities are realized. In 1998 Hurricane Mitch swept through Nicaragua, as well as other Central American countries, causing many deaths and displacing thousands of people. In the aftermath large amounts of aid poured into the country to finance reconstruction efforts. Fearing the possibility of exacerbating gender inequality and anticipating an opportunity for challenging the existing gender status quo, the women's movement has worked to promote a gender sensitive reconstruction.

The Women in Reconstruction Conference, a Central America-wide meeting of activists in Tegucigalpa, Honduras, declared that one of the principal aims of the process is to 'interpret the concept of "reconstruction" from the perspective of a new ethical citizenship that includes the transformation of discriminatory structures, the elimination of poverty and the full participation of women and other socially marginalised groups' (Women in Reconstruction 1999: 1)

One of the most active and innovative NGOs in Nicaragua is the Movimiento Comunal Nicaragüense (MCN). As Pierre La Ramée and

Erica Polakoff maintain: 'Certainly there is no nongovernmental organization quite like the Movimiento Comunal elsewhere in Latin America in terms of its scope and vision of community development' (La Ramée and Polakoff 1997: 196). In the context of a neoliberal state that has increasingly shed its responsibility for the provision of social services the MCN plays an important role in Nicaraguan society. Anna Fernandez Poncela argues that: 'When social services are reduced or eliminated, women, conscious of their roles in their families and the communities, are the ones to protest and attempt collectively to fill the gaps' (Fernandez Poncela 1996: 56). Thus it is not surprising that women constitute the majority of participants in the activities of the MCN and are active in its leadership.

Founded in 1978, the MCN is a community-based organization working throughout Nicaragua at the neighbourhood, municipal and national levels. The movement grew out of the struggle against the dictatorship when neighbourhood-based groups called Civil Defense Committees began to organize clandestinely in support of the revolutionary insurrection. In addition to a military role, the CDCs provided an alternative to the crumbling state structures in the dying days of the dictatorship (Ruchwarger 1985). After July 1979, when the Sandinistas came to power, these groups were unified as the Committees for the Defense of Sandinismo and were absorbed as a branch of the revolutionary government.

As with other popular movements which worked with the new state, there was a strain between the CDSs in their role as the representatives of community-based interests and their function as part of a state machinery. On the one hand the incorporation of community movements into the state and party structure gave a platform for and legitimacy to the livelihood claims of participants. Furthermore, the revolutionary state provided the possibility of wider social transformation that would improve the access of all Nicaraguans to basic goods and services, the demands for which were the basis of much community activism. On the other hand the weakness of this structure for the CDSs, and popular movements more generally, was the lack of autonomy *vis-à-vis* the state and party.[3]

Since 1990 the work of the MCN has been defined by local communities who set priorities and initiate projects such as communal kitchens, projects for sanitation and potable water, health care, education and property rights (MCN 1999). The MCN's formal statement on the gender question is that all of their 'lines of work, social as well as technical, are crossed by a gender focus' and one of the organization's goals is to 'achieve equality between men and women in political, economic and social rights' (MCN 1999). It is significant that such a clear stance has been taken by the MCN, which has also instituted 'gender training' within the organization and a pledge to bring more women into leadership positions. While this indicates critical reflection in response to feminists within and outside the organization, as with the legislative and policy changes made by the state, implementation is the key to the success of realizing the laudable aims of a 'gender policy'. Although many of the leaders and members are, or were, Sandinista supporters, the organization is avowedly non-partisan. This political neutrality is a difficult stance given the shared history of the organization and the Sandinistas. However, the FSLN, the Sandinista party, has been riven by splits, with different factions claiming to represent the true legacy of the revolution, and so there is no easy alliance between a cohesive revolutionary party and a popular social movement. Furthermore, because it has attempted to 'pick up the pieces' dropped by the neoliberal state, it has arguably become more of a service provider than a social movement.

In reflecting on what she sees as its unrealized potential Sofia Montenegro argues that it could 'take all the aggregates of the people that it works with, and move beyond a vision of victims or beneficiaries, to the idea of taking each one of them and making a political subject of them, to take them to the possibility of changing their reality' (Montenegro 1998). The MCN in its various incarnations has been a space for personal and collective transformation, particularly as participants seek to understand and change their class-based oppression. It remains to be seen how the organization will move forward with its new gender-aware strategy; certainly the dramatically increased profile of gender-specific activism, particularly on the issue of violence against women, will have an impact on this process.

'We Have a Right to Live Without Violence'[4]

In the early years of the revolution violence within the home was rarely a subject for public discussion. However, women's groups began to speak out about the problem and to petition the state to put into place legal and institutional mechanisms to combat it. Research conducted by the Women's Legal Office (OLM) and the Office on Family Orientation and Protection (OPF) in the mid-1980s confirmed that domestic violence was a widespread phenomenon that pervaded all sections of Nicaraguan society. In a random sample of women between the ages of 25 and 34, it was found that 44 per cent had suffered beating within the home. The OLM saw the prevalence of domestic violence as a consequence of power inequalities between men and women that naturalized particular male and female roles and behaviours. So challenging domestic violence involved not merely addressing individual instances of violence against women but also questioning gender subordination and the idea of the home as a 'private' domain outside the arena of public scrutiny (Collinson 1990: 17). The promulgation of a new constitution in January 1987 set out a broad set of social and economic rights, establishing for the first time the principle of equality before the law and in the workplace. Furthermore, it established rights not only in the public sphere but also in the private. In particular, article 36 mandated the right of all Nicaraguans to physical and psychological security and stipulated that behaviour that jeopardizes this is a criminal offence, thus giving constitutional status to the right to live without violence. The revolutionary government's March 1987 'Proclamation on Women' reiterated and extended the Sandinistas' commitment to women's emancipation as an integral part of the revolutionary process. The document explicitly addressed the issue of violence against women and children and pledged to introduce stiffer penalties for such offences (*Envio* 1987; Collinson 1990: 17).

The first official survey to address the problem of intra-family violence was the 1998 National Demographic and Health Survey of over 13,600 Nicaraguan women. It concluded that three out of every ten women in Nicaragua in a current or previous partnership had suffered some type of physical or sexual violence at the hands of their partner. One out of ten women had been the victim of sexual abuse. Furthermore, one in five women had suffered from domestic violence in the past twelve months and of these, more than three out of ten had suffered violence while pregnant. The survey suggested that women with low levels of education experienced the greater sexual and physical violence – however, women from all social classes were affected (*Envio* 1998: 22).

One of the most dynamic groups in the contemporary women's movement in Nicaragua is La Red de Mujeres Contra la Violencia, the Women's Network Against Violence. The Network grew out of the January 1992 National Conference for Women, where participants identified violence as one of the most important problems facing Nicaraguan women. The theme of this conference was 'unity and diversity' and it was with this spirit that the Network was set up as a non-hierarchical organization open to all women or groups of women working towards ending domestic and sexual violence against women and children. The Network is not affiliated to any political party and does not profess or require its members to share any particular political position.

Despite its non-partisan stance, one of its basic principles is that violence is not a personal or private problem but rather a social and political one. Violence against women emerges from unequal power relationships between men and women. Hence combating it requires addressing the gender inequality that is at its root. In this way the Network has played a fundamental role in placing issues of domestic and sexual violence on the political agenda. The Network has grown to include 170 local and regional groups across Nicaragua and hundreds of individual members. The goal of the Network is to combat physical and sexual violence against women. To this end it has acted on a number of different fronts, working with different governmental bodies, including the Ministry of Education, the Institute of Women, the police and the Supreme Court of Justice, as well as collaborating with international and other national NGOs. Following the Network's successful lobbying and campaign work, Law 230 was passed, prohibiting physical, sexual and psychological violence in families. The Network currently provides training for lawyers in the application of this new legislation. A unique feature of Law 230 is its criminalization of psychological abuse, which is classified as insults, threats and forms of humiliation that cause psychological damage. If a women is suffering psychological abuse, she is now able to report this to the police and to be examined by a psychologist to evaluate her emotional state. The psychological evaluation is admissible as evidence that can be presented and adjudicated on in a court of law. As a response to the demands of women's collectives the government established 'Women's Commissars' in police stations. These provide legal and counselling services to women who have been raped or suffered physical or psychological violence (*Barricada Internacional*, 1993: 7).

Men Against Violence

Alongside women's activism on this issue there is a small but growing number of 'men's groups' that aim to provide men who have been violent towards their partners and children with the forum to understand and work to change their behaviour. Oswaldo Montoya, a commentator on male violence, argues that to some extent men are victims of the same patriarchal culture that underpins domestic violence. Although men are more powerful than women they are unable to freely express emotion and weakness and such feelings are often displaced into violent activities (Hilton 1999).

The analysis provided by many of the men's groups attributes male violence in part to Nicaragua's recent violent history. Vast numbers of men have participated in military activities in the past 20 years, with very little in the way of counselling to help them deal with these experiences. This, coupled with poverty and the resulting powerlessness, has encouraged men to seek greater authority and dominance within the home. As a consequence Montoya identifies a 'very acute crisis of masculinity' whereby many men have developed pathological behaviours that manifest themselves in violence against women and children. While this approach may have therapeutic value, research on domestic violence in Nicaragua and elsewhere has indicated the prevalence of the phenomenon amongst all socio-economic groups (Hilton 1999). Raquel Carmen del Aguirre of the Women's Network emphasizes that domestic violence is 'not due primarily to the situation of poverty' which grips Nicaragua but rather due to 'a whole culture which has traditionally discriminated against women' (del Aguirre 1999).

Zoliamérica Narváez Speaks Out

In March 1998 Zoliamérica Narváez publicly accused her stepfather, former president of Nicaragua Daniel Ortega, of sexual abuse. She has given detailed testimony of the abuse, which she claims began at the age of eleven and continued for a number of years after this.[5] Narváez argues that, through a process of emotional recovery, she has gained the 'consciousness' to 'claim my right to my identity' and to speak out about the wider issue of intra-family violence (Narváez 1998: 12). She is seeking to have criminal charges brought against Ortega, who has thus far been protected from prosecution because as a current member of the National Assembly he has parliamentary immunity. Ortega denies the charges and, taking on the mantle of the victim, describes the accusations as his 'Calvary' brought on by political enemies anxious to thwart his efforts to 'defend the poor' and diminish his revolutionary legacy (Nitlapán-*Envio* Team 1998). Yet there has been no concerted effort on the part of his political opponents to strip Ortega of this immunity. Sofia Montenegro argues that 'no man, even his worst enemies would speak against Daniel Ortega' and that a 'gentlemen's agreement' not to take up the subject has prevailed, providing an opportunity to 'observe how the patriarchal system works' (Hilton 1999). The Women's Network is campaigning to strip Ortega of his immunity not just because of Narváez's right to justice, but also because the Ortega case is emblematic of the impunity with which crimes of violence and sexual abuse are committed against many other Nicaraguan women and children. To this end its current campaign slogan is: 'I have the right to justice. No more impunity.'

Human Rights for Women

Both the Women's Network and the Nicaraguan Human Rights Commission have used human rights discourses to campaign against domestic violence. This strategy poses some fundamental challenges to the idea of human rights as it is conventionally understood. Discussions of human rights have generally focused on civil and political rights – the freedom 'from' (torture, unlawful arrest, etc.) and freedom 'of' (assembly, religion) – the rights of the individual with respect to their state as named in the

UN Universal Declaration of Human Rights. These have generally been emphasized in liberal democratic states. Social and economic rights – for example, the right to an education, the right to employment – have tended to be seen as less important and enforceable, but still these also rest on an individual right 'to' something provided by the state in the public sphere. Anti-domestic violence campaigns that utilize a human rights framework are demanding something altogether different from states – that is, for the rights in the private sphere to have the same status as those in the public sphere. This is a conceptual shift, for, as Elizabeth Jelin has argued: 'The human rights paradigm rests on an implicit differentiation between public and private life: The civil and political rights of individuals are not recognized in the private sphere of family relationships' (Jelin 1996: 179).

Anti-domestic violence campaigns have managed this in two ways. First, because specific legislative provisions against domestic violence do exist, when incidences of domestic violence are not prosecuted by the courts, this is challenged as a human rights violation. Here a woman's right to report domestic violence and to have her accusation tested by the criminal justice system is seen as a basic human right. Women's groups have contested the fact that women have differential access to the criminal justice system. Violeta Delgado from the Women's Network argues: 'We all have the right to justice. It is a basic right to be defended, a basic human right, because "all people are equal before the law and have equal rights". We should not forget this right because if we do not claim it and we don't defend it we will lose it' (Delgago 1998). Second, women's groups in Nicaragua have been part of a wider sustained process of social and economic resistance on the part of women's movements globally. This is augmenting and expanding the existing UN Universal Declaration of Human Rights. The rights that have been elaborated are: gender equality, freedom from violence, the right to the free expression of sexuality, reproductive rights including the access to safe and legal abortion, the right and responsibility to raise children and to support them financially and emotionally even after the breakdown of a partnership.

The efforts of anti-domestic violence campaigns both to lay claim to existing rights and to work to expand these needs to be seen in relation to wider struggles around citizenship and rights in Latin America. Because of the processes of 'democratization' popular movements and states across Latin America are defining what citizenship and rights are and will be. This is far from being an unproblematic process; nevertheless, in many different contexts struggles are contesting what it means to be a citizen, what 'rights' people should have and what role the state should take in securing these. A key concept that has emerged from these debates is the idea of 'a right to have rights' (Dagnino 1998).

In many Latin American societies human rights discourses were first mobilized in the face of grave forms of state violence against individuals in the form of torture, assassinations and disappearances. In Nicaragua, however, they were involved in defence of the state in the context of the Contra war, where the International Court of Justice found the USA guilty of illegally mining Nicaraguan ports. Here a concept of rights was deployed in relation to an individual and her/his state and to a sovereign state in relation to another respectively. Nicaragua's revolutionary experiment of the 1980s marks it out from the rest of Latin America in terms of the deployment of human rights discourses, and this has shaped present debates.

Conclusion

The post-1990 era has also been a time of changing economic forms of organization – international lending agencies entered with the development money that had previously been denied, but it was to be tied to structural adjustment programmes. The conditions for devolving the responsibilities of the state were in line with the ideological commitments of the new government. Hence the privatization of the state was in line with dismantling the Sandinista apparatus and the privatization of previously state-owned property. In Nicaragua an overlap in the roles and functions of political actors has been a persistent problem.

The institutions of the 'modern' Nicaraguan state are relatively recent and are in the process of dramatic change and reformulation. The present form of representative government dates back only to the mid-1980s. The integralism of the 1980s, with its preoccupation with constructing expressly revolutionary institutions and identities, has given way to attempts to formalize and specify the content of the rights and responsibilities of the citizen and the state. Here there is significant disagreement. The gender-specific rights, for which many women's movements are calling, question the patriarchal forms of organization generally within the family as well as the political sphere.

In debates on domestic violence in Nicaragua competing discourses and imagery have come into play. The Women's Network Against Violence and the Nicaraguan Human Rights Commission have constructed a moral imperative to combat domestic violence with recourse to the moral banner of women's human rights. Both the right and sections of the left (for example, supporters of Daniel Ortega's immunity from prosecution) draw upon traditional notions of the sanctity family as a private space in which the state should not intervene.

A number of the debates that have emerged in the Nicaraguan context will be familiar to feminists in other parts of the world. One of the key themes is the task of achieving unity while respecting diversity. For the Nicaraguan feminist movement this is relevant to the task of building bridges not only between women of different class and ethnic backgrounds but also between women of different political affiliations. That Nicaragua has a tradition of political violence makes this task all the more complicated. Amazingly, coalitions within the feminist movement have managed to include not only women who were supporters of the revolution but also women who sided with the Contras.

The efforts of anti-domestic violence campaigns both to lay claim to existing rights and to expand the present framework need to be seen in relation to wider struggles around citizenship and rights in Latin America. Here, processes of 'democratization' have set the stage on which popular movements and states across Latin America are defining what citizenship and rights are and will be. This is not an unproblematic process, as various actors struggle over what it means to be a citizen, what 'rights' people should have and what role the state should take in securing these. In this way women's activism in Nicaragua is redefining the meaning of 'human rights'.

Notes

1. For more analysis of legislative changes in the 1980s see Collinson 1990; Stephens 1990.

2. This attempt to reintroduce Catholic morality has extended to changes in sex education policy where abstinence and the sanctity of the traditional family have been taught since 1990 (Ocón and Pasos 2000).

3. For an excellent and detailed discussion of the CDSs and the MCN see La Ramée and Polakoff 1997.

4. This slogan has been widely used in Nicaragua by the Women's Network.

5. For more on the Zoliamérica case see *La Boletina* 1998.

Bibliography

Alvarez, Sonia E. (1998) 'Latin American feminisms "go global": trends of the 1990s and challenges for the new millennium', in S. Alvarez, E. Dagnino and A. Escobar, *Cultures of Politics, Politics of Cultures: Re-visioning Latin American Social Movements*, Boulder, CO: Westview Press.

Barricada Internacional (1993) 'Women's Commission formed', *Barricada Internacional*, 13(360) (April).

Blandón, María Teresa (1994) 'The impact of the Sandinista defeat on Nicaraguan feminism', in G. Küppers (ed.), *Compañeras: Voices from the Latin American Women's Movement*, London: Latin America Bureau.

La Boletina (1998) 'Entrevista con Zoliamérica Narváez', special supplement, *La Boletina*, 36 (August–October), http://www.puntos.org.ni/boletina/bole36/index.html

La Boletina (2000) 'Debate feminista', *La Boletina*, 42 (April–June), http://www.puntos.org.ni/boletina

Chinchilla, Norma (1985–86) 'Women in the Nicaraguan Revolution', *Nicaraguan Perspectives*, 11 (Winter).

CODA (2000) 'Working with the Nicaraguan Communal Movement (MCN)', http://www.cit.org.uk/mcn.htm

Collinson, Helen (ed.) (1990) *Women and the Revolution in Nicaragua*, London: Zed Books.

Dagnino, Evelina (1998) 'Culture, citizenship, and democracy: changing discourses and practices of the Latin American left', in S. Alvarez, E. Dagnino and A. Escobar, *Cultures of Politics, Politics of Cultures: Re-visioning Latin American Social Movements*, Boulder, CO: Westview Press.

del Aguirre, Raquel Carmen (1999) 'The Nicaraguan Women's Network', Central America Women's Network Public Meeting, London, 24 February.

Delgado, Violeta (1998) 'Tengo derecho a la justicia, no más impunidad', *La Boletina*, 36 (August–October), http://www.puntos.org.ni/boletina

Drew, Allison (1995) 'Female consciousness and feminism in Africa', *Theory and Society*, 24.

Envio (1987) 'Church–state relations: a chronology – Part II', *Envio*, 6(78) (December).

— (1997) 'Women's movement fights Ministry of Family bill', *Envio*, 16(189) (April).

— (1998) 'Intra-family violence', *Envio*, 17(207) (October).

Fernandez Poncela, Anna M. (1996) 'The disruptions of adjustment: women in Nicaragua', *Latin American Perspectives*, 23(1) (Winter): 49–66.

Hadgipateras, Angela (1997) 'Women's rights in Nicaragua – Aleman's fundamentalist agenda', *Central America Report* (Winter).

Harris, Hermione (1987) 'Introduction', in A. Angel and F. Macintosh, *The Tiger's Milk: Women of Nicaragua*, London: Virago.

Hilton, Isabel (1999) *Crossing Continents: Disaster and Disillusion in Nicaragua*, Radio 4, 25 March.

Huerta, Juan Ramón (1999) '¿Movimientos sociales diezmados en Nicaragua?', http://www.ciberdiario.com.ni/files/entrevista1.htm

Jelin, Elizabeth (ed.) (1990) *Women and Social Change in Latin America*, London: Zed Books.

— (1996) 'Women, gender and human rights', in E. Jelin and E. Hershberg (eds), *Constructing Democracy: Human Rights, Citizenship and Society in Latin America*, Boulder, CO: Westview Press.

Kaplan, Temma (1992) *Red City, Blue Period: Social Movements in Picasso's Barcelona*, Berkeley: University of California Press.

La Ramée, Pierre M. and Erica G. Polakoff (1997) 'The evolution of the popular organizations in Nicaragua', in G. Prevost and H. E. Vanden (eds), *The Undermining of the Sandinista Revolution*, Basingstoke: Macmillian.

Latin American and Caribbean Committee for the Defense of Women's Rights (CLADEM) (1998) 'A Declaration of Human Rights for the Twenty-first Century', *Envio*, 19(230) (September): 38–41.

Linkogle, Stephanie (1996) *Gender, Practice and Faith in Nicaragua*, Aldershot: Avebury.

López Vigil, María (2000) 'The silence about incest needs to be broken', *Envio*, 19(230) (September): 15–25.

Meza Basaure, María Eugenia (1999) 'Violence against women: a centuries-old plague', *Envio*, 19(227) (June).

MCN (1999) 'Principales temáticas de trabajo a nivel de la comunidad y en sus instancias dirigentes', http://www.ciberdiario.com.ni/files/entrevista1.htm

Molyneux, Maxine (1981) 'Socialist societies old and new: progress towards women's emancipation?', *Feminist Review*, 8 (Summer).

— (1984) 'Mobilisation without emancipation? Women's interests, state and revolution in Nicaragua', *Critical Social Policy*, 10(4).

Montenegro, Sofia (1998) 'Interview with Midge Quant', 30 April, http://www.ibw.com.ni/~cgenica/SOFIAM.html

Narváez, Zoliamérica (1998) 'This is my history' *Envio*, 17(200) (March).

Nitlapán-*Envio* Team (1998) 'Stormy weather ... can't get our poor selves together', *Envio*, 17(206) (September).

— (1999) 'Crossroads at the century's end', *Envio*, 18(221).

— (2000) 'After the pact: the die is cast', *Envio*, 19(222–223) (January–February): 3–13.

Ocón, Maria Dolores and Myra Pasos (2000) 'Nicaragua Equity, a women's struggle', Instituto del Tercer Mundo – Social Watch, http://www.socwatch.org.uy/1998/english/reports/nicaragua.htm

Randall, Margaret (1981) *Sandino's Daughters: Testimonies of Nicaraguan Women in Struggle*, London: Zed Books.

— (2000) 'Rethinking power from a feminist vision', *Envio*, 19(222–223) (January–February): 19–29.

Rowbotham, Sheila (1992) *Women in Movement: Feminism and Social Action*, London: Routledge.

Ruchwarger, Gary (1985) 'The Sandinista mass organizations and the revolutionary process', in R. Harris and C. Vilas (eds), *Nicaragua: A Revolution Under Siege*, London: Zed Books.

Saporta Sternbach, Nancy, Marysa Navarro-Aranguren, Patricia Chuchryk and Sonia E. Alvarez (1992) 'Feminisms in Latin America: from Bogotá to San Bernardo', in A. Escobar and S. E. Alvarez (eds), *The Making of Social Movements in Latin America: Identity, Strategy and Democracy*, Boulder, CO: Westview Press.

Schirmer, Jennifer (1993) 'The seeking of truth and the gendering of consciousness', in S. Radcliffe and S. Westwood (eds), *Women and Popular Protest in Latin America*, London: Routledge.

Stephens, Beth (1990) 'Developing a legal system grapples with an ancient problem: rape in Nicaragua', *Women's Rights Law Reporter*, 12(2).

Wieringa, Saskia (1994) 'Women's interests and empowerment: gender planning reconsidered', *Development and Change*, 25.

Women in Reconstruction (1999) 'Exercising Power for Equality' (Executive Summary), trans. Anna Turley and Marilyn Thomson, The Central America Meeting, Tegucigalpa, Honduras, April.

9

Sexual Politics in Indonesia: From Soekarno's Old Order to Soeharto's New Order

Saskia E. Wieringa

Ever since the putsch of 1 October 1965 that brought General Soeharto to power, the Indonesian state has waged a war of sexual imaging. By posing the government against 'communist whores', the army, under General Soeharto, was to be presented as the virile saviour of a nation on the brink of destruction. Not only did ex-President Soeharto's New Order state legitimate itself by its destruction of the Communist Party of Indonesia (PKI, Partai Komunis Indonesia), as Rex Mortimer and other scholars have suggested (Mortimer 1969), the military also orchestrated a campaign of slander and sexual innuendo against the PKI's women's organization Gerwani (Gerakan Wanita Indonesia, Indonesian Women's Movement). The underlying sexual politics integral to this process of legitimation have been largely ignored, even though the campaign of vilification was to be pursued for more than thirty years. It was pursued for so long because it represented a powerful supportive logic sustaining Soeharto's rule right up until his fall in mid-1998. Even in the last days of Soeharto, politically active women such as Megawati Soekarnoputri (who, as Soekarno's daughter, could not openly be accused) were labelled as subversive and a threat to state stability (see Langenberg 1996).

A consequence of the sexual accusations falsely hurled at Gerwani was to be the destruction of what had been one of the most powerful women's movements in the world (Wieringa 1995). Not only was Gerwani banned and destroyed, the remaining women's organizations were brought under strict government control. The state even set up its own mass women's organizations, under the umbrella of Dharma Wanita (Women's Duty), which were intended to re-subordinate women, rather than to emancipate them (Wieringa 1985, 1988 and 1995). The feminist organizations in Indonesia that were set up in the mid-1980s had to manoeuvre very carefully to avoid being called *Gerwani baru*, 'new Gerwani'. Long after the PKI had been destroyed in one of the bloodiest transitions to power in modern times, the spectre of communism, especially as animated by its women, was still invoked to justify the harsh repression of any democratic anti-government forces in the country.[1]

I will introduce the women's organization Gerwani and disentangle its role, real and alleged, in the so-called 'events of 1965' (as the 1 October putsch and its aftermath are often called in Indonesia). I will then discuss the extraordinary consequences of the portrayal of the PKI as a moral poison enacted through its women by the construction of an official government legend about the rise of the Indonesian army out of the injuries and deaths it suffered in 1965.

Gerwani

The women's organization associated with the PKI (Wieringa 1985, 1988, 1992, 1993 and 1995), Gerwani, or Gerwis,[2] as it was called between 1950 and 1954, was set up by a group of young women who wanted to fulfil their ideals of the Indonesian revolution. Unlike members of other women's organizations, such as Perwari,[3] they did not withdraw into what was commonly seen as women's terrain, the struggle for social issues, but they kept up a presence in the political arena. The initial emphasis of its members on a marriage law based on monogamy dwindled after President Soekarno's polygamous marriage with Hartini in 1954. The focus shifted to a struggle for equal labour rights for women and for equal responsibilities with men in the struggle for full national independence and socialism. Rights for women and children, including crèches and the creation of the 'revolutionary family', remained central themes throughout Gerwani's history. Full national independence and peace as defined by the WIDF[4] were other major issues. After the 1954 congress of the organization it followed the 'mass line' the PKI had already set in place. Thousands of cadres were being trained. Members went into the villages and neighbourhoods to discuss the daily problems with peasant women and urban women, especially women labourers. A major effort was made to combat illiteracy among women.

In the escalating political tensions of the early 1960s, Gerwani members participated actively in the 'one-sided actions' the Indonesian Farmers' Front (BTI, Barisan Tani Indonesia) organized to implement the land reform laws. Together with Gerwani's efforts to get women's political rights[5] established this greatly antagonized conservative forces in the countryside.

In its later years Gerwani's feminist wing was to lose out to its communist wing and the ties between Gerwani and the PKI and between these two organizations and President Soekarno were to become stronger. The women's organization propagated a model of militant motherhood in which mothers were responsible for the moral education of their children, to make them worthy members of the 'true Manipol[6] family'. These families were intended to become 'strong fortresses' against the influence of imperialist culture, and to help Soekarno and the nation to achieve Soekarno's vaguely defined revolutionary goals, which in the last years of the Old Order included the campaign of Confrontation with Malaysia. Gerwani also organized some anti-price rise demonstrations.

Gerwani differed from other women's organizations of its time in several significant ways and was to stray from the women's *kodrat*, a religiously inspired code of conduct based on women's intrinsic 'nature'. While all women's organizations had displayed a considerable amount of political activism during the prolonged struggle for Indonesia's independence, most of their members felt they should leave the political arena once that goal had been reached (Vreede-de Stuers 1960; Wieringa 1995). Women's anti-colonial activities were tolerated only in so far as they could be associated with women's motherly qualities in giving birth to the nation and with the preferred model of wifehood, as faithful companions of their warrior-husbands.

The best description of how revolutionary men of those days saw women's participation in the national struggle is provided by Soekarno himself in his book *Sarinah*, which was originally published in 1947. Basing his ideas on socialist approaches to the 'woman question', especially on the writings of Bebel and Zetkin, Soekarno wrote that only after the national revolution was won would women no longer suffer from the 'patriarchal illness' they had had to endure for so long. Under male supervision, more specifically his supervision, women should occupy themselves with the revolution as the 'second wing of our national garuda'[7] (Soekarno 1963: 255–7).

After independence, apart from Gerwani, most women's organizations busied themselves with activities commonly classified as 'social', and withdrew behind the thresholds of their homes and social clubs. Soekarno himself ignored most of the feminist views he had so ardently defended in *Sarinah*, especially after his marriage with Hartini.

The *kodrat* of Indonesian women prescribes that they should be meek, passive, obedient to the male members of the family, sexually shy and modest, self-sacrificing and nurturing, and that they should find their main vocation in wifehood and motherhood. An illustration of Gerwani's resistance to this *kodrat* is provided by the following lines of a poem written by a supporter of Gerwani: 'no longer / are we gilded posies / engaging when compliant / exquisite when yielding / enchanting when submissive / to hell 'tis our duty to go / to heaven permitted to follow'.[8] The Indonesian term *ibu* means both wife and mother. Indeed, the association of women as in relation to their husbands and children is so pervasive that young unmarried women are generally seen as 'potential wives' (Tiwon 1996). This ideal of femininity can incorporate a certain degree of economic autonomy.[9] Notwithstanding traditions such as the 'lady soldiers' at the royal palaces of Central Java (Kumar 1980), Javanese women in particular are supposed to be like Sumbadra, the shy and obedient wife of the *wayang* (shadow puppet play) hero Arjuna. Gerwani, on the other hand, upheld a model of womanhood that was more in line with the figure of Srikandi, Arjuna's warrior-wife. Although the organization never questioned the primacy of women's motherly role, it propagated a model of militant motherhood, fusing women's maternal functioning with political activism. This was contrary to what conservative forces in society upheld (Wieringa 1995).

The 1 October 1965 Coup

The change from Soekarno's Old Order state to the New Order of President Soeharto was introduced by the so-called 'October 1965 events', instigated by the 30 September Movement.[10] The propaganda campaign that followed linked communism (and later liberal, critical thinking in general) with women's frightening sexual powers once unleashed. This is associated with Islamic concepts of sexual disorder,[11] and also with a pre-Islamic, Hindu world view. Both in the *Kakawin Bharata Yudha*, one of the major texts related to the popular Javanese *wayang* play and in certain *hikayat* (Malay stories) there are scenes in which crowds of frenzied women forsake husbands and children (Tiwon 1996). I suggest that Gerwani was singled out as the ideological repository of resistance against the virile order of the military and of conservative forces in society because of its insistence on women's political activism. This was seen as an unacceptable form of rebellion. Fatima Mernissi has argued that women's disobedience is much feared in the Muslim world, because its consequences are enormous. She observes that:

> rigid sex-role stereotyping is so fundamental to hierarchical order, that when women challenge the status quo, they threaten not only patriarchal power (their relation to the husband) but the very existence of the entire system and more specifically God's claim to obedience. (1996: 111–12)

Mernissi's statement is based on Morocco, but her views can also throw light on how gender has been part of the politics of Indonesia and especially of Java, which has a similar rigid system of gender ideology, women's *kodrat*.

My account of events in the last months of 1965 is based on an analysis of print media and on interviews with participants. It restores the sexual politics that have been largely missed out of the history of the period. By mid-1965 tensions in Indonesian society were reaching a climax. In the countryside the unilateral actions of the PKI-associated Farmers' Front, which demanded the rapid implementation of the recently introduced land reform laws, had thoroughly disturbed social relations. Rising levels of inflation caused increasing poverty. The relationship between the army leaders and the PKI became increasingly tense, with President Soekarno leaning more than ever towards the PKI side. Only the nation's leader seemed able to keep the competing factions together. The PKI was particularly worried that the president might not be able to protect them much longer in view of the six murder attempts that had been made on him already (May 1978). Rumours of his illness therefore caused great unrest.[12]

In this tense situation several middle-ranking officers of the army, led by Colonel Untung, staged a military putsch. They wanted, so they testified later, to protect the president against plans of an alleged Council of Generals, which, so they had come to believe, intended to overthrow Soekarno on Army Day, 5 October. Also, they were discontented with the corrupt and decadent lifestyle of some of those generals, in particular Yani (Crouch 1978). The plans of the officers were discussed in several meetings of the PKI politburo,[13] during which some limited support was promised to the plotters.

During the putsch six generals and one lieutenant were killed and their bodies were thrown into a deep well known as Lubang Buaya (Crocodile Hole), at a training field for volunteers of the Malaysia campaign, which had been used mainly by volunteers[14] of the PKI-affiliated youth organization and Gerwani. This field lay on the grounds of the military airport, Halim. Before the day was out General Soeharto's forces had managed to cajole and threaten half of the rebel forces into submission (Crouch 1978). In the meantime President Soekarno had decided not to appoint General Soeharto, who was next in line to replace the murdered chief of staff, General Yani, possibly because he considered him too 'strong-willed' (Anderson and McVey 1971). Instead he appointed a junior general, Pranoto Reksosamudro. Soeharto ignored the orders of his president. He issued his own radio announcement that he had taken over the army leadership to restore security and order (Crouch 1978: 132). Two weeks later Soekarno was compelled to replace Pranoto by Soeharto. Thereafter followed the propaganda campaign, the massacre and mass detainment.

Broadly speaking there are three interpretations of the events in October 1965 that marked the end of the 'Old Order'. The army version is that the PKI was the *dalang* (puppeteer) behind the coup, through its Special Bureau. The fullest account of the army view is given by Notosutanto and

Saleh (1968).[15] The PKI, on the other hand, maintained initially that it was an intra-military affair. This version was supported abroad by a paper circulated since 1966 authored by two social scientists from Cornell University, Anderson and McVey. A third interpretation is that Soeharto and possibly the CIA were behind a conspiracy to break the power of the PKI. Holtzappel (1979), Scott (1985), Utrecht (1970) and Wertheim (1979, 1991) have elaborated this view. This interpretation stresses the class aspects of both the coup and the propaganda campaign that followed it, pointing out that most victims fell in the areas where peasant unrest had been most common.

I suggest another interpretation: that Soeharto has shown himself to be both a ruthless and very ambitious man and a person able to wait patiently for the right moment to strike. The information he had received[16] may have convinced him that the coup was so clumsily planned, with so little actual support, that it would be too risky to support it, while it could very easily be put down. He would then come out as the great saviour of the nation and Soekarno would have had no other choice than to appoint him chief of staff. The start of the propaganda campaign that formed the second, 'real' coup may have been when Soekarno appointed a junior officer to army chief instead, which humiliated and enraged Soeharto and made him realize that his only access to power lay in the removal of President Soekarno, and that in order to replace the president, his most powerful support group at the time, the Communists, had to be destroyed (Wieringa 1995).

Gerwani and the 1 October 1965 Coup

In the middle of the 1980s I interviewed some of the main surviving Gerwani leaders who had just come out of prison, as well as some ordinary members who had been associated with the events around 'Lubang Buaya'. Just released, they found themselves in an atmosphere of innuendo and accusations in which they and their former organization had become associated with amoral, anti-religious conduct, with sexual perversions and atrocities, based on the slander stories the army constructed of what had happened in the night of 30 September and 1 October 1965.

My reconstruction of what actually happened at Lubang Buaya is the following: some seventy women, most of them young girls from the youth organization, others from the trade union and the farmers' front, and a few Gerwani members, including some wives of soldiers, were assembled at Lubang Buaya by the plotters. Gerwani as an organization was left out of the plans. What happened then? What about the wild accusations that were later hurled at them, of 'naked, sexual dancing', of having 'severed the penises of the generals', and of having their 'eyes gouged out'? How did the generals die (Anderson 1987)? One of the assembled women told me the following story, which was corroborated by other interviews I held with surviving members of Gerwani and the youth organization:

> A few days before the coup I was picked up by a female party member to be engaged in some extra activities at Halim. She never disclosed what was up, but as usual I joined. Once there I was asked to sew stripes of various colours on uniforms to distinguish friends from enemies. It was a lot of work and we worked until late at night. So on the morning of October 1st I was sleeping heavily when we were woken up by shouts. It was still dark outside and we were all frightened. We ran to the open space where we saw a group of soldiers dragging those kidnapped generals. It was quite a noise, for they kept shouting 'kabir'[17] at them. In fact that was quite a common word, we used it all the time. The soldiers hit the generals and finally they were shot and thrown into the well. The soldiers were enraged, they even rained bullets on them when they were already dead. Only then, terrified, we also walked to the well. Afterwards they started circulating stories about dancing and sexual perversions, and cutting off penises. All that is nonsense. Those generals were deadly scared, they couldn't even get them up! And the girls were scared too, they huddled in a corner!

The army went to great length to construct the stories they decided to circulate. Witnesses were 'quoted' in the papers, photographs were shown. There were television broadcasts and radio programmes on the horrors said to be committed at Lubang Buaya. How did the military go about that? One of the volunteer girls who had been present at Lubang Buaya:

> I was sixteen and was a member of the Pemuda Rakyat [the PKI's youth organization]. I had been trained at Cipete and had joined many exercises for the Malaysia confrontation, so when I was asked to come to Lubang Buaya I naturally joined. I witnessed the soldiers kill the generals and ran home afterwards. I was arrested at nine o'clock in the morning and put in prison for two weeks. I was beaten and interrogated. They forced us to undress and to dance naked in front of them while they took pictures. Then I was released. After a little while I was captured again, and released again. In total I was captured five times before they finally decided to keep me in prison. That was at the beginning of November 1965. I was released in December 1982.

The campaign had a slow start.[18] While the autopsy results had become available to the authorities, they were not made public. The report only became known widely when Anderson got access to it and published it in 1987. The autopsy demonstrated that the wounds found on the bodies of the killed generals and lieutenant were either gunshots, or resulted from heavy, dull traumas, possibly caused by clubbing with the butts of guns or the damage likely to occur from a fall into a 10-metre well. All the genitals were intact, all eyes were in their proper sockets, and there were no traces of cuts with razors. As General Soeharto himself had ordered the report to be prepared it is unlikely that he had not been informed of its results before the burial (Anderson 1987).

The first indication of the way in which the deeper layers of the Javanese-Islamic consciousness would be manipulated is on 11 October. A small article appeared in the *AB*, headlined 'Spirits in broad daylight'. The word used for spirit was *kuntilanak*, the name of a spirit of a woman who has died in childbirth and who appears as a beautiful woman with a hole in her back. In this hole she stores kidnapped children. This is a devil-like spirit that hovers around at night. 'It has been reported', the story continued, 'that people belonging to[19] (the word used is *kalap*, meaning 'possessed by an evil spirit') Pemuda Rakyat and Gerwani, umbrella organizations of the PKI-Aidit,[20] are committing several terrorist acts. Unknown women have visited the houses of our Heroes, wearing veils as if they belonged to Islamic organizations. Their movements aroused suspicion, for it was clear they were Gerwani members. Fortunately their evil plans became known before they could commit any evil actions towards the families of the Heroes of the Revolution.[21] We have to be very careful' (*AB*, 11.10.1965).

The same day an article in the *BY* reported on the condition of the bodies of the generals found in the well. Contrary to what the autopsy revealed, the paper wrote that 'eyes had been gouged out, and of some generals the genitals had been cut off' (*BYM*, 11.10.1965). Other papers took up the campaign as well. It was reported that the Indonesian Council of Churches expressed its feelings of great distress, as 'it truly could hardly believe that certain persons in our Pancasila state are capable of executing actions such as rapes which are beyond human boundaries' (*SH*, 9.10.1965). The *Duta Masyarakat* carried a short article entitled 'Gerwani was immoral'. After mentioning that Gerwani members 'touched the genitals of the generals and exhibited their own', the article continued:

> even, according to sources which can be believed, Gerwani danced in front of their victims naked, which act reminds us of cannibalist ceremonies executed by primitive tribes centuries ago. Let us leave it to the women to judge the womanly morality of Gerwani, which is of an immorality worse than animals. (*DM*, 12.10.1965)

In November the first press conferences were reported in which prisoners 'testified' about their experiences. The *AB* of 3 November carried a picture of two young, scared girls, with the statement of a male member of the youth organization that he saw '30 Gerwani members shouting, torturing and playing with the already unconscious General Yani' (*AB*, 3.11.1965). The following day the *BY* carried a story about beautiful Gerwani members who were ordered to sell themselves:

> Documents have proven the existence of a 'Black Cat' group which have been entrusted with burning the houses of non-communist people, as well as the woods, and with destroying vital installations. Linked to this was a group called 'Black Button' consisting of Gerwani members with beautiful faces who had to sell themselves and align themselves with the leaders of other parties to induce them to support the PKI programme. (*BY*, 4.11.1965)

Then all papers featured prominently the 'honest confession' of 15-year-old, three-months pregnant Djamilah, nicknamed the 'Srikandi of Lubang Buaya'. It was reported that both her husband and Djamilah herself were members of the Tandjung Priok branch of the youth organization. On 29 September she was picked up by a PKI leader for some exercises in Cililitan. She is reported to have confessed the following story:

> That day and the following day we exercised ... and at about three o'clock we were woken up ... we were instructed to crush the kabir and Nekolim.[22] There were some 500 people collected there, 100 of whom were women. The members of Gerwani, including Djamilah, were issued small knives and razor blades ... From far we saw a short fat person entering; he was in his pyjamas. His hands were tied with a red cloth and a red cloth was also tied over his eyes. Our leader Dan Ton ordered us to beat up this person, and then they started stabbing with those small knives at his genitals. The first one, as we noticed, to beat and stab the genitals of that person was the chair of Gerwani Tandjung Priok, called S., and Mrs Sas. Then other friends followed ... after that we ourselves joined in torturing that person. All 100 of us joined in this activity ... Then he was dragged to the well by men in uniform ... but he still wasn't dead. Then a uniformed man ordered Gerwani to continue. The Gerwani women continued as before, stabbing and slicing his genitals and his body until he was dead.

I have four accounts of this story, *AB*, 5 November, *DM* and *SH*, 6 November and *BY*, 7 November 1965. It is striking that the wording is exactly the same in all four articles. This suggests that the text was prepared beforehand. Two papers carried identical pictures of Djamilah. The source of the story was stated to be the army. It seems that the army didn't trust the 'honest confession' of Djamilah enough to let her tell the story herself to the press. This account was highly inflammatory and it became widely known. After this story the slogans of the students and other groups who were demonstrating against the PKI and Soekarno included *Gerwani Tjabol* (Gerwani Whores), *Gantung Gerwani* (Hang Gerwani) and *Ganjang Gerwani* (Crush Gerwani).

Islamic leaders spurred on the massacre that now began to unfold. The Islamic reform movement Muhammadiyah held an emergency meeting on 9–11 November at which it was declared that the 'extermination of the Gestapu/PKI and the Nekolim is an obligatory religious duty' (Boland 1982: 146). This call for a holy war was subsequently echoed by many Muslim leaders, who justified the killings as 'the will of Allah'.[23]

Then in the papers a picture appeared of a frightened girl called Sujati, nicknamed Jossy. A fierce-looking bearded man in a uniform was towering over her. The subscript said that she confessed to having been involved in shooting one of the kidnapped officers, General Yani, both in his home and at Lubang Buaya.[24] 'This Gerwani member[25] and high school student is another proof', the papers reported, 'of the evil acts of the Gestapu/PKI, poisoning our young buds ... We should never again allow our new generation which is still clean, to be poisoned and provoked by the traitors of our nation' (*AB*, 19.11.1965).

President Soekarno tried in the meantime to stem the tide of violence. He decided to publish the results of the autopsy on the bodies of the generals which, as Anderson's article clarified (1987), revealed that the reports stating that the genitals of the generals were cut off and their eyes gouged out were false. He called on the journalists to keep themselves to the facts and to refrain from publishing lies. Only one paper published this announcement (*SH*, 13.12.1965).

But to no avail. A few days later the same paper carried the 'confession' of Saina. This 17-year-old 'member of Gerwani', 'with a child and husband' told the investigating team that she had been 'injected several times while training for six and a half months at Lubang Buaya after which she felt wild sexual urges'. According to the head of the Interrogation Team of the Pepelrada[26] West Java, Major A. Danamihardjo S.H., Saina, during the six and a half months of training, 'had been competing together with 199 other Gerwani members to sexually serve 400 men'. Saina had often been injected 'which had aroused her to engage in these indecent acts'. She had told the team that 'Aidit had once given a speech at the camp that PKI volunteers did not need to feel constrained by religious rules but that they should have free sex amongst each other'. To the question as to how it was possible that she 'as a woman could engage in murdering the Generals', Saina explained that 'she could engage in such acts after hearing a speech of Aidit in which he explained that women should be as courageous as men' (*SH*, 8.12.1965). Women's 'courage' and their independent behaviour is thus directly associated with sexual perversion and murder.

It is striking that after these 'confessions' none of the women who had been present at Lubang Buaya and who had been detained was ever brought to court. In December the campaign lost its vigour. Most of the killing in Java had been done, although in Bali the worst killing took place in the second two weeks of December 1965 (Vickers 1989; Schulte Nordholt 1991; Robinson 1995 and 1996).

Creation of Disorder

The above material points to the importance of an analysis of sexual politics behind the events of late 1965, a dimension that, as pointed out above, has been almost totally neglected by the established scholarship. Some authors[27] ignore the significance of the presence of women at Lubang Buaya. Others (Utrecht 1970; Wertheim 1979) present the massacre as a revenge for the actions of the farmers' front. McVey holds that the 'high degree of social tension in the countryside made it easy for the liquidation campaign to become a major massacre' (1971: 28).

Apart from Cribb (1990), Southwood and Flanagan (1983) and Leclerc (1991), who mention the accusations against Gerwani, only Langenberg (1990) discusses the sexual aspects of the propaganda campaign preceding the massacre in some detail. The manipulation of gender ideology was, however, a much more central factor in the birth of the New Order state than these authors maintain.

In my view the significance of the campaign lies in the deliberate manipulation of the collective cultural and religious conscience of the Indonesian population on which Soeharto built his road to power. To do so, the PKI and Soekarno had to be eliminated. But because of Soekarno's great popularity and the large following of the PKI that was not an easy task. Another reason to go slowly and first prepare a 'mental transition' is put forward by Soeharto himself in his autobiography. He explains that a military coup would have been much faster, but that that might have entailed the danger of a counter-coup.[28] It seems that a climate of disorder was deliberately created exploiting the deep anxieties of a population that was already badly shaken by the political and socio-economic tensions of the period. This disorder struck chords with the fear of the uncontrolled sexual powers of women, a religiously inspired apprehension that women's disobedience will endanger the entire social system, Hindu notions of all-female maniacal crowds and the male horror of castration. Assisted by the army, and especially the troops of Sarwo Edhie (Crouch 1978; May 1978; Robinson 1995; Utrecht 1970), Islamic youth groups were the major killers,[29] assisted in some places, especially in Bali, by members of the conservative wing of the PNI.[30] As Utrecht reports, Hindu Balinese saw the killing of people associated with the PKI 'as the fulfillment of a religious obligation to purify the land' (Robinson 1995: 300). Robinson argues that the killings in Bali were spurred on by a campaign mounted by the local military and police authorities

> who began to resort to the language and techniques developed by national military and party propagandists to inflame passions against the PKI ... Later investigations purportedly revealed that Gerwani members in Bali had been instructed to 'sell' themselves to ABRI men in order to obtain weapons for the PKI, and having done so, to murder and castrate the soldiers they had seduced. (1996: 133–4)

Soekarno Replaced

The traumatic 1965–66 period in Indonesian history marks the change from the Old Order of President Soekarno to the New Order of President Soeharto.[31] Ostensibly the New Order preaches a 'return to the Pancasila[32] and the constitution of 1945', that is, to the state philosophy Soekarno drafted and the first, democratic constitution of the Republic. In reality the New Order state is built on a militaristic and patriarchal model of discipline and repression in which any reference to social inequality, including women's subordination, is denounced as being inspired by or related to 'communist subversion'. The myth of the birth of the New Order was consciously created by General Soeharto and his allies and has been continually re-created during his presidency.

The slander campaign against Gerwani and the PKI in 1965 not only facilitated the actual change of power, but also laid one of the ideological foundations for the military rule of the New Order. As Mortimer writes, 'the legitimacy of the Soeharto government rests strongly upon the acceptance of the political public that the PKI committed treason against the state and that by encouraging communists and trying to shelter them even after their treason Soekarno forfeited his right to lead the nation' (1974: 420). The form this 'treason' took, however, was not just the putsch by Colonel Untung and his fellow plotters. It was the assault on the very basis of morality and religion and thus of the social order itself that Gerwani was accused of. Since then, any resistance to the military has been blamed on some 'PKI remnant', or the 'latent danger' the PKI is said to represent. It is made clear what that would lead to: chaos in the state and at home, women's sexual powers unleashed, the minds of children poisoned and innocent Muslim men seduced or even castrated.

Persistence of these Strategies in Contemporary Indonesia

All through Soeharto's reign the PKI was associated with these two words: *penghianat*, 'traitor' and *biadab*, 'primitive', 'pagan'. The PKI was thus excluded from the nation and even from human culture as such. The regime constructed a monument and museum at the site of Lubang Buaya. The well itself was under reconstruction when I last visited Jakarta in 1994. It was being turned into a marble shrine complete with a temple roof intended for the veneration of anti-communism. The enormous museum is called 'Museum Penghianatan [Betrayal] PKI'. On its two vast floors models of wood and papier mâché showing every incident in which the PKI has been involved since 1945 behind glass windows. It is the museum of the victors of 1965–66, intended to create the impression of a treacherous, murderous and thieving PKI, which is all the time confronted by the sincere, invincible army, the true defender of the people. It also contains huge murals of photographs, composed of pictures taken, among other places, at Lubang Buaya. Strikingly enough the pictures of the bodies of the generals, terrible enough as they are, show no signs of razor-blade cuts, and there are no bloody patches on the place where the castrations should have taken place. All the genitals, as far as visible, are intact.

The monument on the same site is called 'Monumen Pancasila Sakti [sacred] Lubang Buaya'. It is a huge semi-circular construction in front of a pillar and a statue of the Garuda, the national bird. Statues of the slain generals and lieutenant in a vigorous pose, and in full military attire, are placed on a platform. Below them the history of Indonesia since 1945 according to Soeharto is presented in a mural. It is here that the full ideological weight of the way the New Order regime was built on the subordination of women and the manipulation of sexual symbols becomes clear. The centre part of the mural is devoted to the events at Lubang Buaya. The generals are being clubbed and thrown into the well. They are surrounded by representations of women. To the left three women are standing. One of them is dressed in a very provocative way and argues defiantly with a man. Both of them are ugly. Beside her two dancing women are arranged, one of whom with a wreath of flowers (representing the so-called 'Dance of the Fragrant Flowers'). Above the well one woman is portrayed, leaning against a tree. She is clad in uniform trousers and a blouse that clearly reveals her full breasts. A knife hangs on her belt. Her posture again is defiant. More to the right the scene is dominated by the overpowering figure of General Soeharto. Under his left arm two women are standing, heads down, attitude demure, one of them carrying a baby. The figure of General Soeharto has intervened and turned those defiant, seductive, dangerous and castrating women into the very symbols of obedience and motherhood. The last scene shows the all-powerful General and President Soeharto in front of what is presumably a courtroom. The absolute military and legal power is his (see also Leclerc 1991).

Conclusion

Communism as expressed by the PKI in the 1950s and 1960s confronted religious, and especially conservative, Muslim and Hindu groups in many ways. But I suggest that apart from the class struggle, the fear of the bold and free way in which Gerwani women spoke up and fought for what they perceived to be their interests struck a deep chord of anxiety in these conservative parts of the population. This facilitated the military man-oeuvres to organize the mass murders. This anxiety had definitely sexual overtones and it was these fears that the campaign Major-General Soeharto mounted spoke to. In my view, conservative parts of the population, especially military and conservative men, became so terrified of what they saw as the castration of their voice by articulate Gerwani members that they translated this fear into the castration of that other organ of male power over women, their penises. Afraid of becoming speechless because of the voice Gerwani gave to women, the conservative parts of the Indonesian public were ready to believe the myth of the sexual castration of military men. The restoration of order by General Soeharto meant the return to male domination, with women obediently following the women's *kodrat* that Indonesian patriarchy has long constructed. Women's political ambitions were to be discredited and channelled into the powerless organ-izations the state had established for them.[33]

The central element of the ideological fury unleashed around women's involvement in the murders of Lubang Buaya is that Gerwani, in its 'communist', 'perverted' madness, had the major hand in torturing and killing the generals, dancing naked, cutting off their penises. The truth as I see it is that women members from the PKI youth organization, Pemuda Rakyat, and Gerwani had indeed been assembled at the training camp. Gerwani as an organization, however, was not involved and the accusations of sexual debauchery are totally unfounded.

The military's lies surrounding the events at Lubang Buaya played into certain deeply held fears of the population, namely that the 'Communist Beast' would pervert 'their' women and that these politically and sexually powerful women would castrate them. This manipulation of the con-sciousness of the Javanese and Balinese masses has been so successful that it has become one of the major ideological underpinnings of the New Order state. However, the sexual politics that contributed to the attack on Gerwani has been largely ignored. This has not only affected how the massacres have been assessed and interpreted. It has also made it impossible to gauge how conceptions of gender and sexuality formed in these horrific circumstances continue to have ramifications today.

Only a few weeks after President Soeharto stepped down in mid-1998 feminist organizations mounted a demonstration against the state-controlled women's organizations such as Dharma Wanita. Now that Soeharto has finally been forced to step down, more than thirty years after the 1965 putsch, students, women's groups and other opposition groups still have to remove the ideological shackles that have ensured obedience to the New Order government for so long. It is my hope that a deeper knowledge of the way in which the Indonesian population has been manipulated by a combination of military power, fear of the 'Communist Beast' and allegations of women's depravity may help in creating the ideological climate in which a new, democratic Indonesia can be built.

Notes

1. See for instance Cribb and Brown: 'Sections of the government continue to warn publicly against the "latent danger" said to be presented by the presumably underground PKI, while unexplained disasters, such as major fires, are often blamed on the communists' (1995: 147).

2. Gerakan Wanita Indonesia Sedar, Movement of Conscious Indonesian Women (Wieringa 1995).

3. Persatuan Wanita Republik Indonesia, Women's Federation of the Indonesian Republic.

4. WIDF is the Women's International Democratic Federation, a federation of socialist women's organizations, residing in East Berlin until the fall of the Berlin Wall. Only in its last years did Gerwani de-emphasize the peace issue, in the wake of the anti-Malaysia campaign (Wieringa 1995).

5. For instance, the struggle to get women accepted as village leaders.

6. Manipol, Manifesto Politik, Soekarno's speech on Independence Day in 1959, is the ideological basis of Guided Democracy.

7. Garuda is the name of a bird in the popular Hindu epic *Ramayana* that has become the national symbol.

8. Sugiarti, originally in 1962, translated in Wieringa (1995: 172). The poem plays with a Javanese saying: *surga nunut, neraka katut* (follow [your husband] to heaven, get dragged [with him] into hell). There are few analyses of the concept of women's *kodrat*. One of the best sources are the letters the Javanese princess RA Kartini wrote at the beginning of the century (the best edition is the one provided by Jaquet in 1987). See also Tiwon (1996).

9. Since the publication of Hildred Geertz's *The Javanese Family* in 1961 there has been a lot of debate on women's supposed autonomy versus their subordination. See for some views on gender ideology Mather 1985, Sears 1996a; Sullivan 1994; Wieringa 1995; Wolf 1992.

10. See for instance Anderson and McVey 1971; Crouch 1978; Gunawan 1968; May

1978; McVey 1971; Mortimer 1969, 1974; Pauker 1969; Pluvier 1973; Southwood and Flanagan 1983; Târnquist 1984; Utrecht 1970; Wertheim 1979, 1991.

11. According to Mernissi the Arabic concept of *fitna* refers to the kind of disorder and chaos that is associated with women's sexual attraction, making men lose their self-control (1975: 4). In Indonesian *fitna* has come to mean slander in general. The concept most commonly used in Indonesian to denote uncontrolled (sexual) impulses is *hawa nafsu*.

12. See also Cribb and Brown (1995: 97). They conclude that 'Indonesian people were ready to believe that a demonic force was responsible for their plight' (1995: 104).

13. See testimonies of Peris Pardede (Gunawan 1968), Nyono and Sudisman (for instance Crouch 1978; May 1978; Mortimer 1974: 419).

14. Other organizations, for instance religious groups, had organized training camps for their volunteers as well. It was thus not only the 'leftist family' that had its young members trained.

15. In 1974 Notosutanto became the head of the History Section of the Armed Forces (Klooster 1985: 134–6). For the army view see also DSTNIAD 1982 and LSIK 1983.

16. Colonel Latief, one of the plotters, met Soeharto on the eve of the putsch. See for instance Wertheim 1979, 1991.

17. Acronym to denote capitalist bureaucrat. This word was especially used to discredit the army officers who had become the managers of confiscated Dutch and British properties, and who had amassed great wealth. It is also an Arabic word meaning 'great', and usually refers to Allah.

18. For the development of the campaign against Gerwani I mainly made use of direct army sources, that is the papers *Angkatan Bersenjata* (*AB*, Armed Forces), *Berita Yudha* (*BY*, Army News) and *Duta Masyarakat* (*DM*, Envoy of Society). These newspapers had a general and broad circulation. For most articles referred to below the army is directly stated as the source. Another newspaper referred to is the Protestant *Sinar Harapan* (*SH*, Ray of Hope). Unfortunately I had no access to the radio programmes that were the major transmitters of news to the masses of the population, as well as to the television broadcasts.

19. The word used is *kalap*, which means 'possessed by an evil spirit'.

20. Aidit was the chair of the PKI.

21. This refers to the military men killed on 1 October. Soekarno had them promoted and called them the 'Heroes of the Revolution'.

22. These terms are part of the rhetoric of the last years of Soekarno's Old Order. *Nekolim* refers to neo-colonial forces.

23. See Cribb (1990) for the role of Islamic youth groups. Schwarz refers to the involvement of Islamic youth groups in the killings as a *jihad*, or Islamic holy war (1994: 21).

24. According to May, Yani was captured by a squad of some 200 palace guards who shot him in his house. He died in the truck that brought him to Lubang Buaya (1978: 95). This story is corroborated by an account of Yani's death in *BY*, 5.12.1965.

25. Neither Jossy nor 'Saina', see below, had belonged to Gerwani, as my sources testify (Wieringa 1995).

26. The Pepelrada were the Regional Authorities to Implement Dwikora (Pengusaha Pelaksana Dwikora Daerah). They were abolished in July 1967 (Crouch 1978).

27. For instance, the early account of Gunawan (1968). But see also Pohan (1988),

who provides one of the most sophisticated analyses of this history from a 'progressive' Indonesian perspective. Pohan dwells at large on the 'creeping coup' that brought Soeharto to power but ignores the impact of the campaign of slander waged against Gerwani.

28. See Soeharto 1991, Chapters 24–26. In his autobiography he ignores the mass killings. When he speaks of violence in this context he refers only to military action against other military units, not against civilians.

29. Manai Sophiaan, a well-known nationalist leader in Soekarno's days and Indonesian ambassador in Moscow in 1965, quotes an interview in *Editor* of September 1993 (no. 49, volume VI/4) with the chair of one of the major Islamic parties at the time, the Nahdatul Ulama, K. H. Abdurrachman Wahid. Wahid said that 'Islamic people alone slaughtered 500,000 ex-PKI'. As there were also many non-Islamic people involved in the killing, Sophiaan suggests that the estimate of Amnesty International of about a million people killed during the massacre may be correct (1994: 311).

30. The massacre was heaviest in East Java, Central Java and Bali. For Bali see Crouch (1978: 152), Schulte Nordholt (1991) and Vickers (1989). Robinson recently provided evidence that in Bali notions of Gerwani's sexual depravity were imported from Java before the army started organizing for the killings (1995 and 1996).

31. The major step in this change of power was the instruction Soekarno was manipulated into giving to Soeharto, in which Soeharto was entrusted with wide powers to restore orders. The instruction has been given the acronym of 'Supersemar', after its title 'Surat Perintah Sebelas Maret' (Instruction of 11 March). But it has also another connotation: Semar is a principal *wayang* figure, both a God and the main servant of Arjuna. Soeharto then purged the highest body in the country, the MPRS (Majelis Permusyawaratan Rakyat Sementara, People's Provisional Consultative Council), of supporters of Soekarno. In March 1967 when the MPRS met, Soeharto was promoted to acting president.

32. The Pancasila contains the following five principles: belief in one God, respect for human values, nationalism, democracy and social justice.

33. See Wieringa (1985) for an elaboration of this point.

Bibliography

Amnesty International (1977) *Indonesia, An Amnesty International Report*, London: Amnesty International.

Anderson, Ben (1987) *How Did the Generals Die?*, *Indonesia*, 43: 109–35.

Anderson, Benedict R. and Ruth T. McVey (1971) *A Preliminary Analysis of the October 1, 1965, Coup in Indonesia*, Ithaca, NY: Modern Indonesia Project, Cornell University, Interim Report.

Boland, B. J. (1982) *The Struggle of Islam in Modern Indonesia*, The Hague: Martinus Nijhoff.

Cribb, Robert (ed.) (1990) *The Indonesian Killings of 1965-1966*, Clayton, Victoria: Monash University Centre of Southeast Asian Studies.

Cribb, Robert and Colin Brown (1995) *Modern Indonesia: A History Since 1945*, London and New York: Longman

Crouch, Harold (1978) *The Army and Politics in Indonesia*, Ithaca, NY and London: Cornell University Press.

DSTNIAD (1982) Pemberontakan G30S/PKI dan Penumpasannya, disusun dan diterbitkan oleh Dinas Sejarah Tentara Nasional Indonesia Angkatan Darat, Bandung.

Geertz, H. (1961) *The Javanese Family. A Study of Kinship and Socialization*, New York: Free Press.

Gunawan, B. (1968) *Kudetß, Staatsgreep in Djakarta, de Achtergronden van de 30 September-Beweging in Indonesien*, Meppel: Boom.

Holtzappel, C. (1979) 'The 30 September Movement: a political movement of the armed forces or an intelligence operation?', *Journal of Contemporary Asia*, 9(2): 216–39.

Kartini, R. A. (1987) *Brieven aan Mevrouw R.M. Abendanon-Mandri en haar Echtgenoot met andere Documenten, bezorgd door F.G.P. Jaquet*, Dordrecht: Foris (1st edn 1911).

Klooster, H. A. J. (1985) *Indonesieners schrijven hun geschiedenis*, Dordrecht: Foris.

Kumar, Ann (1980) 'Javanese court society and politics in the late eighteenth century: the record of a lady soldier, Part I: The religious, social and economic life of the court', *Indonesia*, 29 (April): 1–46.

Langenberg, Michael van (1990) 'Gestapu and state power in Indonesia', in R. Cribb (ed.), *The Indonesian Killings 1967-66*, Clayton, Victoria: Monash University.

— (1996) 'How might the Soeharto era conclude?', *Inside Indonesia*, 48.

Leclerc, Jacques (1991), 'Sang et volupté à Lobang Buaya', ECIMS, mimeo.

LSIK (1983) *Rangkaian Peristiwa Pemberontakan Komunis di Indonesia, 1926–1948–1965*, Jakarta: Lembaga Studi Ilmu-Ilmu Kemasyarakatan (LSIK).

McVey, Ruth (1971) 'PKI fortunes at low tide', *Problems of Communism* (January–April): 25–37.

Manai Sophiaan (1994) *Kehormatan Bagi Yang Berhak*, Bung Karno Tidak Terlibat G30S/PKI, Jakarta: Yayasan Mencerdaskan Kehidupan Bangsa.

Mather, C. (1985) '"Rather than make trouble, it's better just to leave": behind the lack of industrial strife in the Tangerang region of West Java', in H. Afshar (ed.), *Women, Work and Ideology in the Third World*, London and New York: Tavistock, pp. 153–83.

May, Brian (1978) *The Indonesian Tragedy*, Singapore: Brash.

Mernissi, Fatima (1975) *Beyond the Veil: Male-Female Dynamics in a Modern Muslim Society*, New York: Schenkman.

— (1996) *Women's Rebellion and Islamic Memory*, London: Zed Books.

Mortimer, Rex (1969) 'The downfall of Indonesian communism', *Socialist Register, 1969*: 189–218.

— (1974) *Indonesian Communism under Soekarno, Ideology and Politics, 1959–1965*, Ithaca, NY and London: Cornell University Press.

Nugroho Notosutanto and Ismael Saleh (1968) *The Coup Attempt of the 'September 30 Movement' in Indonesia*, Djakarta.

Pauker, Guy J. (1969) *The Rise and Fall of the Communist Party of Indonesia*, Santa Monica: RAND Corporation.

Pluvier, Jan (1973) *Djakarta 1965, "Djakarta", Djakarta '65 – Santiago '73*, Odijk: Sjaloom, Kosmo-Story no. 35.

Pohan, Y. (1988) *Who were the Real Plotters of the Coup against President Soekarno's Government?*, Amsterdam: Indonesia Media Foundation.

Robinson, Geoffrey (1995) *The Dark Side of Paradise: Political Violence in Bali*, Ithaca, NY: Cornell University Press.

— (1996) 'The post-coup massacre in Bali', in Daniel S. Lev and Ruth McVey (eds), *Making Indonesia: Essays on Modern Indonesia in Honor of George McT. Kahin*, Ithaca, NY: Cornell University Southeast Asia Program, pp. 118–44.

Schulte Nordholt H. (1991) *State, Village and Ritual in Bali: A Historical Perspective*, Amsterdam, VU University Press.

Schwarz, Adam (1994) *A Nation in Waiting: Indonesia in the 1990s*, St Leonards: Allen & Unwin.

Scott, Peter Dale (1985) 'The United States and the overthrow of Soekarno', *Pacific Affairs* (Summer): 237–64.

Sears, L. J., (ed.) (1996a) *Fantasizing the Feminine in Indonesia*, Durham, NC and London: Duke University Press.

— (1996b) *Shadows of Empire: Colonial Discourse and Javanese Tales*, Durham, NC and London: Duke University Press.

Soeharto (1966) *Setahun Penghianatan GESTAPU/PKI, Setahun Lobang Buaya*, Jakarta: Jajasan Lembaga Penjelidikan Islam, pp. I–V.

— (1991) *My Thoughts, Words and Deeds: Autobiography as told to Dwipuayana and K. H. Kamadhan, trans. Sumadi Mutiah Lestiono*, Jakarta: Citra Lamtoro Gung Persada.

Soekarno (1963) *Sarinah: Kewadjiban Wanita Dalam Perdjoangan Republik Indonesia*, Djakarta: Panitya Penerbit Buku-buku Karangan Presiden Soekarno.

Southwood, Julie and Patrick Flanagan (1983) *Indonesia, Law, Propaganda and Terror*, London: Zed Books.

Sullivan, Norma (1994) *Masters and Managers. A Study of Gender Relations in Urban Java*, Clayton Virginia: Allen & Unwin.

Tiwon, S. (1996) 'Models and maniacs: articulating the female in Indonesia', in L. J. Sears (ed.), *Fantasizing the Feminine in Indonesia*, Durham, NC and London: Duke University Press.

Törnquist, Olle (1984) *Dilemmas of Third World Communism: The Destruction of the PKI in Indonesia*, London: Zed Books.

Utrecht, Ernst (1970) *Indonesien's Nieuwe Orde, Ontbinding en Neokolonisatie*, Amsterdam: van Gennep.

Vickers, Adrian (1989) *Bali, A Paradise Created*, Berkeley, CA and Singapore: Periplus.

Vreede-de Stuers, Cora (1960) *The Indonesian Woman: Struggles and Achievements*, The Hague: Mouton.

Wertheim, W. F. (1979) 'Whose plot? – new light on the 1965 events', *Journal of Contemporary Asia*, 9(2): 197–216.

— (1991) 'Indonesien in 1965: Wanneer gaan de Archieven open?', *Derde Wereld Jrg*, 9(5) (February): 33–56.

Wieringa, Saskia (1985) *The Perfumed Nightmare: Some Notes on the Indonesian Women's Movement*, The Hague: Institute of Social Studies Working Paper.

— (1988) 'Aborted feminism in Indonesia: a history of Indonesian socialist feminism', in S. Wieringa (ed.), *Women's Struggles and Strategies*, Aldershot: Gower Press, pp. 69–90.

— (1992) 'Ibu or the beast: gender interests, ideology and practice in two Indonesian women's organizations', *Feminist Review*, 41: 98–114.

— (1993) 'Two Indonesian women's organizations: Gerwani and the PKK', *Bulletin of Concerned Asian Scholars*, 25(2): 17–31.

— (1995) 'The politicization of gender relations in Indonesia: the Indonesian women's movement and Gerwani until the New Order state', PhD thesis, University of Amsterdam.

Wolf, D. L. (1992) *Factory Daughters: Gender, Household Dynamics, and Rural Industrialization in Java*, Berkeley, University of California Press.

10

Creating Alternative Spaces: Black Women in Resistance

Pragna Patel of Southall Black Sisters interviewed by
Paminder Parbha

How and why was Southall Black Sisters set up?

The founding members of Southall Black Sisters were a group of Asian and African-Caribbean women active in the anti-racist movement in Britain. They met initially in their homes and were involved in some early campaigning work. The year they started, 1979, in Southall saw mass demonstrations and community mobilizations against racism. The National Front tried to march through Southall to provoke the community. Their meeting in the town hall was not banned and the police came out in force, not to protect the community, but to protect the National Front members. It was a seminal moment in the history of Southall and in the history of Asian resistance against racism in this country. Those Asian and Afro-Caribbean women who formed Southall Black Sisters were very much part of that anti-racist movement where one saw a heightened political consciousness around the term 'black'. In resisting racism in Britain ideas were being borrowed from the US civil rights and black power movements. Around the same time there were many consciousness-raising groups of feminists and black women were beginning to come together, for example the Brixton Black Women's group, which was one of the first to be set up.

Southall Black Sisters was formed by articulate, strong women, who felt comfortable with the term 'black' and comfortable calling themselves feminists. They were not able to find a natural home for themselves in the anti-racist movement, partly because it was so preoccupied with taking on the state and state racism, but also because of its sexism and its failure to address specifically the needs of women. On the other hand, black women were aware that the feminist movement was not really conducive to understanding the racial dimensions of gender discrimination and subordination. (I would say this still remains the case). So black women didn't feel at home in the wider feminist movement either.

I have to stress, because I think this is also true for us now, that by setting up as an autonomous black women's group, the idea was not to separate themselves off from the anti-racist movement, but it was to make space within the anti-racist movement for black women to be able to feel comfortable about talking about issues that affected them. At the same time the women who started Southall Black Sisters saw the autonomous spaces they were developing as a way of strengthening the anti-racist movement, not weakening it. One of the constant criticisms of groups like ours from within the anti-racist movement is that we are being divisive and diverting from the real struggles, which are the struggles against racism. We've always maintained, however, that actually struggles against racism are not one-dimensional, and that opposing injustice is also relevant. As black women, race isn't the only force that shapes our lives.

It's not a question though of saying we're racially subordinated, we're gender-subordinated and we're having a hard time. It's really trying to understand the complexity of the lives that black women or minority women in this country lead. You can't understand that by looking at their lives just through an anti-racist lens, or just through a gender discrimination lens. The analysis has to go beyond that. We have to try and look at the ways in which gender, race and other social divisions which lead to discrimination intersect. That's not easy for people to grasp; people find that very difficult.

You can still go along to feminist events and find black women are just added on as an afterthought. I was at a conference recently on inter-agency approaches to domestic violence, the title of my presentation had been given to me, 'Issues for Black Women', and the first point I needed to make was that these were not in fact 'issues for black women', but actually issues for *all* women. It is important to bring race into the general debate, not to ghettoize it in some workshop, some corner of the conference, and leave it to the black women to discuss among themselves. And in the anti-racist movement, we still can have a hard time bringing a gender perspective in, because we're seen as divisive. Nonetheless whatever we do, we keep on trying to say that the experiences of the women who come to our centre demand a much more sophisticated analysis, a more complicated framework through which to understand their experiences.

What's your involvement in the organization?

I got involved in Southall Black Sisters in 1982. I'd come fresh out of college and my parents lived in Southall. As I said earlier, there was a heightened awareness about being positive about being black, and for me, like many blacks who had grown up in this country experiencing racism, that was really exciting and new. I tended to have a negative view of myself and was feeling confused about where I fitted in. Suddenly to find all these black people saying, it's good to be black, we should be proud to be black, was just really exciting. I needed to be in that environment, because I felt that that was going to be where I would flourish, where I would feel at home.

Also, as a woman growing up in what was probably a typical Asian household, there were certain aspirations for you; the problem was that marriage was seen as the most that you could aspire to, really. I remember growing up thinking there had to be something more to life than that – gut feelings of feminism. In my household I'd fought my battles and refused to get married and so when I heard about the group Southall Black Sisters, I was kind of bowled over. The excitement about being with a group of people from one's own background, but developing a new way of thinking about things was so important. Some of them were younger than me, they were out, they were bolshie, they were feisty, they weren't afraid of anything, and they were selling feminist newsletters on Southall High Street – wonderful. And I thought, yes! that's how I want to be. So I started going to meetings and getting involved.

But, unfortunately for me, the group of women that had formed Southall Black Sisters wanted to move on. They all wanted to develop personally in their own way. Some went into academia, one became a solicitor, others went on to develop careers in writing, and so on. All of them were leaving, when I joined, so in a sense I inherited an empty shell. Nonetheless the legacy I inherited, of looking at race and gender issues together was a very rich legacy and this framework has remained the foundation of our thinking. But because by 1982 they had all left, I had to start from scratch and bring new women in. We managed to secure funding from the then GLC and we set up the first black women's centre in West London. I'm now the longest-serving member; until very recently we have had three core full-time workers. If we get funding we will have another. We have volunteers coming and going, a management committee and users' meetings where campaigns and issues get discussed. Some of the women who use the centre are also represented on the management committee.

What's the focus of Southall Black Sisters' work?

That's an interesting question! When we set up the centre, we had no idea what we were going to focus on. In fact we had long, agonizing debates about whether we should even call ourselves Southall Black Sisters. It was an up-front radical, feminist image; sisterhood was in currency at the time, black was a hip term. Although the name now sounds anachronistic, we won't let it go, because of what it represents for us. But there was a lot of debate within the group. Calling ourselves Southall Black Sisters was all right when we were a group meeting in each others' homes, which was not going to be publicly threatening. But were women going to be permitted to come to an advice service, a provision centre, with a name like that? We also considered providing so-called 'safe' services – sewing, cookery, perhaps at best some employment training, that the community would feel non-threatening. But we decided to do advice and advocacy and campaigning because that was really where the need was not being met. There were lots of women's groups in the community devoted to providing those traditional services anyway, so we just felt, why duplicate what's there anyway? Moreover we didn't want to duplicate traditional women's work. We wanted to create an alternative space for women. So we decided to choose the latter option, quite boldly calling ourselves Southall Black Sisters Centre and saying that we were an advice, campaigning resource centre.

At this point we did not know whether women would come or what difficulties they would come with. But we were to realize very quickly that the problem that they were bringing to us again and again, because their need was not being met anywhere else, was violence in the home. The centre has always been demand-led, and violence in the family in all its forms, ranging from domestic violence to sexual violence to forced marriage, has been the bulk of our work. Though related problems are immigration, homelessness, housing, social security, policing, it remains the case that most of our work is to do with violence in the family and violence against women and children. This was the gap that we were to fill because state agencies, social services and other organizations were not meeting the needs of women while indigenous community organizations set up as part of the self-help movement – welfarist organizations or workers' associations, which were very male-dominated – were not taking up women's issues. It was in neither the state's nor the community's interests to take up issues affecting women.

It has remained the case that advice, case work, advocacy and campaigning remain the key, the real focus of our work. Over the years, due to some high-profile cases and campaigns, we've attained a national profile, so we get demands from around the country from women as well as people ringing up on their behalf. Increasingly we're focusing on advocacy. We are being advocates for women who otherwise have no voice, not just because of language difficulties, but because of their position – their powerlessness in the family, in the community, and in the wider society. It's important to represent and to meet their needs on an individual level and through group action.

The problem is that being advocates for these women is proving to be very threatening to the state. Despite all these discourses about rights, about individual choice and so on, the state doesn't really want to encourage people being advocates for those who really are marginalized. For example, we have constant battles with the police, who cannot cope with groups like us. We try to intervene on behalf of women who get no form of protection and no redress from the police, and who feel they have to turn to us to mediate their needs. The police find us deeply threatening and see our criticisms about them as too radical. In the wider Women's Aid movement it is quite common now for a lot of partnership efforts and inter-agency work to involve the police and the local state. However, whenever we've made criticisms about the police, based on our casework experiences that can be substantiated about the way women have been treated, we are told that we are anti-police or that we are 'political'. It's interesting how our comments are regarded as 'political', whereas other women are not 'political'. So they separate us off from the wider movement and feel that we are somehow women they can't really work with, whereas the others they can. This is partly because of institutionalized racism and partly because the inter-agency partnership consensus-building set-up the state encourages to deal with issues like domestic violence involves compromising and consensus politics. But we do not accept that the police, the women's groups and the individual women on the street are equal players – we can't forget the power relationships.

You mentioned that the work you've been doing has been metamorphosing in response to the issues that you've encountered through your case work. Could you say how the sources of support and conflict have shifted and how this has affected the alliances that SBS has made?

This is very difficult; those who are your enemies can be your friends for a while, and then, later on, turn out to be your enemies after all.

In the initial stages Southall Black Sisters had very little support in the local community. The left saw us as divisive and women's libbers – sort of Western women, while the traditional community, the religious, conservative elements, saw us as home-wreckers, home-breakers, out to destroy the culture, the norms, the community, again Western and corrupting. We were attacked from all sides, physically and verbally. The threats have been more pronounced at certain moments, for instance when we came out in support of Salman Rushdie. Over the years we've had arson attacks on our building – fortunately these were when nobody was there. It's been very difficult to know who is behind them; whether it's irate individual husbands whose wives have gone missing who know that we might have provided refuge for them, or white racists who want to see us burnt down. We don't know, though I suspect it's the hostility within the community.

But having said that, 21 years later, community perceptions have changed somewhat. When we started, domestic violence was definitely a taboo subject in Southall. It is now accepted that the issue exists, and one measure of our success is the fact that even religious organizations and the indigenous organizations now claim to take domestic violence on board. It is on their agenda, although their solutions could be different, because they may be more into keeping the family together. Still, the fact that they even acknowledge the issue means there can be space for support.

Community support depends very much on what issues are involved in a case. For example we did the campaign around Kiranjit Ahluwalia, a Sikh woman, who killed her husband after ten years of violence. She felt that there was no way out. Hers became a high-profile case, because the media suddenly latched on to the issue of women being violent and the bias within the criminal justice system in which it appeared men were treated more leniently than women. Many ordinary people in the community, including men, supported the campaign, and when she was released, a lot of people went and congratulated her. We didn't get visible support from religious institutions, but then we didn't expect that, but the case wasn't controversial in the way it might have been a few years earlier.

In contrast in an earlier case during the mid-1980s we had a serious clash with a welfarist organization which helped the first migrants into the community to deal with problems to do with housing, education, work and immigration. They had access to the levers of power at the local state level, and were able to use their power with the local council to initiate a campaign to shut us down. Some of them were trustees of the local community centre, where a number of women workers had been sexually harassed. Southall Black Sisters, along with another group, Southall Monitoring Group, had joined together to form a campaign to raise the issue of sexual harassment in the workplace, and we wanted to hold these leaders to account. They were trustees of this community centre, they were employers of these women, we wanted to know what measures were they putting into place to deal with this issue. Of course, they didn't like that confrontation. They didn't like the fact that we were trying to hold them publicly to account. Their arguments were that we were outsiders. They attempted to delegitimize us and our work by placing us outside the norms of the community. They called us middle class (which as it happened wasn't true of all of us), and Western. They tried to get the council to stop the funding to the organization because they maintained we were destroying the very fabric of culture and religion in the community.

Looking back now it was a very exciting moment, because it was the users of the centre who took control. They were the ones who said, we will not allow this to happen. The campaign to save the centre wasn't worker-led. It was led by the women themselves – women from various religious, ethnic backgrounds in the Indian sub-continent, African, Caribbean and Arab women demonstrated outside the town hall. They were the ones who came up with the slogans: 'Save Our Centre', 'Where will women go?', 'SBS do a good job'; slogans that said the centre was theirs and that closing it down would mean they would be denied essential services to which they felt they had a right. This mobilization of the users really raised political awareness about the workings and the failures of local democracy, when there is close collusion between community leaders and local council.

Yet this same Association was to support us on the Kiranjit Ahluwalia case and they also backed our campaign on abolishing the one-year rule within immigration law, which prevents women who have insecure immigration status from escaping from a violent marriage. While in the early days Southall Black Sisters were placed on the outskirts and marginalized as the outsiders, through the sheer hard work and commitment of the women who run and use the centre, we've come to occupy a less marginal place. Whether they all like us or not within the community, they cannot any more ignore us. We're there, and we've shown that we're there to stay.

Our natural allies should be those who are fighting against injustices and inequalities, but what's left of the anti-racist movement is a ground of great tension and battles. Obviously we work together, but many joint campaigns have been held up, because of a continuing unwillingness to look at gender issues. Even now much of the anti-racist movement remains gender-blind, both at the academic and at the activist level, and that's a major battle for us. We go on joint demonstrations, for example, against the far right or against racist attacks such as the nail-bombings in Brixton and Brick Lane. There are moments of course when people come together and we see ourselves very much as part of the anti-racist movement. What we're saying is that the anti-racist movement would be strengthened by bringing in a gender analysis. Not all people experience racism the same way; women can experience racism differently. It's a simple point, but it's one that's not quite, I think, understood.

In the Southall area our relations with the left have been most difficult when we've taken up questions of religious fundamentalism and bigotry. Our campaigning for Salman Rushdie wasn't just about Salman Rushdie's right to write, but because we recognized, as women from various religious backgrounds, that the threat to prevent him from being critical of his religion and of his culture actually constituted a bigger threat for us as women. For we too were being critical from within, dissenting from within by demanding the right to autonomy, personal and otherwise. We knew if that could happen to Rushdie, how much easier it would be to silence women. We could see that such a political climate would endanger women organizing and this recognition of the connections made us come out in support of Rushdie. Freedom of expression has a special meaning for women; it represented freedom to choose how you want to live and to have control over your bodies and minds. When we came out publicly in support of Salman Rushdie, many on the progressive left couldn't ally themselves with us. I think the left was caught on the hop. They were preoccupied with the anti-racist struggle, with external threats to the community and this fight against anti-racism became a fight for the preservation of cultural identity. It was therefore very difficult for them to be critical. Whereas as women, we've had to take on external threats, to safeguard the right of the community to exist as a whole, while being critical from within. We had been defending the rights of the most marginalized groups within the community to have a right of existence and the right to be legitimately counted as part of the community. We had no choice, because it is the families, the religious institutions, the whole patriarchal system of power, that keeps women subjugated. We knew from our own experience that in the context of fighting racism, it is a very tricky thing to do to raise these issues which are internal to the community without appearing to be siding with the racists, and colluding with the racist media representations of our communities, cultures and identities.

Realizing that the first thing we had to do was to form alliances with women from all religious backgrounds, we formed Women Against Fundamentalism (WAF). There were women from English, Irish, Jewish backgrounds, Asian women who were Hindus, Sikhs and Muslims along with many others – Iranian women from Muslim backgrounds, for example. We formed the group with the aim of looking at the political use of religion in all our religions, and linked that with the role of women in the religious fundamentalist movement. Obviously there were incredible similarities in all these movements about how they viewed women as the custodians and inheritors of cultural and religious values and traditions.

We also recognized that in the British context, we could not look at the rise of the religious fundamentalist movements without analysing and understanding what the British state was doing. Fundamentalism in minority communities was in part a reaction to racism and one manifestation of institutionalized racism was the imposition of Christian assemblies in schools. This is supposed to be a multi-cultural, multi-racial society, yet the state was signalling that Christianity was going to be the dominant religion, which everyone had to integrate and adhere to.

In Women Against Fundamentalism feminists were sharing a common agenda, understanding that each woman's experiences are located differently, but also understanding that we can somehow surmount those differences to arrive at a common agenda for change. That was a very important moment, because in the mid- to late 1980s feminist politics were riddled with identity politics. You kind of huddled around and formed groups according to your identity. Women Against Fundamentalism consciously worked against forming groups on the basis of who we were rather than what we wanted to achieve. It is important to understand where each of us was coming from, but we have to find ways of going beyond that in terms of being able to sustain an alliance.

Other allies have been radical feminists, especially in relation to our work around battered women who kill and the criminal justice system and imprisonment. Radical feminists have been active around violence against women for many years and have also an analysis about how and why violence occurs. When we started to campaign around domestic violence, for example in the Kiranjit Ahluwalia case, it was radical feminists who mobilized, who came on the demonstrations outside the court of appeal, and who packed out the public galleries. They joined us in demands for changes in the law and in the criminal justice system. Having said that, it's not an easy alliance. We cannot afford to look at the world just through a gender lens. As black women, we also have to look at the world and how it's racialized. There are going to be occasions when we ally with men, on issues of inequality and injustice, and we understand how demands we make as women may have an affect on certain male groups who are marginalized, refugee men or immigrant men. So we can't afford to see everything just in terms of 'patriarchy' – 'the patriarchal system'. We have to also consider other systems of power, and bear in mind how power relations intersect and what they mean for the women that we work with.

We attempt to work with groups who are not obvious allies. For example, recently Southall Black Sisters have been campaigning around Zoora Shah, a Pakistani Muslim woman who was subjected to violence and abuse for ten years, and is serving a life sentence in prison. She lost her court of appeal case in 1998, and since then we've been struggling to bring the tariff of her life sentence down from 20 years. Twenty years is an excessive tariff akin to that given on a terrorist charge or armed robbery. The decision about the tariff's length is made by the home secretary, not the judiciary. So we had to lobby Jack Straw. We decided he was going to listen more to Muslim community leaders than feminists so we set out to get Muslim organizations to support us. We'd never really worked with traditional forces, so it was a very interesting dilemma for us. The first question was what language do we use? If we used our normal terms, the feminist language of choice and autonomy, we weren't going to get very far. So we had to couch our case in a humanitarian language of compassion.

We were not seeking an alliance, we could never sustain an alliance with those who believed the family must be maintained at all costs, we were just trying to get support from them. Even so very few would willingly, openly defend her, though we put it in terms of: enough is enough; she's spent a long time in jail; she has children; her children have suffered; and she recognizes she's done wrong; for compassionate reasons she needs help in order to be released. A number of the religious leaders, particularly from Bradford Council of Mosques, agreed the British legal system was racist. But they believed it was inhuman to allow this woman to die slowly in jail over 20 years. They thought she should have been executed quickly; according to this aspect of sharia law she would have been stoned to death. However, as British Muslims they were obviously not asking for sharia laws to be implemented. So they recognized the racism. But they did not acknowledge the violence that she went through or the obstacles that she faced in trying to get out of that violent situation. They were not aware of the causes of that violence, and why she did what she did in the end, out of desperation. They could not see that people like them were the very obstacles that she, and many women like her, have to overcome in leaving a violent or abusive relationship. Their response was to use anti-racist language to promote a particular agenda. People within anti-racist movements say, you've got to take these people with you, you need to enter into dialogue with them. That's fine, we're not opposed to dialogue, but the point is women need immediate protection. We cannot enter into a dialogue which compromises women's rights. These are the people who have power, and who maintain their power in particular ways and who have such traditional views. Where is the meeting point there?

But alliance building remains vital to us. During the nail-bombing, we made alliances with the gay and lesbian communities, because we recognized immediately that it's not just an issue of racism. Those who want to maintain power over others will discriminate in many ways and seek to subjugate all kinds of people. One of my problems with the civil rights movement at present is that I think there is room to broaden it and seek alliances with all sorts of groups that feel powerless within this society and have experience of inequality.

It's a generic question but what do you think are the key issues for Asian women in Britain today?

I would say the most vital issue is the lack of representation. Asian women lack a voice at the level of the local and the national state. Those who claim to speak on their behalf are people who have very little interest in women's issues or indeed in social justice issues. The voices of women are going unheard. For instance my colleague Hananna was recently involved, on behalf of SBS, on the Home Office Working Party on forced marriages, which was led by people whom the government consider to be the representatives of the communities. It was a real example of multi-cultural politics. On the Working Party, you had representatives of the so-called Hindu, Muslim and Sikh communities. The state always regards communities in a homogenized, monolithic way. Because it doesn't recognize the internal divisions it allows self-appointed leaders to represent the interests of an entire community, which inevitably they don't. People like us were involved, but Hananna had a very hard struggle within the group to maintain some semblance of a feminist agenda and the language that she used was very much in a human rights framework.

There was an internal battle in the Working Group about women's voices being heard. SBS argued that those women who had worked around the issue of forced marriage and who knew what the practical issues were ought to be heard, and that women who had gone through forced marriages should be able to say what their demands were. The Home Office had spent an awful lot of time going up and down the country talking to community leaders and religious institutions about the issue of forced marriage. We insisted they talk to the women themselves. We had to organize a major meeting in Southall of women who use the centre, so they could hear first-hand what it was like to be forced into a marriage, and what the community dynamics were that kept women in these abusive relationships.

Multi-cultural politics assume that within minority communities every-one is the same and that all have one world view. They don't allow for the fact that there is dissent within communities, that people want to have their own personal interpretations of what their culture is, and some want to retain certain aspects, others want to retain other aspects, and some want to reject it altogether. Women like us are not seen as authentic voices of the community, whereas those community leaders are. So inevitably the weight that we carry is not as equals. Whether people are in any way accountable to their communities has never been an issue for the state. Nor do these people need to have any track record in working around women's issues. They are leaders and therefore the state regards their voices as important. Today's context of multi-cultural politics means that you are no longer categorized as Asians, now you are officially recognized in public policy as Muslims, as Sikhs, or Hindus. 'Black' was a political, consciously adopted term but identity has become increasingly fragmented now. So I think who gets to represent whom, whose interests are being represented, whose voices are being listened to are vital questions for Asian women in this country.

Do you see links between women's movements globally and the black feminist movement in Britain?

I don't think enough links and connections have been made between black women's activism here in Britain and movements taking place elsewhere. SBS has been involved in a number of forums on human rights and UN meetings where women from around the globe will come and present an account of their activism and there has been support for practical struggles. But how do we link these conceptually? I'm only beginning to re-think this. But I believe we need to look at how race and gender inequality intersects as systems of power and how certain groups, even within the category of 'women', are marginalized further.

I was at a UN conference recently in Croatia in which women from around the world were talking about how race and gender interconnect in very specific contexts of conflict. You had, for example, *dalit*[1] women, fighting for the right to equality within the caste system and describing how they were particularly targeted as *dalit* women through rape by the police or upper-caste landlords. In Bosnia and in Rwanda, women were raped as part of ethnic cleansing in order to defile their communal ethnic identity. This was only seen as ethnic conflict, and it was forgotten that women within those ethnic communities were targeted and suffered *as women*. Women from both Bosnia and Rwanda were saying that in a post-conflict situation women were not only picking up the pieces but also having to deal with the trauma of rape. Strategies for peace need to take into account how you deal with and overcome trauma as well as seeking ways of preventing atrocities from happening again.

Other women at this forum were talking about the impact of structural adjustment programmes and the multinational corporations on marginalized women. Globalization and free market economy policies are having a particularly devastating effect on, for example, indigenous women. So it's not just a question of poverty being feminized; there are certain groups of women who are particularly vulnerable. They work in situations where there is no state scrutiny, no protection for them as workers, and where the conditions are slave-like. We need a conceptual analysis which will enable us to understand how the strategies of those in power are affecting the most marginalized of groups, including women who are racialized or ethnicized in particular ways.

This leads into the question of how you approach feminism. Do you see differences between black feminism and white feminism?

I think that the feminist movement has failed to look at how these different systems of power can interlock to bring about powerlessness within certain sub-categories of women. When it is admitted that women are not a homogeneous mass it tends to be done in a tokenistic way, for example adding black women's issues at the end, or having a few workshops

for black women to go to. It's not just a problem in relation to black
women, there is this continuous compartmentalization of the way in which
we analyse things. We have to develop a framework, which cross-cuts
patriarchal power, racial supremacy, power based on heterosexual lifestyles,
or age or being able-bodied.

When you go to feminist or anti-racist conferences, there's a feeling of
déja vu – you've been here before. Yet we're facing new political threats all
the time. The collapse of communism has meant that there's a vacuum in
terms of how people identify themselves politically, what they want to
belong to. This vacuum in terms of wider political mass movements is
currently being filled by the revival of religious fundamentalism, which is
providing an alternative ideology to Western liberalism. But on the other
hand a space has opened up for opposition based on human rights and so
the left is talking more and more in the language of human rights. Human
rights is a very individual discourse and as a consequence one individualizes
rather than thinking in terms of mass mobilizations. So there are problems
with it. Nonetheless, that's the oppositional terminology at the moment.
If you want to oppose, you present your arguments in a human rights
framework, that's the discourse that's available. In my view, despite its
snags, it's not to be dismissed, and we do use it. The Human Rights Act
is going to be important to us as a weapon in our armoury. It is a means
of holding the state and indeed the community leaders to account.

I think that it's important now not to compartmentalize race, not to
compartmentalize gender; whenever we talk about issues, whether it's
domestic violence, mental health, housing, whatever it is, we must develop
an analysis which is capable of being inclusive and of tackling the underlying circumstances that produce the life that we witness.

*While many younger women are prepared to support Asian women's centres and
to take part in activity on specific issues, they often would not identify themselves
as feminists. Why do you think this is?*

It's part of the wider process. In this post-feminist climate a lot of
women who identify with the feminist ethos and principles wouldn't identify
themselves as feminists. I think it's partly a reaction to labels. We're past
the collapse of communism, but in the British context, we have a legacy
of Thatcherism that we've had to contend with. She said, quite categorically,
that there was no such thing as society, there are only individuals, whose
main aim was to make as much money as possible and look after themselves.
That's the kind of self-interested consumer legacy that's been left and has
been difficult to shake off. It's de-politicized a lot of things. The drive
towards consensus politics at the moment also contributes. For example, I
feel that the whole debate around domestic violence has been de-politicized

in many ways and so have the issues around police and police accountability, even though in the Stephen Lawrence case anti-racist activists brought police accountability back on the agenda.

You're right, the young women who come to the centre and take part in activities wouldn't call themselves feminists. I don't know what they would call it, girl power or whatever. It's obviously not as political as calling yourself feminist, but that is what there is and that is what we have to work with. Perhaps all this means finding a new language, but at the present time humanitarianism has replaced other political languages. The feminist talk of autonomy and choice is now expressed in terms of human rights. We'll talk about domestic violence as a violation of women's human rights. We've been successful as feminists, black and white, in raising feminist demands within the human rights framework. We're also getting the human rights framework to accept some of the feminist principles that we've established.

Could you elaborate on how this human rights discourse relates to your work in SBS?

The human rights framework has enabled us to oppose those interpretations of multi-culturalism which exclude women. Some aspects of multi-culturalism of course are progressive, in the sense that they promote tolerance and accept diversity. It is better than previous models of assimilation, where the only way minority communities could be integrated into this society was if they shed all aspects of their identity and integrated and adopted the dominant identity. The problem is that while multi-culturalism presents itself as the democratic model, it has had anti-democratic consequences in practice, particularly for marginalized women. This is a major obstacle which SBS has been up against.

The multi-cultural approach has become the dominant approach in social policy, and increasingly in the law. In the name of tolerating diversity certain issues are accepted as being part and parcel of one's culture and one's community traditions. So forced marriage or domestic violence are seen as part and parcel of your cultural baggage and therefore the state won't intervene. The community leaders say don't interfere, you leave it to us and the tacit contract between them and the state is that the state expects them to maintain the status quo and not upset the wider power relations. In return some kind of communal autonomy is allowed but what that means is largely governance over the family. The community leaders can then use the multi-cultural terrain on which to make a series of demands about non-intervention. So Asian women who go to the police or to social services, for example, and say: 'Look, I'm being forced into a marriage, I don't want to be, please help me' will be told: 'Well this is your culture, this is how things are done, and we are being culturally sensitive here, and we cannot intervene.' In other words, those women go unprotected; their rights go unasserted, and they have no recourse in terms of protection or redress.

Southall Black Sisters have had to counter this manifestation of multiculturalism – the hands off, leave them to it approach with a human rights discourse. Our position is that these may be cultural practices, but they are nevertheless human rights abuses. We are beginning to use the kinds of human rights principles that are enshrined in the European Convention, for example the right to live free from inhuman, degrading treatment and torture, the right to privacy, even the right to life itself.

A terrible indicator of the abuse of women's human rights is the fact that Asian women's suicide rates in Britain are up to three times higher than the national average. These statistics are astonishing and if they were occurring in the dominant community undoubtedly a lot more would be done about them than is being done. At present, even if there are suspicious circumstances, they are likely to be labelled suicide. Nobody enquires into why these suicides happen, what brings them about. The inquest system, in establishing the cause of death, will not look into *why* a woman is driven to suicide, but only *how* she died. We are beginning to ask coroners' courts to address a series of questions in relation to the deaths of Asian women. Did she really wish to die or was she killed? Are there suspicious circumstances? – which there often are. Or indeed was she driven to suicide? Was there a history of domestic violence and abuse? A lot of Asian women commit suicide because they feel there is no other way out. They'd rather commit suicide than bring shame and dishonour to themselves. In many cases they are driven to suicide by both the abuse itself and then by the cultural constraints which prevent them from seeking help or speaking out. In such cases we want it to be stated by the coroner that the woman was driven to suicide by inhuman and degrading treatment. That would be a very important acknowledgement of what actually is going on and would send a signal that these are not just neutral suicides. The human rights discourse can thus be a means of suggesting that there's a lot going on behind every individual death. There's a history behind each one, a history to understand.

The Human Rights Act could also be a means of challenging abuses which occur in cases where the police are failing to protect women who have suffered from domestic violence and who, as a result, suffer further violence and whose lives may be at risk. At present the UK government does not recognize that domestic violence is a violation of women's human rights, so there are the legal technicalities which would have to be overcome. But there are also wider questions. Along with other feminists, we have come up against the terms in which human rights discourse has been conceptualized. It is predicated on notions of public and private: since only that which is public can be held to account, private bodies such as the family or private actors, husbands or other male relatives are regarded as within the private arena, outside public scrutiny, and the state abdicates its responsibility. Many of the abuses women suffer are within the area of life defined as 'private' and so Southall Black Sisters are trying to find ways of using the Human Rights Act to make the state accountable. This has obvious theoretical repercussions and connects back to your point about international links. There have been important questions raised in Strasbourg about women who have suffered abuse such as rape or domestic violence, and who have turned to the police unsuccessfully for protection. The argument that the police should be held to account in such cases redefines the role of the state in relation to individual rights. This formulation of human rights is not just about the state itself refraining from violating someone's rights, but is about the state putting measures into place to prevent violation of rights. It puts a positive obligation on the state to remedy the situation.

We have a number of cases where the police have failed to protect women, which we would like to try and frame within the context of the Human Rights Act. There are some signs of human rights being redefined in personal relationships – for example, the Home Office Working Party Report on forced marriages recently acknowledged that forced marriage is an abuse of women's human rights.

I have no illusions. I can see that a human rights discourse could be used in some contexts to maintain power. Nevertheless, politically it is becoming increasingly important for us as a weapon in engaging with the consequences of the multi-cultural consensus. It focuses attention on the individual when the individual is being marginalized and silenced and it provides a means of blurring the line between the public and the private which can hold the state responsible. I think the language of human rights is useful. We have to find creative ways of using it, and we will.

Note

1. *Dalit*, meaning oppressed or broken, is the name used to describe persons who were previously known as untouchables under the Hindu caste system.

11

Individual and Community Rights Advocacy Forum: Campaigning for Women's Rights in Papua New Guinea

Orovu Sepoe

Most commentators on the national political scenario in Papua New Guinea highlight the existence of a 'robust democracy', evident through freedom of speech and expression, freedom of assembly, a multi-party system as well as regular and popular elections of parliamentary representatives. A closer look will reveal that this so-called robust democracy is controlled and managed by a small elite who have become the predominant actors, and the primary beneficiaries, in the areas of governance and business. Only a small percentage of Papua New Guinea's citizens are conscious of their civil, political, social and economic rights. The vast majority of people are illiterate and/or subsistence rural dwellers. They remain on the margins of a modern political system introduced through the process of colonization. In practice the constitutional rights guaranteed to all Papua New Guinea citizens tend to be restricted to a minority of the privileged. An even closer look at this minority will reveal that the key players are men. Women therefore constitute the majority among the marginalized.

In the absence of any real and concrete public responsibility towards promoting and protecting human rights in Papua New Guinea, non-governmental organizations (NGOs) have come to fill in this political vacuum. Among these is the newly formed Individual and Community Rights and Advocacy Forum (ICRAF) which aims to protect and promote the human rights of women in Papua New Guinea. It is too early to assess the impact of ICRAF, so I will focus on the process of addressing human rights issues, examining the rationale behind its formation, the activities in which it has been engaged and the strategies it has employed.

Human Rights of Women in PNG: An Overview

The Constitution of the Independent State of Papua New Guinea zealously upholds and guarantees protection of human rights for its citizens. Yet in its application of these same legal rights, there have been numerous cases of abuse and discrimination. Different sectors of the community experience this discrimination in different ways.

The fanfare of celebrating Papua New Guinea's Silver Jubilee in 2000 had little meaning for the vast majority of women, since they experience more discrimination and abuse of their human rights than men. For instance, a high-profile forum on violence against women, held on the occasion of the Silver Jubilee, highlighted persistent neglect and inaction on the part of government since the country's independence in 1975. Violation of economic, social and cultural rights continue to be pronounced and prevalent at all levels of society and amongst different categories of women.

Regular and systematic measures to address human rights issues have yet to be firmly established in Papua New Guinea. One such measure would require the mainstreaming of gender issues in policy-making processes. Mainstreaming is essentially about integrating gender issues into the normal operations and activities of government departments and agencies. There is little indication of this process occurring in Papua New Guinea. Most of the formal activities concerning women's rights fall squarely in the hands of the only department assigned for social development, namely the Department of Home Affairs, and women's organizations, in particular the PNG National Council of Women (NCW) and the PNG Women in Politics (WIP).

Women in Papua New Guinea collectively and individually advocate, organize and negotiate with established structures of power to gain access to decision-making structures and processes, but with very limited success. Structural constraints pose many difficulties for the exercise of their democratic rights. Many factors affect their effective participation in national development: among these are traditional/cultural attitudes; legal rights; access to financial resources; violence; illiteracy; and poor health – in 1997 female life expectancy was only 57.3 years.

Collective Experience of Persistent Inequality

Women's relatively disadvantaged situation in Papua New Guinea provides an impetus for activities and programmes geared towards achieving gender parity and social justice. Numerous assessments of women's status in the country consistently point out the low status and poor condition of women – for example, the National Goals and Directive Principles recognizes the importance of achieving women's equality and their development, but reality shows otherwise. Classic indicators of low female literacy rate – estimated at 34 per cent – and high mortality rates speak volumes about women's lives. Producing approximately 80 per cent of food for domestic consumption, women are overlooked in agricultural policies and their implementation, and in training. Women's access to credit is very limited and major cash crop and mining projects offer little opportunities for women. They make up only 17 per cent of the formal workforce.

The low status of women is indeed a major development issue. Successive governments have proceeded at a snail's pace towards increasing women's effective participation, and although there is a National Women's Policy which has received endorsement from the government, the reality has yet to match up with official statements.

At the top levels of national leadership, women almost disappear. This leadership pattern is, of course, common throughout the world; however, in the context of Papua New Guinea, women's absence is also a feature of the entire political system.

It is evident within the formal electoral process. The 1997 election saw only two female candidates out of a total of 55 candidates elected into the National Parliament. Why have female candidates been less successful than male candidates not only in the 1997 election but in successive elections since independence? What can be done to see greater numbers of women in the highest decision-making arena? These are the key questions posed and critically debated in many women's forums. In a workshop held in 1996, prospective candidates discussed the problems they encountered in their preparation for the 1997 national election. Fifty per cent of participants cited lack of finance, lack of knowledge of the reform, little knowledge of Parliament and the legislative process, the electoral system, the public service procedures and overall structures and processes of government.

A crucial factor that needs to be taken into account in considering women's political and social participation is the diversity in women's positions. Women are not a homogeneous group, and this affects the forms that their participation takes, and their chances of success. Women's political experience is largely confined to the informal political processes, through their membership in many NGOs and community-based organizations. In formal structures of government, women generally have had very little or no experience at all. An exceptional minority of key actors actually hold the thread that links the informal and formal spheres of politics.

Women generally feel marginalized or neglected by the government. The political rights of women have yet to be enforced and actively promoted.

Fine Words on Human Rights

A plethora of mandates (international, national and regional) intended to promote gender inequality exist, yet the actions of successive governments since independence in 1975 have not reflected the principles embodied within these mandates. There is a huge gap between the formal rights that have been drawn up and the activities of government agencies.

The Convention on the Elimination of All Forms of Discrimination Against Women (CEDAW) covers all aspects of human rights of women. The government has yet to enforce, implement and apply these in national laws and statutes, and in governmental activities. It is therefore valid to state that women's *de jure* equality has yet to be secured in Papua New Guinea.

In September 2000, the UN Millennium Declaration, among other principles, affirmed human rights, democracy and good governance. Most crucial is the fact that member states endorsed, affirmed and resolved to fully respect and uphold the Universal Declaration of Human Rights. By this declaration, heads of states and governments effectively 'committed' their respective governments:

- To combat all forms of violence against women and to implement the CEDAW.
- To work collectively for more inclusive political processes allowing genuine participation by all citizens in all member countries.

Increasingly, at an international level, equality between women and men is accepted as a human right and women's rights are regarded as human rights. It is, moreover, widely acknowledged that the realization of equal rights and equal opportunities depends on the equal participation of women and men in national, regional and international bodies and policy-making processes.

The World Conference on Human Rights affirms the Charter of the United Nations on Human Rights and specifically recognizes the rights of women and girl children as integral to universal human rights. That is, the rights of women and girls are universally valid and unilaterally non-discriminatory.

On the part of governments, the action required is to promote and protect, through ensuring that information about human rights is disseminated to all sectors of society and women in particular. Governments are ultimately responsible by acknowledging promotion and protection of human rights as a legitimate role or function or purpose of governance. Likewise, the international community has to ensure the same.

The Women's Desk in ICRAF: Translating Words into Action

The Individual and Community Rights Advocacy Forum (ICRAF) is appropriately labelled 'the rights forum' in Papua New Guinea. It is a non-profit, non-governmental organization established in 1992 to address issues relating to human rights, environmental destruction and land rights in the country. It operates with a skeleton staff comprising professionals, in particular lawyers, community workers and counsellors, and a handful of administrative and volunteer staff.

The broad objectives of ICRAF include the provision of legal services in the areas of human rights abuse or discriminatory practices and environmental issues. It also carries out awareness and educational campaigns, and monitors the abuse of human rights and environmental destruction. In terms of these activities, the Forum has done a great deal. The impact of these activities is, however, not tangible or easy to measure in terms of the achievement of 'goals'.

There are two programme desks: the Women's Desk and the Land and Environment Desk. Both programme desks carry out activities in advocacy, workshops, print and electronic media, awareness campaigns, protests, petitions, court injunctions, networking, coalitions and partnership with like-minded NGOs.

ICRAF conducts its programmes in the protection and promotion of human rights, community land and environment in three main ways. Some level of legal aid is offered to those seeking to protect their natural environment, particularly the rainforest, from massive destruction and exploitation. Para-legal training and awareness is provided to the community in general, also specifically with a special emphasis on NGOs and land-holders' and women's groups. This serves as a means of mobilizing the community and getting people more involved in the protection of human rights, land issues and the environment. Activities of state agencies, corporate bodies and individuals are monitored and investigated as a means of ensuring that these organizations and individuals are respecting their obligations under the law and that these activities are not undermining people's rights and destroying their environment.

Public advocacy, lobbying and campaigning come out of these three components of the organization's work. Campaigns can arise from investigative monitoring activities. They also develop as a result of initiatives taken by the government. They respond to issues that threaten individual and community rights, endanger the environment or negatively affect social and cultural relationships between people. They involve advocacy and lobbying around proposed legislation or lobbying and campaigning for corrective actions in instances where investigation has confirmed breaches of rights or threats and destruction of the environment.

The key professionals in implementing the programmes are the lawyers, whose main tasks are the provision of legal aid, legal opinion and participation in the delivery of para-legal training and awareness. The respective

Programme Desks organize and co-ordinate the activities in training, advocacy, awareness-raising and monitoring.

The participants in ICRAF activities come from a cross-section of civil society. They include women's groups, churches, landowner groups and other NGOs that share similar agendas or are involved in community/grassroots development or community awareness, or are engaged in activities geared towards protecting and promoting social justice, sustainable economic models and environmental protection, awareness and advocacy.

The need to take action against violence against women, raising awareness about domestic violence and assisting victims (both women and children) of domestic violence has become a crucial component in the Women's Desk's efforts to improve the status of women. In direct response to the escalating cases of violence against women throughout the country, a Women's Refuge and Crisis Centre has been set up to cater for the needs of victims of violence.

ICRAF also has a Resource Centre, which produces and distributes information handouts and pamphlets and runs its own resource library. Training awareness materials for its various activities are also developed at the resource centre addressing the issues: 'What is domestic violence?'; 'How can I get help?'; 'How to get maintenance and custody for married women'; and 'How to get maintenance and custody for unmarried/single mothers'. The Resource Centre's services are delivered in schools, workshops in local communities, conferences, radio programmes and other forms of media.

The ICRAF Women's Desk: 'Women Working for Women and the Community'

This Programme Desk recognizes the basic principle that 'Women's Rights are Human Rights', while being aware of the context of gender relations within which abuses and threats to human rights occur. Hence attempts are made to involve both men and women in workshops and forums to raise awareness and take action against women's human rights abuses.

The Women's Desk aims specifically to promote women's rights in social, cultural, political and economic development, to monitor the abuse of women's rights and to provide counselling and legal aid for abused women.

The Women's Desk seeks to empower women to defend their rights in four main ways. Legal aid is offered to women facing domestic violence or sexual violence and to women seeking protection from gender discrimination. Awareness workshops and para-legal training are provided to the community. The activities of state agencies, corporate bodies and individuals are monitored as a means of ensuring that these organizations and individuals are respecting their obligations under the law and not undermining the situation of women and children. The programme also involves advocacy and lobbying around discriminatory laws and practices or for actions where investigation has confirmed breaches of rights.

The ICRAF Women's Refuge and Crisis Centre

The lack of government support for initiatives to address violence against women and children and its failure to provide services for victims of violence have prompted greater activity on the part of non-governmental, community and church-based groups. Even so, few of these groups target women alone and very few are directly concerned with violence towards women. Programmes related to the abuse of children are covered in specialized agencies already targeting women. Activities in this sector are in the areas of awareness-raising, refuge centres, counselling services and legal aid.

The high rate of violence against women prompted the setting up of a Women's Refuge and Crisis Centre in April 1996 in the capital of Papua New Guinea, Port Moresby. It caters for victims of violence, in particular women and children. It gives support through counselling, legal advice and aid. It aims to raise awareness about violence against women and children, to empower clients by teaching basic living skills, and to work towards improving the status of women. Two weeks' crisis accommodation is provided, during which time clients undergo training in basic life skills and conflict-resolution skills. In offering a much-needed service, ICRAF's

---

Box 10.1 Disseminating Information on Domestic Violence

No one has the right to hit, bash or threaten you or your children.

No one has the right to touch or force you or your children into sexual contact.

THIS IS A CRIME!!

No matter who: husband, boyfriend, relative: the law is the same.

YOU CAN GET HELP!!

Contact:

THE ICRAF WOMEN'S REFUGE/CRISIS CENTRE FOR COUNSELLING, TEMPORARY SHELTER AND LEGAL ADVICE.

message is delivered in a precise and sharp manner, as shown in the information pamphlet in Box 10.1.

In several provinces similar refuge centres have been set up, in Simbu, East Sepik, Eastern Highlands and East New Britain. Other organizations that work in the area of violence include the Salvation Army, Catholic Family Services, Life Line, and the Young Women's Christian Association (YWCA).

The statistics shown in Box 10.2 indicate the magnitude of the task undertaken by ICRAF and counterpart NGOs, which can only do so much with very limited resources.

Box 10.2 ICRAF Statistics on Cases of Violence

Seventy-seven per cent of ICRAF Women's Desk cases involve women seeking assistance from domestic violence.

Of this group 40 per cent also involve cases of violence against children.

Of the women seeking assistance from domestic violence:

- 40 per cent are from customary marriages;
- 40 per cent are from *de facto* relationships; and
- 20 per cent are from statutory marriages.

Ninety-five per cent of domestic violence cases involve families with children.

Eight per cent of cases involve child sex abuse.

Eight per cent of family cases involve child abduction.

Seventy-nine per cent seek maintenance for their children.

Eighty-four per cent seek custody of their children.

Sixty-six per cent of married women seek maintenance for themselves.

Forty per cent of women living with domestic violence also experience sexual assault including rape and other violent sexual acts.

Eighty-five per cent seek Peace Order and Good Behaviour Bonds from the District Court.

Forty-two per cent of women living with domestic violence seek a divorce or dissolution of marriage.

Five per cent experience sexual assault.

Sixty-five per cent of domestic violence cases are alcohol-related.

Twenty-seven per cent of ICRAF cases are women from the ICRAF Refuge and Crisis Centre.

Conclusion

Despite many constraints, non-governmental organizations and women's groups play a crucial role in protecting and promoting the human rights of women through grassroots activities, networking and advocacy. The Papua New Guinea National Council of Women and the Papua New Guinea Women in Politics, and groups within NGOs such as the Individual and Community Rights Advocacy Forum carry the responsibility themselves, but their efforts urgently need support from the government. The organizational capacity of ICRAF, for example, to carry out crucial activities is severely handicapped by lack of support from the structures of power.

Funding for ICRAF activities has been raised primarily by church-based agencies overseas; Bread for the World, based in Germany, and the International Church for Cooperation (ICCOP) based in the Netherlands. Sporadic assistance has come from major development agencies such as the European Union, the UNDP and foreign embassies.

Funding constraints therefore pose the greatest problem for implementing ICRAF programmes. Since the Forum's establishment there has been no public funding to support its activities. The government does acknowledge in official statements 'partnership' with NGOs for addressing development problems, but has nothing to offer in this assumed relationship. In fact it takes a back seat when it comes to social issues. This attitude is prevalent at all levels of society in Papua New Guinea and even in the government's own agencies.

The most fundamental underlying constraint is the lack of political commitment from the government to protect and promote the human rights of women. This is evident in the lack of funding support for ICRAF activities and its own activities to complement NGO initiatives.

Given the extent of the problems faced by women in Papua New Guinea, there is a need to set priorities. In my view, the key issues are violence, literacy and public decision-making. NGOs can play a useful part in addressing these issues. However, the activities of NGOs tend to overlap and if scarce resources are to be effectively utilized their programmes require streamlining. The network of NGOs already in existence could also be strengthened through this process of rationalization. Otherwise, the competition for scarce resources among NGOs can have a detrimental effect on their worthwhile services.

The stakes are high for national development as well as for the lives of women and girl children in the years to come, unless the government takes positive steps to integrate human rights into the activities of its agencies.

Successive governments since independence have been signatories to declarations and conventions to protect and promote women's rights as human rights, yet have neither abided by this nor offered any concrete support to implement these at the global, national and regional levels. The evidence of negligence on the part of government in relation to women's needs and rights is incontestable, and pressure could be applied by resorting to the Optional Protocol.[1] This could serve as a means to force the government to implement the international rights agreements to which it has been a signatory.

The women of Papua New Guinea have relentlessly struggled and continue to struggle for their rights, yet are up against male dominance and control of the state resources and policy-making processes. A new political space has been created for this struggle in the context of NGO activism and women's collective action. However, NGOs lack the power to call the state to account. Using the constitutional guarantees as their point of entry, the dominant power structures are gradually being made to adapt to women's demands and needs. Given the choice of working either within existing structures or through new forms of organization to achieve changes, Papua New Guinea women are utilizing both avenues to make their claims on state and society.

Collective awareness of persistent inequality in decision-making at all levels of government has prompted women, individually and collectively, to become agents of building a more inclusive and representative democracy committed to attaining betterment of society. They continue to negotiate a tough and narrow path to a shared role in decision-making in a supposedly democratic system of governance.

In the course of my research I conducted interviews with Powes Parkop, chairman of the Board of Directors, ICRAF, 1992–97. Parkop is a prominent human rights lawyer who still fights legal battles to protect and promote human rights in Papua New Guinea with Lady Hilan Los, the Women's Desk co-ordinator since 1997. Lady Los is a social work graduate, married to a Supreme Court judge, Sir Justice Kubulan.

Note

1. The Optional Protocol, an independent human rights treaty added to the UN 1979 Convention on the Elimination of All Forms of Discrimination Against Women (CEDAW), provides a framework for individual women and women's groups to report violations of their rights.

Bibliography

Commonwealth Ministers Reference Book (1999/2000) Kesington Publications in association with the Commonwealth Secretariat.

Country Strategy Note: 1997–2001, UNDP.

Draft United Nations Millenium Declaration, The Millenium Assembly of the United Nations, September 2000.

Individual and Community Rights Advocacy Forum Women's Desk information pamphlet.

Individual and Community Rights Advocacy Forum Women's Refuge/Crisis Centre information pamphlet.

Individual and Community Rights Advocacy Forum, 'The Rights Forum', information pamphlet.

Papua New Guinea Law and Justice Baseline Survey of Community Initiatives. Australian Agency for International Development (AusAID), May 1997.

Platform for Action and the Beijing Declaration; United Nations Fourth World Conference on Women, September 1995.

Sepoe, Orovu (2000) *Changing Gender Relations in Papua New Guinea: The Role of Women's Organisations*, New Delhi, UBS Publishers.

12

Implementation of the Gender Demands Included in the Guatemala Peace Accords: Lessons Learned

Clara Jimeno

The recent history of Guatemala demonstrates how social change and democratization can be achieved through action within civil society. Women's organizations, which had become active during the long period of civil war, were to play a new role in the peace negotiations and in the ongoing process of implementating the Peace Accords that ended armed conflict between the government/army and the guerrilla forces.

The extension of democracy into everyday life thus had its roots in the resistence to repression. The Assembly of Civil Society (ASC) was a body created by the Marco Accord[1] in January 1994 to develop proposals for the negotiation table. The Assembly comprised eleven organized sectors[2] from civil society, one of which was the Women's Sector. The Sector was formed as a coordinated body by women's organizations.[3] It became their direct and permanent link with the peace negotiations and expanded as new organizations joined, although one of its weaknesses has been the low representation of Mayan women.

Guatemala is a multi-cultural society in which the indigenous population constitutes the majority (60–70 per cent). It is also a country of extreme disparities of wealth that has marginalized sectors of the population, among them poor women and indigenous peoples. Following a CIA-sponsored coup in 1954, the status quo was propped up by armed repression that hampered any political participation from within civil society. This nurtured a revolutionary movement that confronted one of the most repressive regimes in the history of Central America.

Government repression resulted in the emergence of a guerrilla movement in 1960–61, and a 36-year civil war was to ensue (1960–96). The guerrilla forces combined in 1982 to form the Guatemalan Revolutionary Unity (URNG), and by the early 1980s there was also a widespread movement for an end to human rights violations. This, along with support from the international community, eventually led to the peace process launched by President Vinicio Cerezo in 1986. Finally, after many years of negotiations between the army, the government and the URNG, the Peace Accords were signed in December 1996.

The Background to Women's Participation in the Peace Accords

Social movements played an important role in the peace process in Guatemala and one result was to be the inclusion of gender in the Peace Accords.

Guatemala has a history of violations of human rights and lack of democracy. However, during the revolutionary period, the promotion of civil society organizations led to the granting of women's right to vote and the creation of the first women's organization. The repression that followed included the execution and 'disappearance' of thousands of civil activists, stripping the social movements of a potential leadership, as well as the possibility of exercising their right to self-development.

Women united against the violence affecting the country, and contested the violations of their human rights in both the political process and the private sphere of the family. Mayans, who constitute 60 per cent of the population, combined to fight against the long tradition of discrimination and exclusion against indigenous peoples. This was to have a double impact on women who were both indigenous and female. Breaking women's traditional exclusion meant facing many challenges: from the economic elite, the conservative clergy, male patriarchy and also some segments of civil society.

Since men, especially indigenous males, were the majority of the victims of the civil war, Guatemalan women have had to fill the void. In the villages and among the internally and externally displaced peoples, women, particularly indigenous women, were to assume the leadership. These conditions created the potential for women's mobilization and their achievements were to be remarkable.

Women's organizations began to develop during the 'limited political' opening in the 'return to democracy' of 1985, when the army formally relinquished some of its power. The 1980s constituted a benchmark because women took a leadership role in the politics of the country and formed their own organizations. They were the first to rise during the armed repression of the 1980s and to demand an end to violence and respect for human rights, nationally and internationally. The leading organizations in this process were the Mutual Support Group (GAM) and the National Co-ordination of Guatemalan Widows (CONAVIGUA). The former was composed of women, mainly Mayan, who had become widows as a result of the armed repression.

During the 1980s women's organizations began to spread in different sectors in the capital city, in the rural areas and in internal refugee camps (Communities of Population in Resistance – CPRs), as well as in refugee camps in Mexico. Also women in exile, who were mainly marginalized illiterate indigenous peasants, began to organize. The political development of women in exile led them to important positions in the Permanent Commissions of Guatemalan Refugees. These Commissions negotiated and organized their return from Mexico. As a result, refugee camp-based organizations were formed in Mexico and were brought back to the country. Two examples were Mama Maquin and Ixmucane. Other organizations included dispersed refugee women in Mexico, for instance, Ixchel Flower of Hope and internal refugee women's organizations such as the Organization of Women in Resistance from Ixcan. These groups played an active role in the General Assembly of the Communities of Population in Resistance, which negotiated the reintegration of the internal refugees into civilian life.

Examples of organizations emerging in the capital city during this period include the Group for the Improvement of the Family (GRUFE-PROMEFAM), Tierra Viva, the only explicitly feminist organization in the country and the Council of Mayan Women. Mayan women have been particularly discriminated against because of their culture and level of poverty and the development of their organizations has been of vital importance. Nevertheless, political space for the participation of Mayan women within civil society organizations, including women's organizations, has continued to be constrained.

All these women's groups face daunting problems. The majority of women in Guatemala live in the most deprived conditions at the bottom of the economic ladder. In these circumstances it is very difficult to develop their capacities to participate politically. The unequal and marginal conditions affecting Guatemalan women in education, health, housing, access to land and adequate incomes hinder their participation. While the UNDP's gender-related development indicator of 0.603 (1998) placed the country as a whole, at the middle level, it revealed a greater degree of inequality existing in certain regions. Seventeen of the country's 22 provinces had indicators lower than 0.500 in 1995 and women in the rural areas were particularly affected, especially indigenous women (UNDP 2000; ECLA/UNDP 1998).

Not only do women need adequate standards of living in order to participate in democratic processes, they are also burdened by their triple work day (work, home and public life). This places them at a distinct disadvantage *vis-à-vis* men and limits their political participation. Women's organizations have been strengthening women's political participation, building the skills to access decision-making positions and vote in elections. They have also demanded respect for women's human rights. As Cathy Blacklock in *Reading Political Practices* observes, this is a slow process whose 'long term goal ... is to develop women's ability to participate politically, to contest the development of civil society and the deepening of democratization in Guatemala (1994: 5).

While women's organizations have been bringing the voice of the excluded to the forefront, they have not been able adequately to represent the multi-cultural diversity of the country or to involve a large percentage of the female population. This under-representation is the result of the recent development of women's organizations, the fragmentation of civil society, social and ethnic exclusion, rural marginalization and the lack of resources.

The women's groups have not yet achieved a sense of cohesion, due to the absence of a common platform and the lack of a functional organizational infrastructure. However, a positive advance has been the social policies developed by the Women's National Forum, a consultative body that operates between the government and civil society. Also, since 1999 the Women's Sector has been reaching out to the rural areas and has broadened its membership to include the diverse ethnic communities.

On the one hand, women's organizations continue to be linked to the popular movements and to operate within civil society. On the other hand, women's organizations are building national and regional coalitions to address women's specific issues and support the implementation of the Peace Accords.

While women's organizations are playing an important role through increasing gender awareness and mobilizing women, they lack support from other organizations in civil society. So although women's organizations have defended the demands of civil society as a whole, they are still fighting for gender demands in isolation. Only a limited number of civil society organizations have integrated gender equality into their work and mandate. Deborah Stienstra emphasizes that 'the advancement of gender equality has been hampered by the fact that it has too often been relegated to women's groups alone ... Gender equality requires the participation of many more and it needs to be recognized as an organizational priority (Van Rooy 1999: 81).

However, Guatemalan women's organizations have made strong international links. One example is the Co-ordination of Women's Groups Nuestra Voz (Our Voice), formed in Guatemala with the support of Nuestra Voz from Vancouver, which supports Guatemalan women organizing in their communities and builds awareness in Canada about their struggle for equality, justice and peace. Nuestra Voz in Guatemala became part of the

Women's Sector, which participated in the peace negotiations and is involved in the ongoing implementation of the women's demands. Between 1991 and 1994 Nuestra Voz in Vancouver was greatly helped by the participation of Sandra Moran (in 1991–94), a leader of the Women's Sector. In 1994, she returned to Guatemala and formed the Co-ordination of Women's Groups Nuestra Voz.

Women's groups also grew in the new political spaces created by the peace negotiations and the implementation of the Peace Accords. Examples include the Women's Sector and the National Women's Forum, where civil society and government institutions worked together for the first time and began to dissolve the legacy of confrontation between civil society and the state. For the first time indigenous and non-indigenous women were to be represented on a large scale. The Forum outreached to 25,000 women from all over the country. Much of this achievement was the result of the work of the organizations participating in the Women's Sector, which organized women in the rural areas.

However, the existence of these formal mechanisms for women's participation does not ensure real participation in promoting gender issues because there can be manipulation from the state or a lack of gender awareness among women themselves. For example, congresswomen who belonged to the political party formerly in power, the National Advancement Party (PAN), expressed their opposition to gender terminology included in the proposal to create the National Women's Institute. PAN is a 'modernizing' right-wing party, which initiated privatization in Guatemala.

The National Women's Institute was to serve as the overseer of national policies for the development of women. This body was never to be approved, despite a commitment from President Portillo. In the face of opposition he retracted his commitment and created the Women's Secretariat in May 2000 instead. This is an advisory and coordinating body, but the Secretariat is not able to develop policies or implement international commitments regarding gender issues.

President Portillo, who was elected in November 1999, is a populist from the radical right-wing party, the Guatemalan Republican Front (FRG). He shares power with Efrain Rios Montt, leader of the party and a former army general accused of genocide while in power.[4] Though Rios Montt opposed the establishment of the National Women's Institute, President Portillo's social policy statements have endorsed gender issues in general terms. This inclusion of gender can be traced to the Peace Accords and the subsequent lobbying by women's organizations.

Guatemalan women's organizations have taken the responsibility of monitoring the implementation of the Peace Accords, with the aim of ensuring that gender equality is integral to the process of addressing the problems that led to the civil war. However, it is evident that the Peace Accords do not resolve the structural problems affecting the country, including the highly concentrated levels of land tenure and income. For instance, the Inter-American Development Bank reports that 10 per cent of the Guatemalan population receives 50 per cent of the total income (America Latina Frente a la Desigualdad 1998).

Moreover, the implementation of the Peace Accords has been a slow process partly because social inequality was further intensified by the privatization policies of President Arzu. Furthermore, high levels of violence and impunity persist, claiming the life of Bishop Juan Gerardi in April 1998, only two days after he presented a report on human rights violations. Hurricane Mitch and the November 1999 general elections affected the rate of implementation of the peace process as well, while the defeat of the public referendum on constitutional reforms hindered the legal foundation of the Peace Accords.

This defeat revealed the need for all groups in civil society, including the women's organizations, to develop new strategies. With hindsight it was apparent that there had been a lack of information to voters and a low voter enumeration rate (only 40 per cent of women were registered to vote). The deeply rooted abstensionism in the society had not been add-ressed: only 18.5 per cent of registered voters went to the polls and the media offensive launched by conservative forces remained unchallenged. Nor had any programmes been put in place to eliminate the barriers preventing women from voting. Even so, it was noticeable that, in contrast to the capital city, the referendum won majority approval in the rural areas, where most indigenous people live. These results showed the rural population's increased awareness of the Peace Accords' relevance for the identity and rights of indigenous peoples and they reflect the hard work of rural organizations representing Mayan peoples, women, peasants, co-operatives and communities of returnees.

The Achievements of Women's Organizations

Alliances among women's organizations The autonomous contribution of women's organizations in the peace process is an indication of the advancement of women's political participation. Initially women's organiza-tions participated in the peace process within other sectors, such as the labour unions and popular movements. However, in May 1994, the Women's Sector was created and women achieved independent political participation in the negotiations.

It was the first time that women had coalesced as a negotiating body and was to prove a difficult process. In order to obtain political clout, women had to overcome their differences to achieve a strong unified stand on various issues. The integration of different perspectives has been challenging and, as Lorena Robles notes, they have had 'to do a lot of consciousness raising amongst [themselves] because ... [members] come with prejudices of [their] own sector, be it labour, Mayan or whatever' (1995: 7).

The crucial contribution of the Women's Sector has been to ensure that gender demands be included in the Peace Accords and to monitor their implementation through bodies such as the National Women's Forum, but it also works at the grassroots. The Women's Sector has increased its membership and diversified its composition. Some of its new members are women from political parties and religious organizations as well as from gender programmes located in the National University San Carlos, the Dolores Bedoya Foundation and the Centre for Legal Action and Human Rights (CALDH). By 1999 the Women's Sector had representatives from 17 out of the 22 provinces of Guatemala.

After successfully integrating its gender proposals into the Peace Accords, the Women's Sector continued to work in consolidating the role of women's organizations. It came out empowered by its participation in the Assembly of Civil Society in 1999 with a firm commitment to developing a multi-ethnic, multi-cultural, multi-lingual identity and turned to the task of monitoring the Peace Accords.

As a result of the intervention of the Women's Sector, the Peace Accords recognized equality between women and men at home, at work, in productive activities and in social and political life. The government committed itself to promoting and supporting women's participation, particularly in the rural areas, and to eliminating discrimination and sexual harassment of women. In addition, it pledged to support women's access to jobs, training, land, credit, technology, housing, education and health. Most significant was its commitment to promoting women's participation at all levels of decision-making, as well as creating and strengthening government institutions responsible for promoting women's participation. Another important pledge was to provide gender awareness training to public servants responsible for implementing programmes and laws addressing women's needs and rights.

The gender demands emanating from the Women's Sector have also permeated the left-wing Guatemalan Revolutionary Unity (URNG)'s class-based analysis of inequality and exploitation. The URNG, which united all guerrilla groups in the country, was to modify its position on gender and incorporate a substantial part of the Women's Sector's demands in the 'Proposal to a Society' it developed for the peace negotiations. In this document, the URNG asserts that Guatemalan women must be guaranteed conditions of equality and full participation in political, civil, economic and social sectors. The URNG also states that all forms of gender-based discrimination that constitute obstacles for the exercise of women's capacities should be eradicated.

In December 1998, the URNG became a political party and created the Commission of Women's Political Issues. Two members of the Commission were Lola, the only woman member of URNG's National Executive Committee, and Silvia Solorzano, a former member of the URNG's International Relations Commission. The Commission's objectives are to promote women's participation in the party's executive body and to support women candidates in the election process. The URNG particularly emphasizes the political inclusion of grassroots women.

Joint work with government institutions   The National Women's Forum was set up in 1997 to ensure that women's demands were included in the Peace Accords. It received most of its funding from the United Nations Development Programme. It came into being as a result of a complex process of discussion around civil society participation in the consultation process.

Some members of the Women's Sector have criticized the National Women's Forum for its incapacity to respond to the creativity and experiences of grassroots women's organizations. However, it was not developed as a government institution; the Forum's coordinating committee consists mainly of civil society representatives. Moreover, the majority of these representatives are Mayan women. This major achievement was not accomplished without struggle.

The initial proposal for the Forum's organization, aiming to build a democratic structure, was rejected by the government after long discussions. Instead, a hierarchical structure was put in place with a co-ordinator appointed by the government. This was challenged by the Women's Sector. The result was the implementation of a Co-ordinating Committee with a majority of civil society representatives. Out of a total of ten members, six were from civil society organizations, one of them from the Women's Sector and four from governmental institutions. The result was a broad, plural and representative body through which for the first time in Guatemala diverse groups of women participated in the development of national policies addressing women's inequalities.

The Forum's crucial contribution in the consultation process was to divide the country into linguistic areas. This allowed women from different administrative divisions to participate in their own language in the consultation process. The Women's Sector played a major role in achieving a more representative structure for these consultations by securing bottom-up representation at local, regional and national levels that were organized in eight different linguistic communities.

Reflecting on this process of democratization, Sandra Moran from the Women's Sector said: 'As women, we are making use of one more space ... and for sure, we will come out better organized and with new ways to struggle. This will help us to continue challenging the conservative atmosphere that, little by little, is gaining more space in Guatemala and the world' (Nuestra Voz 1999: 4).

From March 1999 the Forum developed proposals for women's civic, political, social and economic equality and its Plan for the Equity of Opportunities 1999–2001: Promotion and Development of Guatemalan Women was approved a few days before President Arzu left office in December 1999.

The Forum's proposals outlined basic needs for housing, land tenure, health, education, work, income-generation projects and credit. They also addressed violence against women and its implications for women's development. The Forum put a great deal of emphasis on the civic and political participation of women. It called for the promotion of women's organization and participation in decision-making through:

- national programmes to sensitize the population, train public servants dealing with women's issues and promote research on women's civic and political participation;
- a gender approach in educational programmes;
- the decentralization and simplification of the electoral processes;
- a restructuring of the citizen's identification system;
- an infrastructure to reduce the burden of women's domestic work;
- institutions and public policies for women's development; and
- mechanisms for the full exercise of women's citizenship.

The Forum has encouraged the participation of women in the revived urban and rural development councils. These had been created by President Cerezo to decentralize government decisions and were disbanded during the civil war. The councils never really involved citizens at a local level, nor did they engage women in participation. The Women's Sector has been strengthening women's organizations in the rural areas to enable them to take part in the reformed councils and present proposals in them.

Two highly controversial topics were raised in the National Assembly of the Forum: women's right to choose their sexuality and to control their own body. The discussion of sexual preference and abortion was restricted by the content of the Peace Accords, which had included only sexual education, a demand achieved after great opposition. Other difficulties were the cultural diversity of the Assembly and the lack of information about sex and reproductive issues, especially in the rural areas. These combined with blatant homophobia and the conservative and religious condemnation of the women raising these issues. When I interviewed her in 1999, Lucia Quina from CONAVIGUA stated that to act on women's reproductive rights, especially abortion, was still difficult.

Nevertheless, the National Assembly did agree that people's sexual preference must not be a cause of discrimination and that illegal abortion was a cause of maternal death. Within the conservative and traditional context of Guatemalan society, these are significant advances.

While women's reproductive rights had been put forward by the Women's Sector in the process of negotiations, they were not included in the Peace Accords, due to lack of support from the government, the left organizations, the URNG and the army regarding these issues. They continue to be the topic of intense debate in the Women's Sector. When I conducted a series of interviews in 1999 a founder of Tierra Viva, the feminist organization that has been part of the Women's Sector and active in raising sexual and reproductive rights, Maria Eugenia Lemus said that the weakness and lack of consolidation of the Guatemalan women's move-ment prevented the discussion of women's strategic needs, such as women's sexuality. She stated that this situation was further complicated by the fact that the women's movement had a popular base, not a feminist one. Efforts had been made to link the class struggle to the gender struggle, but, in the process, women's demands around sexuality had been missed out. Lucia Quina from the National Co-ordination of Guatemalan Widows (CON-AVIGUA) agreed that feminism was an unknown word in rural com-munities, but said this was no longer true of the indigenous women participating in women's organizations in the capital city. Olga Rivas, from the Group for the Improvement of the Family (GRUFEPROMEFAM), expressed concern that popular women lacked feminist theory. This vacuum made it impossible to build upon and systematize the experiences of the women's movement. She also pointed out the lack of linkages between women who have this knowledge (usually university graduates) and those who do not (women from the grassroots).

Building a women's social force within the Congress Pressure from women's organizations on gender inequality has been accompanied by the mobilization of working-class and Mayan women. One result was the Women's Commission, which has formed a crucial link between women's organizations and the Congress. Among the women participating in the Commission were the Mayan leader Manuela Alvarado and Nineth Monte-negro, founder of the Mutual Support Group (GAM), which played a crucial role in the struggle against impunity for those responsible for the forced 'disappearances' during the repression. In 1999 the Commission paid tribute to the contribution of several women to the struggle against violence. These included Olga Rivas from GRUFEPROMEFAM, along with others from Tierra Viva, the Guatemalan Women's Group and Women in Solidarity.

The impact of these interconnections between differing kinds of women's organizations has been reflected in legislation that has been debated by the Congress. Examples are:

* The Law Against Domestic Violence, approved in 1996.
* Draft of the Regulations for the application of the Law Against Domestic Violence.
* The creation of the National Co-ordinator for the Prevention of Domestic Violence (included in the Regulations of the Law Against Domestic Violence).
* Draft of the Law Against Sexual Harassment.
* Draft for the creation of the Institute for the Development of Women (the Institute was not approved).
* Reforms to the Civil and Penal Code to eliminate legislation that discriminates against women.
* Draft of a law contesting forced military recruitment, proposing an alternative of choosing between military and social service.
* Reforms to the Labour Code presented by the Women's National Office (Woman and Legislative Reforms Project). Some of the issues addressed by these reforms are sexual harassment in the work place, recognition of women as independent agricultural workers with the right to be paid and the rights of domestic and maquila workers and child labour.
* Reforms to the Electoral Law including a 30 per cent quota of female participation in the political parties' list of candidates.
* Reforms to the Law of the Rural and Urban Councils, to include women's participation.
* Law for the Dignity and Integral Promotion of Women, 1999.

However, the women's organizations are aware that laws are not enough; they have to be accompanied by information and conscientization campaigns, especially in the rural area, as well as by training in gender awareness for the public servants who implement them. Moreover, mechanisms to regulate, monitor and evaluate the application of the law need to be created.

Negotiating support from the Congressional Commissions After a long process of discussion and negotiation in the course of which the Women's Commission obtained support from the Legislative and Constitutional Commissions, the Civil Code reforms addressing women's inequalities in the family were approved. Not only did this mark an important beginning in building support within Congress, it constituted a serious challenge to the conservative and patriarchal values blocking women's demands. The Civil Code reforms seek to eliminate discrimination against women within the family and to give equal rights to both partners. They rule that:

- Both spouses have the right to represent the family.
- Childbearing is a shared responsibility of both parents.
- Both spouses have the right to administrate the family inheritance.
- Each spouse has the right to oppose the other spouse taking actions that could affect the family patrimony.
- Both parents will have custody of a minor or of a child with disabilities.
- The husband does not have the right to prevent his wife working outside the home.

Strengthening women's political participation The creation in 1996 of the Forum of Women from Political Parties meant that for the first time in Guatemalan history women from different political parties joined an organization in which they analysed problems and proposed solutions together. Approximately five hundred women took part in what was to be a remarkable learning process. Dialogue and consensus-building were based on respect for differences. This spirit was personified by the president of the Forum, Flora de Ramos, a deputy from the Guatemalan Republican Front (FRG) and a member of the Congressional Women's Commission.

Prensa Libre reported on 4 March 1999 that the Forum aimed to 'build the capacity of Guatemalan women, without regard for their political affiliation. The objective is to promote them to participate as candidates in the electoral process' (p. 4). The Forum put the case for a minimum quota of 30 per cent female participation in the list of candidates put forward by political parties. Its attempts to improve the representation of women connected to wider efforts to reform the Electoral Law. Unfortunately the Forum was disbanded in 2000, due to the failure of the political parties to fulfil the Guatemalan election law in the 1999 elections. (Four of the seven political parties legally registered disappeared, and PAN was weakened by internal problems.)

Enhancing the participation of Mayan women's organizations In 1999 the Accord of Identity and Rights of Indigenous Peoples created the Office for the Defence of the Rights of Mayan Women, which recognized the double discrimination against indigenous women (through racism and sexism), as well as their specific situation of poverty and exploitation.

While the impact of this body could be limited by the fact that it is under the authority of the Presidential Commission of Human Rights, rather than the Ombudsman Office of Human Rights, which is independent of the government, it is, nevertheless, a real achievement for Mayan women.

The Office is one indication of how Mayan women's organizations are increasing their political participation. Mayan women have become active in the Women's Sector through the Council of Mayan Women and the Coordination of Mayan Women's Organizations. On 8 March 1999 *Prensa Libre* cited Rosalina Tuyuc, a Mayan woman from CONAVIGUA and a deputy from the Guatemalan Front: New Guatemala (FDNG), describing how attitudes have begun to change: 'There has been an awareness process regarding women's political rights. Before, men were the only ones that took the decisions over women's lives.' The newspaper also quoted Manuela Alvarado, a Mayan woman and FDNG deputy, stressing the need to overcome marginalization: 'As women, we have to get organized in order to participate in the decision-making process and abandon that difficult stage that left us out of the political mainstream' (p. 4).

Lucia Quina, from CONAVIGUA, reflected, in an interview with me in 1999, upon the tremendous difficulty Mayan women had had in ensuring that the Office for the Defence of the Rights of Mayan Women be integrated within the Peace Accords. But she was very aware of the danger of Mayan participation becoming tokenistic.

Indigenous women are active on several fronts: while asserting Mayan representation and participation in the society they are also struggling within their communities. Quina regarded the main hindrance to women's development as 'machismo'. For this reason she believed it was strategic to incorporate men in sensitization programmmes that addressed women's human rights.

For Mayan women struggle around gender inequalities, discrimination and sexual harassment is taking place alongside the fight for cultural rights within Mayan communities. The complex dimensions of their resistance makes it particularly important that a commitment to gender equality should be embodied in the conception of Office for the Defence of the Rights of Indigenous Women included in the Peace Accords. This was articulated by Rosalina Tuyuc when she supported the draft bill to set up the Office: 'Today is the moment to comply with the [peace] commitments to eradicate gender discrimination and to give an incentive to the struggle for the promotion of women and equality in Guatemalan society (*Grafico*, 17 October 1998: 7).

Developing regional alliances Guatemalan women's organizations have been part of a wider process of regional and international solidarity. From

1998, regional alliances have been formed by women journalists, women from political parties and women working against violence. They are committed to making women's contributions 'visible' and to developing an approach to equality that integrates class, gender and ethnicity. They have also sought to devise common strategies in response to the challenges of economic integration and globalization that have been having adverse effects upon the lives of poor women. Regional and international networks have also contributed to cultivating women's leadership and their political participation. For example, there have been:

- the first regional meeting of female journalists;
- the Encounter of Central American Women from Left Wing Parties;
- the Forum of Central American Women from Political Parties; and
- the Central American Network Against Violence Against Women.

Barriers to the Participation of Women's Organizations

Mainstreaming gender equality within civil society is a difficult process. Not only have the women's organizations in Guatemala been hampered by lack of support from other movements, they have been under intense pressure to implement the Peace Accords and forced to adjust to rapid political changes in the country. Internal weaknesses also mean that the majority of women's organizations still do not reflect the cultural diversity of the country. Many of them have their headquarters in the capital city; they lack resources and face restricted channels of communication, which limit their capacity to reach women in the rural areas. Conversely, women's organizations from the rural areas cannot establish offices in the capital city, or mobilize speedily.

Rural under-representation and the lack of mechanisms to articulate their concerns nationally are problems for all groups campaigning in Guatemala, but the difficulties are exacerbated for women. Social and economic deprivation combines with women's extra domestic responsibilities and these are compounded by patriarchal attitudes, sexual violence and lack of rights.

There are dilemmas too around seeing and thinking about women's priorities. The assumptions and debates that preoccupy women's organizations in the capital city have a limited reach in the majority of the rural areas, particularly in the isolated ones. While women's strategic needs and reproductive rights are emphasized within the urban context, in the interior of the country women have to focus on their basic needs because of extreme poverty and marginalization. These conditions demand different approaches from the women's movement and strategies to ensure that the work of women's organizations is complementary and that divisions that have developed between groups are reduced.

Guatemalan society continues to be divided by very marked social classes and by racism towards Mayan peoples, both of which have serious consequences for the lives of indigenous women. The Office for the Defence of the Mayan Peoples expressed its concern about the lack of improvements in the conditions of living of the Mayan population, stating that:

> The government has advanced some political aspects of the Peace Accords, but they have been mainly formal and operative. Little has been done to modify the extreme poverty, exploitation, discrimination, exclusion and marginalization of the poor and the Mayan peoples. (Tierra Viva 1999: 11)

A lack of trust and scepticism within the ethnic communities, the results of hundreds of years of subordination, have made the attempts of Mayan organizations to change these conditions harder. Consequently a large number of women still cannot exercise their citizenship rights because they do not have identity documents. A significant number of them lost their documents during the armed conflict. Other women cannot reach the offices that issue them, especially women who live in isolated rural areas. As a result, the women's vote continues to be under-represented in the election process.

An aftermath of military repression has been a 'culture of fear'. While human rights are formally accepted and political repression is no longer supported by the state, a residual danger of political violence has bred a feeling of insecurity in civil society. Several women have been among the targets. Examples are the murder of Maria Victoria Ramirez Sanchez, a sociologist from the Association for the Advancement of the Social Sciences (AVANCSO), in 1999 and the forced disappearance of Mayra Gutierrez, a professor at the National University of San Carlos, in 2000.

Women have thus been affected by the general fear over challenging human rights violations as well as being under pressure not to insist that their rights as women be respected. The interconnections between women's public action and personal and sexual subordination are all too evident – the political repression of women has, for example, included rape. Their participation in the resistance to repression has had consequences too for relations between men and women. A common phenomenon is women activists who are divorced or separated, due to lack of support from their partners, whose patriarchal values have survived the peace process. Consequently, the women's organizations' challenge has to be taken into domestic and sexual relations. Empowering women has to extend to the strategic gender interests that enable them to take control of their own lives.

Many women have displayed considerable personal courage in demanding equality within the family and denouncing domestic violence, rape and sexual harassment. However, change will not be possible until men become more aware of gender inequality. The cost of women taking sole responsibility for the transformation of gender relations was one of the most important issues discussed in the World Forum of Non-Governmental Organizations in Beijing.[5]

It is increasingly being recognized that injustices in the personal sphere are of public concern. Legislation has been drawn up in relation to domestic violence and the issue has become part of the government agenda (the National Programme to Eradicate Domestic Violence), but the institutions that are implementing the programmes lack resources. The Women's Ombudsman Office has a shortage of staff to take care of rape cases, and of forensic doctors and psychologists. Many abused women are now aware of their rights and of the legislation that protects them, but there is no government funding to provide them with shelter in emergency situations. So there is a need to provide adequate funding to institutions working on women's issues.

Conclusions and Lessons Learned

The peace negotiations and the implementation of the Peace Accords opened up political spaces in which women have found new ways of participating. This new terrain is, however, endangered by a lack of credibility surrounding the Peace Accords, especially after the referendum. Few people know about the Accords because the government has done little to communicate the relevant debates and proposals. Information has been mostly conveyed by civil society organizations involved in the peace process, particularly by the Women's Sector.

The National Women's Forum and the Women's Sector have emerged with much greater skills and experience in political negotiation and policy-making. The Women's Sector has also formed connections with rural women's organizations, which has enabled this growing process of learning to spread. An important feature has been the creation of anti-hierarchical structures. However, this vital achievement is at risk because of lack of resources. There is consequently a need for women's organizations to continue lobbying international funding organizations, especially the Consultative Group of International Lenders, to secure resources for the implementation of programmes and projects included in the National Proposal of the Women's Forum.

The grassroots and multi-cultural participation achieved by the Women's Sector represents a real breakthrough. Still, a challenge lies ahead. The next step is to broaden their activities and find ways of consolidating organizational structures so they can survive in the long term. This is particularly important, for the Guatemalan women's movement has had many experiences of women's organizations coalescing around specific issues that have proved to be short-lived.

The Women's Forum needs a more democratic structure in order to ensure that the multi-ethnic, multi-cultural, multi-lingual characteristics of Guatemalan society are represented. The Forum's transition into a permanent institution funded by the government is important, especially in its role as a consultative body. However, this change carries dangers of co-option, which could lessen the autonomy of the movement. The gains made by the women's organizations are thus revealing new problems around consciousness and participation.

It is becoming increasingly evident that there is a need to systematize the experience and lessons learned from the participation of women's organizations in the aftermath of the Peace Accords. These experiences could lead to the development of better methods of working together, just as the lessons learned from the experience of the Salvadorian 1994 Women's Platform were key to the activities of women's organizations, not only in Guatemala but in Central America.

When I interviewed Olga Rivas from GRUFEPROMEFAM in 1999, she made the point that the women's organizations needed to become more coherent and strategic. She observed: 'There is a consensus among women's organizations to concentrate on the Peace Accords. However, it is necessary to redefine the dynamic of women's organizations with strategic planning. We have to open a discussion about what we want to achieve and define strategies. Crucial points of this debate are the development of an agenda for Guatemalan women's development and for strategies that bring women's organizations together.'

Guatemalan women have been engaged in a sustained struggle for an equal and democratic society and their courage in facing the manifold barriers to their political participation needs to be recognized. Three main areas need to be addressed in the future: the socio-economic factors that prevent women's full political participation, gender awareness among women and men and the strength and co-ordination of women's organizations.

Notes

1. Spanish abbreviation for the Accord for the Framework for Democratization in the Search of Peace by Political Means.

2. The ASC sectors included: women, political parties, religious groups, unions and

popular organizations, academics, small business and co-operatives, Mayan organizations, journalists, research centres, human rights organizations, NGOs and CACIF (the Co-ordinating Committee for Commercial, Industrial and Financial Institutions). CACIF opposed the creation of the ASC and refused to participate in the Assembly.

3. At present women's organizations participate in six other co-ordinating bodies: 'Women of May 28', addressing women's health led by the organization 'Tierra Viva', the 'Co-ordination to end Violence Against Women', 'Beijing + 5', 'Cairo + 5' and 'Women's 2000' organizing the World March of Women.

4. Efrain Rios Montt was accused of genocide against Mayan people during his 1982–83 *de facto* government.

5. Beijing: Equality in Diversity 1995 Project of Strategies for Actions Post-Beijing.

Bibliography

Blacklock, Cathy (1994) 'Reading political practices: women's contestation of human rights in Guatemala', paper presented to CPSA Annual Conference, Calgary.

— (1996) 'Contesting democratization in Guatemala: women's political organizations and human rights', PhD thesis, Ottawa.

Economic Commission for Latin America (ECLA/UNDP) (1998) *Guatemala: Los Contrastes del Desarrollo Humano*, Guatemala: ECLA/UNDP.

Facultad Latinoamericana de Ciencias Sociales (1997) ¿Que Sociedad Queremos?, Guatemala.

— (1998–99) 'Dialogo', Guatemala.

Foro Nacional de la Mujer (1997–98) *Report*, Guatemala.

— (1998) *Guia para el Proceso Local y Regional de Elaboracion de Propuestas de los Ejes Social, Economico y Juridico en el Marco de los Acuerdos de Paz*, Guatemala.

— (1999a) *Propuesta de Desarrollo Civico Politico*, Guatemala.

— (1999b) *Propuesta Nacional: Ejes Desarrollo Economico y Desarrollo Social*, Guatemala.

Guatemala News and Information Bureau (1998–99) *Up Date on Guatemala*, San Francisco.

Inter-American Development Bank (IDB) (1998–99), *America Latina Frente a la Desigualdad: Informe de progreso economico y social en America Latina*, Washington, DC.

International Centre Against Censorship (1998) *Popular Participation and the Right to Development*, London.

Nuestra Voz (1999) *Nuestra Voz de Mujer*, 5 March, Vancouver.

Programa Regional la Corriente (1997) *Movimiento de Mujeres en Centroamerica*, Managua.

Robles, Lorena (1995) 'Discussing Women's Role in Civil Society. "Marching in the Streets is not enough"', *Guatemala*, 16(4) (Winter): 6–7.

Sector de Mujeres (1997) *Quienes Somos*, Guatemala.

— (1998) *Consejos de Desarrollo Urbano y Rural (CDUR)*, Guatemala.

Stienstra, Debora (1997) 'Working Globally for Gender Equality', in Alison Van Roy (ed.), *Canadian Development Report 1999: Civil Society and Global Change*, Ottawa: The North-South Institute.

Smith, Susan, Dennis G. Willms and Nancy A. Johnson (eds) (1997) *Nurtured by Knowledge: Learning to do Participatory Action-Research*, New York: Apex Press.

Swift, Jamie (1999) *Civil Society in Question*, Toronto: Between the Lines.

Tierra Viva (1997–98) *Enterese y comente*, Guatemala.

— (1999) *Enterese y comente* (November).

United Nations Development Programme (UNDP) (2000) *Human Development Report 2000*, New York: UNDP.

Interviews with representatives of Guatemalan women's organizations and political parties (1999)

Sector de Mujeres, Sandra Moran (Co-ordinating Commission)

URNG – Silvia Solorzano (Women's Political Issues Commission)

Tierra Viva – Maria Eugenia Lemus (founder member)

CONAVIGUA – Lucia Quina (Board of Directors)

GRUFEPROMEFAM – Olga Rivas (Executive Director)

Index